MASTERPIECES OF THE MODERN THEATRE

A NINE VOLUME SET EDITED BY ROBERT W. CORRIGAN

CENTRAL EUROPEAN THEATRE / *The Game of Love* and *La Ronde* Schnitzler / *Electra* Hofmannsthal / *R.U.R.* Čapek / *The Play's the Thing* Molnár

ENGLISH THEATRE / *The Importance of Being Earnest* Wilde / *Major Barbara* Shaw / *Loyalties* Galsworthy / *Dear Brutus* Barrie / *Enter Solly Gold* Kops

FRENCH THEATRE / *The Parisian Woman* Becque / *Christopher Columbus* de Ghelderode / *Electra* Giraudoux / *Eurydice (Legend of Lovers)* Anouilh / *Queen After Death* Montherlant / *Improvisation or The Shepherd's Chameleon* Ionesco

GERMAN THEATRE / *Woyzeck* Buechner / *Maria Magdalena* Hebbel / *The Weavers* Hauptmann / *The Marquis of Keith* Wedekind / *The Caucasian Chalk Circle* Brecht

IRISH THEATRE / *The Countess Cathleen* Yeats / *The Playboy of the Western World* and *Riders to the Sea* Synge / *The Silver Tassie* and *Cock-a-Doodle Dandy* O'Casey

ITALIAN THEATRE / *Six Characters in Search of an Author* and *The Pleasure of Honesty* Pirandello / *Crime on Goat Island* Betti / *Filumena Marturano* Filippo / *The Academy* and *The Return* Fratti

RUSSIAN THEATRE / *A Month in the Country* Turgenev / *Uncle Vanya* and *The Cherry Orchard* Chekhov / *The Lower Depths* Gorky / *The Bedbug* Mayakovsky

SCANDINAVIAN THEATRE / *Hedda Gabler* Ibsen / *Miss Julie* and *The Ghost Sonata* Strindberg / *The Difficult Hour* Lagerkvist / *The Defeat* Grieg / *Anna Sophie Hedvig* Abell

SPANISH THEATRE / *The Witches' Sabbath* Benavente / *The Cradle Song* Martínez-Sierra / *The Love of Don Perlimplín and Belisa in the Garden* Lorca / *The Dream Weaver* Buero Vallejo / *Death Thrust* Sastre

MASTERPIECES OF THE MODERN IRISH THEATRE

Edited by ROBERT W. CORRIGAN

FIVE PLAYS

THE COUNTESS CATHLEEN

THE PLAYBOY OF THE WESTERN WORLD

RIDERS TO THE SEA

THE SILVER TASSIE

COCK-A-DOODLE DANDY

COLLIER BOOKS, *NEW YORK*

CONTENTS

[5]

THE IRISH DRAMATIC FLAIR

by Robert W. Corrigan

Without the Irish the English-speaking theatre of the past three hundred years wouldn't have been much. From the time the London theatres reopened in 1660 until the angry young men took them over after the Second World War, there haven't been many English playwrights of note who were not Irish. Think how impoverished the Restoration and eighteenth-century drama would be without Congreve, Farquhar, Goldsmith, and Sheridan—all Irishmen! In the nineteenth century all of the best English writers wrote in other forms (and what attempts they made at writing for the theatre were not very successful). English theatre then, such as it was, was popular and diversionary; and, again, the best of its practitioners was Dion Boucicault, an Irishman. Near the end of the century the British theatre began to revive, thanks to the talents and efforts of Oscar Wilde and George Bernard Shaw. Shaw, indeed, pretty well dominated the twentieth-century theatre until shortly before his death. It is hardly necessary to add that Wilde and Shaw were also Irish. It would appear that the Irish have highly developed histrionic sensibilities and a flair for the dramatic.

However, this is not what most people consider the Irish drama to be. Invariably, we think of the Irish literary renaissance and the emergence of the Abbey Theatre with its Lady Gregory, Yeats, Synge, and O'Casey. This is as it should be, but it is a little misleading. The Abbey under Yeats was the first and only flowering of the theatre on Irish soil. As such it was a kind of cultural island which needs explaining. Until Yeats and his colleagues—particularly Lady Gregory, George Moore, and Æ—made a concerted effort to create a national literature, most Irish writers went to England or Paris to make their careers. But these efforts, coming as they did in the last years that Ireland was an isolated and rural land, its people dominated by folk customs and living by an agrarian economy, could not be the the the beginning of anything. The Abbey Theatre was a magnificent monument to a vital but unheralded past. The revolution came in 1917 and Ireland—whether it wanted to or not—had to join the rest of the world. With the coming of technology and industrialization, the spirit of the Abbey died and Ireland's playwrights have had to begin all over again—in exile.

William Butler Yeats was one of the greatest poets of the English language. He did not achieve such stature as a playwright. He might have had he lived at another time. The fact is that the Abbey Theatre soon became a European theatre and not the birthplace of a new Ireland. Yeats could write in more or less conventional modes (witness *The Countess Cathleen*) but they did not satisfy him. As a romantic, he wanted a theatre which would capture the poetic spirit of Ireland's glorious past. But the Abbey audiences weren't interested, and in exasperation Yeats rejected them—at first only a little, and then almost completely. His last plays were aristocratic, esoteric, and could be played successfully only in the rarified atmosphere of a highy cultivated coterie audience. As Yeats retreated to his drawing room, any hopes that the Abbey would become a new "Globe" were shattered. And yet, there is an irony in Yeats' career as a playwright. Although his efforts to create a national theatre failed, he began, in his frustration, to experiment with "new–old" forms, and these experiments have had, and are still having, a tremendous influence on playwrights all over the world. In his attempts to create a purely national drama, Yeats, it turns out, was one of the shapers of the contemporary international theatre.

One of the writers Yeats retrieved from foreign capitals turned out to be the Abbey's greatest playwright. John Millington Synge was in Paris beginning a study of the French symbolist poets when Yeats persuaded him to return to Ireland and write about Irish rural life. It has been often argued that great art usually emerges in periods of decline, that it is an expression of social decadence. Synge's brief career as a dramatist would support this view. Like some of the plays of Sophocles, *The Playboy of the Western World* and *Riders to the Sea* celebrate the values of a world that has either, in fact, disappeared or is about to. There is a spirit of affirmation and life in these plays, but their brightness is like the last shine of a roman candle before it burns out. Christy Mahon "was the only playboy of the western world." And this is the whole point. Ireland was changing fast, and Synge's plays are the final masterpieces of a world that was soon to fall apart.

Sean O'Casey, who followed Synge, was the playwright of this revolution. Ireland had changed, and so had the Abbey. No longer are we in the land of Galway and the Western Islands, but in the *city* of Dublin. Periods of transition are always hospitable to the dramatist (Hebbel had argued that all great drama occurs in periods of transition), and O'Casey's early—and most successful—plays express the turbulence and vitality, the suffering and meaninglessness, of the Irish revolution. But after things quieted down and Ireland became a respectable Anglo–European nation, O'Casey was left resting on his own buoyancy. He had to reject the new Ireland, but he couldn't write about anything else. Thus the long exile to Torquay in England began. Although O'Casey was to try many wild experiments in form and technique, all of his last plays (including the two in this volume) were written in the spirit of the revolution which had long since come to an end. There is a pathetic poignancy in this, and only a man with the spirit of the "Green Crow" could have kept cawing as long as he did, when deep in his heart he probably knew there was nothing to caw about.

But in the plays of each of these giants, the Irish flair for the dramatic is clearly discernible. And their spirit lives on, although now—as I said earlier—in exile. First, there was O'Neill in America and then Denis Johnston; Brendan Behan had it in excess in London; Samuel Beckett has it more quietly in Paris; and some new writers—Patrick Galvin and Donagh MacDonagh—have tried to bring it back to Dublin. All evidence indicates that while the Golden Age of the Irish theatre lasted only a short while, the Irishman's age-old capacity to create a language which sings on the stage has not waned.

MASTERS OF THE MODERN THEATRE

by Robert W. Corrigan

AFTER VISITING the United States in 1835, Alexis de Tocqueville described the kind of literature he believed an industrialized democratic society would produce. "I am persuaded," he wrote in *Democracy in America*, "that in the end democracy diverts the imagination from all that is external to man and fixes it on man alone.... It may be foreseen in like manner that poets living in democratic times will prefer the delineation of passions and ideas to that of persons and achievements. The language, the dress, and the daily actions of men in democracies are repugnant to conceptions of the ideal.... This forces the poet constantly to search below the external surface which is palpable to the senses, in order to read the inner soul.... The destinies of mankind, man himself taken aloof from his country, and his age, and standing in the presence of Nature and of God, with his passions, his doubts, his rare prosperities and inconceivable wretchedness, will become the chief, if not the sole theme of poetry." Any examination of the arts of the past century would seem to indicate that Tocqueville's prophecy has been fulfilled, and it is certainly clear that the theatre's general pattern of development during this time can be best described as a gradual but steady shift away from universal philosophical and social concerns toward the crises and conflicts of man's inner and private life. It is possible to discover foreshadowings of this change in direction and emphasis in the plays of the early nineteenth-century romantics—Buechner, Hebbel, Kleist, Gogol, Musset—but it was not until Ibsen that the theatre's revolutionary break with the past became clearly discernible. In fact, Ibsen's career as a playwright to a large extent parallels both in form and in theme the modern drama's increasing tendency to be concerned more with the conflicts of the individual's interior world than with the significance of his public deeds.

The causes of any revolution are always as difficult to untangle as its consequences are to assess, and any attempt on the part of the critic to describe them will inevitably result in oversimplification. But it is possible to discover certain basic changes in attitude which had been evolving in Europe since the time of Luther and which had begun to crystallize in Continental thought by the second half of the nineteenth century. And the works of the revolutionary playwrights—Ibsen, Strindberg, Chekhov, Shaw, and Hauptmann—were the first to express in the theatre certain of these radical shifts in the way man had come to think of nature, society, and himself. What follows is an attempt to set forth briefly some of the more important aspects of this revolution in the drama which Ibsen referred to as "a war to the knife with the past."

One of the dominant ideas of the modern *Weltanschauung* is the belief that it is impossible to know what the world is really like. Beginning with Luther's refusal to accept that there was any intelligible relationship between faith and works, the sacramental view of experience gradually disappeared. In rejecting the phenomenal world as an outward and visible manifestation of man's spiritual condition, Luther began a revolution in thought which, because of the achievements of science and technology in the past two hundred years, now makes it impossible for man to attach any objective value to the observations of his senses. This insistence on such a clear-cut division between the physical and the spiritual aspects of reality had a profound effect on the modern dramatist. Inevitably, it made him increasingly distrustful of his sensory responses to the "outside" world, and at the same time it tended to negate whatever belief he might have had in the objective validity of his subjective feelings and sensations. The modern artist no longer holds a mirror up to nature, at least not with any confidence; he can only stare at his own image. He becomes a voyeur to his own existence.

Probably no force in the nineteenth century did more to destroy man's belief in an established norm of human nature, and hence begin this process of internalization in the theatre, than the advent of psychology as a systematized field of study. In his book *"Modernism" in The Modern Drama*, Joseph Wood Krutch argued that the basic issue confronting all the dramatists of the past hundred years was the problem of "modernism." Briefly, modernism involves both the conviction and the practice that to be modern is to be, in many important ways, different from anyone who lived before. This does not mean that man has changed; human nature is the same, but man's way of looking at himself has changed significantly. It is this new view of man that creates the problem for the dramatist.

Good examples of this changed perception can be found in Ibsen's *Hedda Gabler* (1890) and Strindberg's *Miss Julie* (1888). Hedda and Julie have the distinction of being the first fully and consciously developed neurotic heroines in dramatic literature. By neurotic we mean that they are neither logical nor insane (in the sense of being random and unaccountable) but that the aims and motives of each has a secret personal logic of their own. The significant thing about both characters is that they are motivated by the premise that there is a secret, and sometimes unconscious, world of aims and methods, a secret system of values which is more important in human experience than rational ones. This approach to character is not, however, the same as the Romantic attitude which affirms the superior validity of the nonrational. We need only read Strindberg's famous Preface to *Miss Julie* or Ibsen's working notes for *Hedda Gabler* to discover that they did not believe, as did the nineteenth-century Romantic poets, that the irrational was a supernatural and unknowable force; rather, in giving detailed account of why their heroines behaved as they did, Ibsen and Strindberg insisted that neurotic behavior and mysterious events are always explainable in terms of natural causes. The significant difference is that neither of these characters can be explained or judged by a common standard; the actions of each character (and by extension, of each human being) are explicable only in terms of that peculiar combination of forces, frustrations, and desires which is unique to himself.

For us living in the middle of the twentieth century there is nothing very new in these psychological ideas; but, coming when they did, they were quite revolutionary, and they have created problems for the playwright which have not yet been solved. By convincingly demonstrating that normal people are not as rational as they seem, and that abnormal people do not act in a random and unintelligible way, psychology has made it difficult, if not impossible, for the dramatist to present his characters in a direct way. In earlier times when it was believed that there was a sharp distinction between the sane and the insane, the irrational "aberrations" of human behavior were dramatically significant because they could be defined in terms of a commonly accepted standard of sane conduct. It seems clear, for instance, that Shakespeare believed Lear on the heath to be insane, while it is equally clear that Macbeth at the witches' cauldron was not. But for the modern dramatist deeds do not necessarily mean what they appear to mean, and in themselves they are not directly revelatory of the characters who commit them. Miss Julie, Hedda Gabler, and Kostya Treplev of Chekhov's *The Sea Gull* are all suicides; but, unlike Othello's suicide, the meaning of each of their deaths cannot be clearly ascertained from the actions that preceded it. The plight of the modern dramatist in this regard becomes apparent when we realize that without Strindberg's Preface or Ibsen's Notebook we could never know for certain what the significance of each heroine's death really was. And the ambiguity of almost every interpretation of *The Sea Gull* is largely due to the fact that Chekhov never made the meaning to Treplev's suicide explicit.

All drama of the past is based upon the axiom "By their deeds shall ye know them." The significance of the dramatic hero was revealed by his deeds, and there was a direct relationship between the hero's overt acts and his inner spiritual condition. The significance of Oedipus, for instance, is revealed by his deeds, not by some explanation that he is suffering from an Oedipus complex; and there is a direct relationship between the act of tearing out his own eyes and his solving the riddle of the Sphinx. Even when a character commits a dissembling deed, it is to deceive the other characters in the play, not the spectators. Certainly one of the chief functions of the soliloquy in Elizabethan drama was to keep the audience informed as to what was going on. Hamlet may put on an antic disposition, but not before he tells the audience he is going to do so. However, beginning in the nineteenth century, the drama began to reflect man's growing distrust in the ability of his senses to comprehend the true nature of reality. Appearances are no longer believed to be direct reflections of ideal reality, like the shadows on the wall of Plato's cave; rather they are thought of as a mask which hides or distorts reality. And by the time of Pirandello, particularly in such plays as *Right You Are, If You Think You Are*

(1916), *Six Characters in Search of an Author* (1921), and *The Mock Emperor* (*Enrico IV*) (1922), appearances not only do not express reality, they contradict it, and the meaning of these plays is not to be found in appearance or reality but in the contradiction itself.

One of the great achievements of the Elizabethan dramatic form was its ability to express several levels of experience simultaneously. The world of Hamlet is both public and private, a world in which personal and familial relationships, fantasy and mystery, and political and psychological conflict co-exist in a state of constant dramatic tension. One of the main reasons why the Elizabethan dramatic form works so successfully is that appearances can be taken at face value. But when the dramatist begins to distrust the validity of his sensory perceptions, it becomes difficult, if not impossible, for him to dramatize the complex totality of experience in a single form. Reality must be broken down into its component parts, and each part can be expressed only in a form peculiar to itself. Admitting individual differences in the works of each dramatist's writing of any given period, it is nonetheless possible to describe with some accuracy the dramatic form employed by the playwrights of the fifth-century Greek theatre, the Elizabethan and Restoration theatres of England, and the French neo-classic theatre of the seventeenth century. But in discussing the modern theatre we must always speak of forms, for there is no single, dominant form in the serious theatre of the past hundred years. It is for this reason that the evolution of the drama since the time of Shakespeare has been so aptly described as a process of fragmentation.

It is likely that every serious dramatist believes it his artistic duty to be true to his presuppositions about the real nature of the world in which he lives. However, once a playwright believes that the meaning of every human action is relative and intelligible only in terms of a unique and subsurface combination of forces, the dramatic events of the plot cease to have meaning in themselves, and they take on significance only as the secret motivations of the characters who participate in them are revealed. (The technique of earlier drama is just the reverse: the motivations of the characters are revealed by the events of the plot.) But how does the dramatist objectify the hidden and unconscious, and what happens to the theatre when he feels obligated to explain and probe into his characters' hidden lives? Explanation is always a dangerous business in the theatre (since the time of the ancient Greeks, exposition has always been the dramatist's most difficult problem), but the moment a playwright assumes that if he explains his characters he has written a play, that danger becomes mortal. All too often the writers of the modern theatre have forgotten that a dramatic situation requires not that we *understand* a character but simply that we *believe* in him. Dramatic action always leads to a judgment; it requires that something shall happen to and through the characters; something that is embodied in the events of which the characters are a part. Whenever the personality of the character, rather than the action of which the character should be a part, becomes the playwright's chief concern, dramatic process dissolves into explanation, and when that occurs, the range of the theatre is drastically reduced, if not unalterably damaged.

One has only to compare the plays of the mid-twentieth century to those of Ibsen, Shaw, or Strindberg to realize just how much the scope of the theatre has been narrowed. However, early evidence of the gradual loss of belief in dramatic heroes, who needed no explaining, can be found in the sentimental bourgeois drama of the eighteenth century. For the first time a character was no longer noble, responsible, or morally significant, and therefore dramatically interesting just because of his birth, position, power, or wealth. As a result, the dramatist was obliged to justify both his choice of characters and the situations in which they are engaged. The Romantic drama of the eighteenth and nineteenth centuries resisted a break with the past and attempted unsuccessfully to perpetuate the forms and figures of earlier times. Certainly the revolt of Ibsen and his contemporaries in the last quarter of the nineteenth century was in some measure due to their conviction that the dramatic conflicts of the Romantic drama were inflated and without significance, and that the nobility of its characters was artificial and contrived. In rejecting the artificialities of Romanticism, the modernists changed the theatre in many ways; but for all their dissatisfaction with their predecessors they were unable to forestall disbelief in the possibility of heroic characters who needed no explaining.

This was largely because as a literary movement nineteenth-century naturalism was so closely related to nineteenth-century biology. Darwin's theories of evolution (*Origin of Species*, 1859) and the discovery of new genetic laws had convinced many writers that man's existence, including his personality, was a phenomenon that could be explained in terms of scientific laws. As a result, increasingly, man's complex biological needs rather than his capacity to make moral choices were thought to be his most significant characteristic. Once such a view was accepted, however, the exceptional man, who because of his position and power had the greatest freedom of choice, ceased to be the fullest embodiment, and therefore the best representative, of those conflicts and choices that most clearly define the human condition. Instead, the lives of the poor—where the role of natural necessity is most readily observable— became the playwright's most suitable subjects. The drama of the common man, then, did not happen by accident, nor did it evolve because some dramatist or group of dramatists wanted it to. Given the problem of creating in a world in which all human actions tend to be explained in terms of psychological or sociological cause and effect, a world in which the possibility of deliberative and moral choice is doubted if not rejected outright, it is difficult, if not impossible, for the playwright to fashion a character of traditional heroic stature.

There is an old saw about no man being a hero to his valet. Neither is he one to his psychoanalyst. Nor can he be one to a playwright who views his actions as behavioral phenomena explicable in terms of some kind of laws—scientific or otherwise. Oedipus, for example, remains a hero of great stature so long as he is not suffering from an Oedipus complex. But once we learn to explain him in terms of repressed hopes and fears, traumatic childhood experience, or a vitamin deficiency in infancy, although he may remain interesting—in fact he may gain a new kind of interest, as Cocteau's *The Infernal Machine* attests—he loses stature. Even if we are able, temporarily to accept the Elizabethan attitude toward heroes, which of us can understand a Hamlet or a Lear? And which of us can forgive an Othello or a Macbeth? But it is precisely because they seem mysteriously beyond our powers of understanding that they remain heroes for us. And it is a belief in a mysterious, unknowable quality in men that substantiates man's sense of his own importance in the universe. However, if a playwright comes to believe that all human actions are in reality predictable behavioral responses, and his moral judgments of these actions can be dissolved by psychological understanding, how can he pattern a tragedy or create characters with stature? If there can be no possibility for an appraisal of personality as such, why should Hamlet's death be any more significant than that of Rosencrantz and Guildenstern?

But the problem does not end here. For once the dramatist dismisses the possibility of passing moral judgments on his characters' actions, he comes face to face with an even more frightening spectre—guilt that has no form of expiation and thus turns into anxiety. It has long been known that art must ultimately fail in its attempt to come to grips with the facts of death. Perhaps this is also true of anxiety. How can there be drama in an Age of Anxiety? What kind of play will be produced when the central conflict is between something and nothing? Many of the arts may be able to express the condition of anxiety; but the theatre, because of the objective reality and irremovable presence of the living actor, and because the drama is essentially an embodiment of the conflict between at least two opposing recognizable and nameable forces, is incapable of dealing with anxiety, or it does so to its own great peril. Beginning with the Watchman in the opening scene of the *Orestia* right on through the ghosts of Elsinore and the tormented heroes of Schiller and Kleist, the theatre has always found a way to transform anxiety into fear; that is, give it a definite object. But when we come to such plays as Ibsen's *Ghosts* and *The Master Builder* and Strindberg's *There Are Crimes and Crimes,* and *The Ghost Sonata,* we discover that although this process of objectification is attempted, it is not totally successful. And when the transformation does not take place, the form and content of drama begin to change in uncontrollable ways, as some of the plays of Beckett and Ionesco, Pinter and Albee will attest. It is difficult enough to find a meaning for man in a world that views a return to nothingness as the ultimate reality, but it is next to impossible to create a dramatic "action" which can encompass the terror of being on the edge of the abyss. Kierkegaard, and more recently Paul Tillich, have declared that this threat of nothingness is the central anxiety of modern man. Many modern playwrights have sought to overcome the despair of this situation by maintaining that the only meaning of life is to be found in that death which is inevitable. But this is not an assertion that gives meaning to any of the particularities of life; in fact, it drains them of meaning. At best, it is a method of redeeming existence from meaningless anarchy by showing that the pattern of life is simple and imperturbable. But such a pattern, though it may appear to conquer chaos, is too abstract to live successfully in the theatre.

In life as we experience it, we are conscious of our physical natures, our social situation, and our unique psychic existence; and we live on all three of these levels simultaneously. For this reason it is impossible for us to act or make a choice without some element of human behavior— what we do out of physical necessity or because of social habit—playing a significant role in our decision. At the same time, because of the simultaneity of our being, it is impossible for us to understand completely the individuality of our actions. But in the theatre we see life as pure deed, that is, life in which the arbitrariness of human behavior has been eliminated and in which the mysterious transformations of individuality have been fixed. Thus, in contrast to a person in life, who is recognized by the continuity of his being and finally can only be known through intuition, a character in a play is an identity who is defined by the coherence of his acts. For this reason the deeds of a dramatic action are always public, and the characters best suited to drama are men and women who, either by fate or choice, lead a public life and whose deeds are of public concern. This explains why kings, princes, and nobility have traditionally been the most suitable subjects for drama. But as the increasing dominance of the machine in modern life has gradually destroyed the direct relation between a man's intention and his deeds, public figures have ceased to be our most appropriate heroes because, as W. H. Auden points out, "the good and evil they do depends less upon their characters and intentions than upon the quantity of impersonal force at their disposal."

Our world, it would seem, has become almost too big for the playwright. Power is too impersonal, great deeds are collective achievements, and the great man is one who is capable of withstanding some of the pressures of a mass society and manages, somehow, to maintain a face and stance more or less his own. Compare, for example, the achievement of a Lindbergh (our last "lone" hero) to that of a Colonel Glenn, who was interchangeable with five other astronauts. Or, how can the power of a Napoleon be envisioned today? In our times power is so enormous that it is barely visible and those who govern are little more than incidental and easily replaceable expressions of that power. Power is like an iceberg; the largest part is submerged—in abstraction, anonymity, and bureaucracy. Government, like modern physics, has lost its physical reality and can be expressed only in statistics and formulae. Indeed, the true men of action in our time, those who transform the world, are not the statesmen and politicians but the scientists. Unfortunately, their most significant actions are not suitable subjects for the theatre, because their deeds are concerned with things, not people, and are, therefore, speechless.

But what are the implications of this for the theatre? Who are the true representatives of a world whose heroes are nameless? As the Swiss playwright Duerrenmatt put it: "Any small-time crook, petty government official, or policeman better represents our world than a senator or president. Today art can only embrace victims if it can reach men at all; it can no longer come close to the mighty. Creon's secretaries close Antigone's case."

That there has been a shift in attitude toward the heroic is easily seen when we examine any one of the many modern adaptations of the Greek tragedies. For example, today most people find Anouilh's *Antigone* much more a reflection of their attitudes and thus more immediately interesting than Sophocles' tragic working of the theme. The characters and the dilemma of their situation seem more human. Antigone is not a hard and almost inhuman girl, with such a monomaniacal fixity of purpose that she rejects all other feelings and desires. In the modern version she is, humanly, both weak and strong. She has a lover in Haemon, whom she rejects; but she is also a helpless little girl who runs to "Nanny" for comfort and strength; as she approaches death, she is afraid and seeks the consolations of even the most callous of guards. Creon is not a blind and power-mad tyrant; he is a businessman king who is caught in the complex web of compromise and expediency which will not allow abstract moral principles to upset the business of government.

However, what the play gains in humanity it loses in tragic force. The sense of Antigone's aloneness and Creon's moral blindness, and of the inevitable destruction implicit in their conflict, has been softened. Anouilh's Antigone is not alone and unloved, and his Creon is not blind. We pity their situation because they are two quite attractive people caught up in a situation which neither of them likes but which they cannot control. They are victims in a disordered world which they have not created and which they have no moral obligation to correct. As the play ends, we are left with an ambiguity that allows for no reconciliation.

One of the most important functions of the hero, both in art and life, is to supply those images, values, and ethical standards which people aspire to and which they would like, if possible, to incorporate into their own lives. It would seem, however, that increasingly our modern industrialized society not only does not need heroes, but it actually suppresses or perverts our need of them. In their important book *Industrialism and Industrial Man*, Kerr, Dunlop, Harbison, and Myers convincingly demonstrate that "like ideologies, the great personality—the one great figure around whom historians so frequently weave their story—began to seem less important. Instead of ideologies and dominant personalties, we became increasingly attentive to the inherent nature of the particular industrializing system and the basic strategy and forces at work within it." Only the system, then, is important, and it fills men's remaining need for heroes by promoting celebrities, those heroes of the surface who play well their constantly shifting roles.

Furthermore, specialization—the key operative principle of an industrial society—produces not only pluralism in our economic system but also a pluralistic deviation of heroic types. However, when there are and can be so many heroic types—one cannot even begin to count all the heroes of the popular imagination—you begin to get a leveling; and with that leveling not only is the stature of heroism diminished, but the individual's sense of his own identity is actually invalidated.

Traditionally, the hero is always best described in terms of those forces that urge him to spiritual redemption. Maxwell Anderson once wrote that "from the point of view of the playwright, the essence of a tragedy, or even a serious play, is the spiritual awakening, or regeneration, of his hero." But the one thing that characterizes the hero of surfaces—and this is certainly in large measure due to industrialization and bureaucracy—is precisely the fact that he lacks the dimensions of spiritual awareness, personal morality, and social responsibility. Paul Tillich wrote in his *The Religious Situation* that "the fundamental value in ethics of a capitalistic society is economic efficiency—developed to the utmost degree of ruthless activity." Such an ethical standard is hardly conducive to the creation of great heroes in the drama.

That we live in an antiheroic age is a commonplace. Carlyle proclaimed its coming in the nineteenth century when he said: "We shall either learn to know a hero . . . when we see him, or else go on to be forever governed by the unheroic." This transformation has occurred; we have accepted it; we are even used to it. Whatever nostalgia we may still occasionally feel is more than adequately taken care of by television. In the place of the hero we have the celebrity, that triumph of the ordinary. In our time, hero worship has become horizontal; indeed, we even look down to a "man like myself."

While the advent of psychology as a systematized field of study may have been the most powerful single force to shape the modern theatre, actually the process of internalization had begun much earlier. For instance, it is clear from Hebbel's essays on the drama that the despair of old Anton's "I don't understand the world any more" in the final scene of *Maria Magdalena* is much more than an expression of the age-old frustration of the parent who does not understand the behavior of his children. It also reflects his dimly understood but tremendously painful realization that it is no longer possible for him to comprehend what the world has become or to imagine what the future will be like. Until the Industrial Revolution, patterns of life were passed on from father to son with the confidence that these patterns would satisfy the needs and desires of each new generation. Such confidence was justified, for life changed so gradually and imperceptibly that when changes did occur they were easily assimilated into the shared life of the community. But by the middle of the nineteenth century the effects of the Industrial Revolution had begun to be felt on all levels of society. Technology, with its ever increasing capacity to transform man's way of living, not only made the future so unpredictable that it soon became impossible for him to imagine what his life would be like twenty years hence, but in its singular concern with the individual's functional qualities technology tended to isolate him from his fellows and invalidate his spiritual values and metaphysical concerns. At the same time, the discoveries of the nineteenth-century archeologists, and the ensuing interest in anthropology, tended to break down provincial and absolutist attitudes concerning human nature. Early anthropologists like Mannhardt, Robertson-Smith, Tylor, and the great James Frazer made it clear that human nature was not something fixed and unchanging but only that kind of behavior exhibited in each culture. In fact, as early as 1860 scholars were demonstrating that human nature is so plastic that it can, as Frazer was later to point out in the Preface to the first edition of *The Golden Bough* (1890), "exhibit varieties of behavior which, in the animal Kingdom could only be exhibited by different species." Furthermore, by the middle of the century, democracy was finally beginning to be established both as a way of life and as a form of government. Today we tend to forget what a revolutionary idea democracy is and the shattering effects that it had upon the values of eighteenth- and nineteenth-century Europe. Alexis de Tocqueville told us long ago: "Not only does democracy make every man forget his ancestors, but it hides his descendants and separates his contemporaries from him, it throws him back forever upon himself alone and threatens in the end to confine him entirely within the solitude of his own heart." In short, by the middle of the nineteenth century every established view of God, human nature, social organization, and the physical universe was beginning to be seriously challenged if not invalidated. And this revolutionary climate had a profound effect on the theatre.

Of all the arts, theatre is the only art that has always concerned itself with human destinies. Dramatic action is historical in the sense that the perpetual present of each moment on the stage is created out of past events and is directed toward a definite, if yet unknown, future. In previous ages the destiny of any dramatic action was significant because the ever-changing events in the lives of dramatic heroes could be meaningfully related to eternity, that is, to some permanent value or idea such as Fate, the Gods, or Heaven and Hell, which transcends the human condition and which is believed in by the dramatist and/or his audience.

In the plays of Buechner and Hebbel we discover the first indications in the theatre of that sense of alienation from both God and Society which underscores the fact that man's belief in eternity had been shaken. And one of the most significant aspects of Ibsen's work (at least after *Peer Gynt*, 1867) is the fact that the realm of ultimate value had either disappeared or has become so mysterious that it has ceased to have dramatic relevance. In its place we find instead a belief in some form of social ideal or societal structure;

first, as the agent of some unknown Destiny, and then as Destiny itself. But when society begins to assume the role of Destiny, that is, is thought of as the determining force for good or evil in the lives of men, man cannot help but feel eventually that the meaning of his Destiny has been drastically reduced. For Society, as Robert Bolt writes in the Preface to his *A Man for All Seasons*, "can only have as much idea as we have what we are about, for it has only our brains to think with. And the individual who tries to plot his position by reference to our society finds no fixed points, but only the vaunted absence of them, 'freedom' and 'opportunity'; freedom for what, opportunity to do what, is nowhere indicated. The only positive he is given is 'get and spend' . . . and he did not need society to tell him that. In other words we are thrown back by our society upon ourselves, which of course sends us flying back to society with all the force of rebound."

Any mind capable of spiritual aspiration seeks in the actions of the dramatic hero that which affirms the vitality of the free will in any given situation. Man's free will may be defeated by the forces of Destiny—in fact, the great plays have always testified that the destroying forces of Destiny are as much a part of the hero's character as his free will; it may be paralyzed and thus incapable of action; it may be submerged by the battle in such a way as to become part of that Destiny; it may even turn out to be an illusion; but it must always be an active force if we are to believe that we are partaking in human greatness. Such a Destiny must be greater than an aggregate of human beings or an expression of social patterns.

Ironically, the revolt of Ibsen and Shaw against the conventional nineteenth-century drama was motivated by a desire to enlarge the range of Destiny in the theatre. In their attempts to present men in his total historical and social setting, they were rebelling against the narrow and private worlds that had been dominating the stage since the Restoration. But in spite of their efforts, nothing could change the fact that in the two hundred years since Shakespeare the world of the spirit had greatly diminished. The Ekdals' attic and Mrs. Warren's drawing room were not—and never could be—the same as Elsinore or Cleopatra's barge.

Nonetheless, the pioneers of the modern drama had revitalized the theatre precisely because they believed that significant social issues should be dealt with in the theatre. Thus for nearly three decades the theatre had a vitality of spirit and a forcefulness of manner which it had lacked for more than a century for the very reason that its context had been reduced. To the playwright writing at that time the human and social problems, which were the source materials of the naturalistic play, appeared capable of solution if only man and society would learn to use their common sense; which usually meant one of two things—the acceptance of a less rigid standard of social morality or the espousal of some form of socialism. But with the collapse of the established social order in the first World War, the validity of these too-easy solutions was impugned, and beginning with the plays of the early German Expressionists (written 1912-1916) the positive optimism of the Edwardian era gave way to a sense of bewilderment, exasperation, and defeatism, only occasionally tempered by the slim hope that the war had brought man to the threshold of a "New Age." The theatre reflects these changes from confidence to doubting and despair, from complacent faith in cherished values to an anxious questioning, from a rigorous but rigid morality to the mystic evangelism, the fanatical polemics, and the frivolous apathy of a disintegrating world. These changes are most apparent in the Jekyll and Hyde theatre of the German Expressionists whose nerve-shattered playwrights alternated between a militant idealism and grotesque nightmares. But one need only compare Shaw's *Heartbreak House* to *Major Barbara*, Pirandello's *Right You Are, If You Think You Are* to *Liolá*, or Hauptmann's *Winter Ballad* to *The Weavers* to realize that the effects of the collapse of the old order were widespread and were reflected in the works of established writers as well as those of the new generation. Immediately after the war the theatre on the continent was dominated by attitudes of emotionalism and cynicism, but these gradually gave way to feelings of frustration, futility, and despair, and by the middle of the 1920's the serious drama of Europe had become almost totally introspective and psychological in its orientation.[1]

[1] Because they were essentially isolated from the main currents of European history in the first two decades of the century, the Irish and American theatres were not immediately effected by the spreading paralysis which was transforming the rest of modern drama. But it is clear from O'Casey's *The Plow and the Stars* (1926) and *The Silver Tassie* (1927) that the Abbey Theatre could not withstand for long the theatre's introspective tendencies,

Obviously, this tendency toward paralyzing introspection has by no means been accepted by everyone writing for the theatre. In fact, a large segment of the modern theatre might be best described as a reaction against the despair and dehumanizing implications of the modernist position. These "resistance movements" have sought to discover the means, both formal and substantive, whereby the possibility and validity of selfhood and human integrity, personal responsibility, and morally significant judgments could be reasserted in the theatre. Some playwrights—especially Eliot, Fry, Betti, and Claudel—have turned to orthodox Christian belief to provide a metaphysical structure for their drama. Others, like Lorca and Synge, have written out of the traditions and value systems of premodern hieratic societies. Probably the largest group of all is composed of those dramatists who have sought to escape the deadly strictures of modernism by turning to classical mythology.

All of these writers shared one common and fundamental attitude: each of them was in some way rebelling against the conditions of the modern world. They were not only conscious of that lack of a sense of community which inevitably occurs in an increasingly democratic society; more important, they were aware of man's growing sense of his own isolation. The modern world, with its growing collectivism, paradoxically tends to throw man back upon himself, while at the same time it increasingly tends to destroy the individual's sense of his own selfhood. This creates an impasse which the modern dramatist, for the most part, has been unable to overcome.

Joseph Warren Beach, in analyzing the problems of modern fiction, describes the reaction of many writers to this condition in this way: "One of the hardest things for man to bear is spiritual isolation. The sense that he stands alone in the universe goes terribly against his gregarious instincts. He has an over-powering impulse to construct a system which will enable him to feel that he does not stand alone but is intimately associated with some force or group infinitely

---

and there was no serious American drama until O'Neill's plays were first produced right after the war. In the twenty years between O'Neill's *Beyond the Horizon* (1920) and *The Iceman Cometh* (1941) the American theatre repeated the Continental cycle in its own terms, and by the beginning of the Second World War all of the Western theatre had reached that No Man's Land between comedy and tragedy, between pathetic aspirations and ridiculous bewilderment, between never-beginning action and never-ending talk.

more powerful and significant than himself." It is clearly
evident in the work of all those playwrights who have re-
belled against modernism that they too are seeking to construct a system that will restore meaning to life and validity
to art. In the end, however, they have not been completely
successful, because they have all too often had to deny the
realities of the modern world in the process. Furthermore,
they have not accepted the wisdom of Brecht's statement that
"when one sees that our world of today no longer fits into the
drama, then it is merely that the drama no longer fits into the
world." By insisting upon values that we may once have cherished but which no longer in actuality exist, the playwrights of
the resistance have not been able to revitalize the theatre or
it's audiences. And most important, they have not succeeded
in stretching the imaginations of men in order that they might
conquer that sense of isolation and despair that pervades the
modern world. And this brings us to the playwrights of the
mid-twentieth century.

In an age dominated by space orbits and telestars, the
fear of nuclear war, the tension of cold war diplomacy, and
the insecurity of a defense economy, our greatest uncertainty
is whether or not in the midst of epochal disorder man has
any good chance, to borrow Faulkner's phrase, of prevail-
ing; and if he does, what kind of man will prevail?

This uncertainty has had a profound effect on our theatre,
and if there is one thing that characterizes the work of almost all of our serious playwrights of the last two decades
it is that their plays express the contemporary theatre's tremendous concern to find a metaphor for universal modern
man as he lives on the brink of disaster—a metaphor that ex-
presses the inalienable part of every man, that irreducible part
of each of us that exists after all the differences have been
stripped away and which is beyond and beneath all that is
social, political, economic, religious, and ideological. In short,
they are searching for a metaphor of man left face to face
with himself.

Such an idea of the theatre has tremendous implications
for the drama, and we are just now becoming aware of them.
First of all, it abolishes the traditional linear plot because
our contemporary playwrights are not interested in present-
ing an action in any Aristotelian sense but are, rather, dram-
atizing a condition. Whenever one asks what the central
action of a Beckett, Ionesco, or Pinter play is, he comes a

cropper; "action" for the contemporary playwright is an artificial concept. He is concerned with showing life as it is, and in life there is no central action, there are only people, and the only thing that is basic to each individual is the ontological solitude of his being. The dramatist's only concern is to create in his plays a situation which will reveal the private drama that each man has inside himself and which is enacted every day in the random, apparently meaningless, and undramatic events of our common routine. "History," said James Joyce's Stephen Daedalus, "is a nightmare from which I must awake." The rapidity of historical change and the apparent powerlessness of the individual to affect Collective History has led in the theatre to a retreat from history. Instead of tracing the history of an individual who is born, grows old, and dies, many modern playwrights have devoted their attention to the timeless passionate moments of life, to states of being. They want to express the paradox, the contradiction, and the incompleteness of experience. They are attempting to suggest the raggedness, the confusion, the complexity of motivation, the "discontinuous continuity," and the basic ambiguity of all human behavior. They are, in short, pursuing the premises of modernism to their fullest and most logical conclusions. The writers of the contemporary theatre are facing the "facts of life." If the dramatic meaning of their plays is that drama is no longer possible, they would contend that any other meaning would be artificial, illusory, false; if the dialogue in their plays consists of meaningless clichés and stereotyped phrases, they would insist that this is the way we talk; if their characters are constantly changing their personalties, these playwrights would point out that no one today is really consistent or truly integrated. If the people in their plays seem to be helpless puppets without any will of their own, they would argue that we are all passively at the mercy of blind fate and meaningless circumstance. They call their theatre "Anti-Theatre," and this they insist is the true theatre of our times. If they are correct, so be it! Then history has again followed its own inexorable laws. The very forces that gave life and strength to the modern theatre have caused its decline and death.

But the theatre is always dying, and with equal regularity, like the phoenix, it is resurrected. No one can say with certainty what its new form will be, but that there will be a future seems certain. First, largely because of the development of college and university theatre programs in this country and the large increase in the number of professional repertory theatres here and abroad, there are more people who have experienced good theatre than ever before. And this enlarged audience wants and needs theatre, and it will not be satisfied for long with the maimed rites of psychological and moral cliché, or impassioned jeremiads from prophets of doom, or the meandering contemplations of writers who are morbidly consumed in introspection and self-analysis. Fortunately, there are audiences who want and need the theatre, and they go to the theatre in the hopeful anticipation that the stage will be capable of accommodating all of the terrible-wonderful emotions and insoluble dilemmas of our shared life together. This demand insistence by audiences on a drama that deals with the significant issues and concerns of our public life will, I believe, force our playwrights to open up new frontiers in the drama and thus extend the boundaries of the theatre. The second great hope of the theatre is that, in spite of the overriding temper of despair and the dominance of antitheatricality in current drama, our playwrights still find human action significant, still find it necessary to write plays, and, in the very act of writing, attest to the miracle of life. We live in one of the most dramatic ages in the history of mankind, and if the past is any kind of reliable guide to what the future of the theatre will be, we have good reason to believe that the theatre of tomorrow can be as dramatic as the world in which we live today.

MASTERPIECES OF THE
MODERN IRISH THEATRE

WILLIAM BUTLER YEATS

1865–1939

WILLIAM BUTLER YEATS, for all his greatness as a poet, never had much influence on the modern theatre. Usually we think of him as one of the leading figures of the famous Abbey Theatre in Dublin and the man responsible for encouraging so many writers to participate in the Irish theatrical renaissance. Yeats' own plays, however, tend to be dismissed as the interesting experiments of a great poet—experiments which were too esoteric and aristocratic to be dramatically viable on the popular stage. And yet, now, better than two decades after his death, it would appear that T. S. Eliot's evaluation of Yeats' contribution to modern poetry might apply equally well to the theatre. Yeats was, in Eliot's words, "one of those few whose history is the history of our own time, who are a part of the consciousness of their age, which cannot be understood without them."

Yeats, with his passionate desire to express great complexity within a dramatic form that was simple, direct, organic, and, above all, compressed, wrote a series of plays that foreshadow the work of Beckett, Ionesco, Pinter, and many other contemporary dramatists. Like them, Yeats was unsympathetic to the full-length play. As early as 1906 he was advocating what was to become the credo of a large number of mid-century playwrights: the fusion of tragedy and farce into a single dramatic form. Finally, in his return to the myths, legends, and forms of Greek and Oriental drama to find an artistic form capable of expressing the chaos of the modern world, Yeats developed a strategy which has been followed in some fashion by nearly every serious dramatist of the twentieth century. In short, although there is no evidence of a direct influence on the playwrights who came after him, it is clear that Yeats was a seminal dramatist; his plays pointed out several new directions which the drama would have to take if it was to be relevant to the modern world. The fact that so many playwrights in our own time are following these paths would indicate that Yeats was a pioneer in the theatre as well as in poetry.

THE TRAGIC THEATRE[1]

I DID NOT FIND a word in the printed criticism of Synge's *Deirdre of the Sorrows* about the qualities that made certain moments seem to me the noblest tragedy, and the play was judged by what seemed to me but wheels and pulleys necessary to the effect, but in themselves nothing.

Upon the other hand, those who spoke to me of the play never spoke of these wheels and pulleys, but if they cared at all for the play, cared for the things I cared for. One's own world of painters, of poets, of good talkers, of ladies who delight in Ricard's portraits or Debussy's music, all those whose senses feel instantly every change in our mother the moon, saw the stage in one way; and those others who look at plays every night, who tell the general playgoer whether this play or that play is to his taste, saw it in a way so different that there is certainly some body of dogma—whether in the instincts or in the memory—pushing the ways apart. A printed criticism, for instance, found but one dramatic moment, that when Deirdre in the second act overhears her lover say that he may grow weary of her; and not one—if I remember rightly—chose for praise or explanation the third act which alone had satisfied the author, or contained in any abundance those sentences that were quoted at the fall of the curtain and for days after.

Deirdre and her lover, as Synge tells the tale, returned to Ireland, though it was nearly certain they would die there, because death was better than broken love, and at the side of the open grave that had been dug for one and would serve for both, quarrelled, losing all they had given their life to keep. "Is it not a hard thing that we should miss the safety of the grave and we trampling its edge?" That is Deirdre's cry at the outset of a reverie of passion that mounts and mounts till grief itself has carried her beyond grief into pure

[1] Reprinted with the permission of The Macmillan Company from *Essays and Introductions* by William Butler Yeats. Copyright © 1961 by Mrs. W. B. Yeats.

contemplation. Up to this the play had been a Master's unfinished work, monotonous and melancholy, ill-arranged, little more than a sketch of what it would have grown to, but now I listened breathless to sentences that may never pass away, and as they filled or dwindled in their civility of sorrow, the player, whose art had seemed clumsy and incomplete, like the writing itself, ascended into that tragic ecstasy which is the best that art—perhaps that life—can give. And at last when Deirdre, in the paroxysm before she took her life, touched with compassionate fingers him that had killed her lover, we knew that the player had become, if but for a moment, the creature of that noble mind which had gathered its art in waste islands, and we too were carried beyond time and persons to where passion, living through its thousand purgatorial years, as in the wink of an eye, becomes wisdom; and it was as though we too had touched and felt and seen a disembodied thing.

One dogma of the printed criticism is that if a play does not contain definite character, its constitution is not strong enough for the stage, and that the dramatic moment is always the contest of character with character.

In poetical drama there is, it is held, an antithesis between character and lyric poetry, for lyric poetry—however much it move you when you read out of a book—can, as these critics think, but encumber the action. Yet when we go back a few centuries and enter the great periods of drama, character grows less and sometimes disappears, and there is much lyric feeling, and at times a lyric measure will be wrought into the dialogue, a flowing measure that had well befitted music, or that more lumbering one of the sonnet. Suddenly it strikes us that character is continuously present in comedy alone, and that there is much tragedy, that of Corneille, that of Racine, that of Greece and Rome, where its place is taken by passions and motives, one person being jealous, another full of love or remorse or pride or anger. In writers of tragi-comedy (and Shakespeare is always a writer of tragi-comedy) there is indeed character, but we notice that it is in the moments of comedy that character is defined, in Hamlet's gaiety, let us say; while amid the great moments, when Timon orders his tomb, when Hamlet cries to Horatio "Absent thee from felicity awhile," when Antony names "Of many thousand kisses the poor last," all is lyricism, unmixed passion, "the integrity of fire." Nor does character ever attain to complete definition in these lamps ready for the taper, no matter how circumstantial and gradual the opening of events, as it does in Falstaff, who has no passionate purpose to fulfil, or as it does in Henry V, whose poetry, never touched by lyric heat, is oratorical; nor when the tragic reverie is at its height do we say, "How well that man is realized! I should know him were I to meet him in the street," for it is always ourselves that we see upon the stage, and should it be a tragedy of love, we renew, it may be, some loyalty of our youth, and go from the theatre with our eyes dim for an old love's sake.

I think it was while rehearsing a translation of *Les Fourberies de Scapin*[2] in Dublin, and noticing how passionless it all was, that I saw what should have been plain from the first line I had written, that tragedy must always be a drowning and breaking of the dykes that separate man from man, and that it is upon these dykes comedy keeps house. But I was not certain of the site of that house (one always hesitates when there is no testimony but one's own) till somebody told me of a certain letter of Congreve's. He describes the external and superficial expressions of "humour" on which farce is founded and then defines "humour" itself—the foundation of comedy—as a "singular and unavoidable way of doing anything peculiar to one man only, by which his speech and actions are distinguished from all other men," and adds to it that "passions are too powerful in the sex to let humour have its course," or, as I would rather put it, that you can find but little of what we call character in unspoiled youth, whatever be the sex, for, as he indeed shows in another sentence, it grows with time like the ash of a burning stick, and strengthens towards middle life till there is little else at seventy years.

Since then I have discovered an antagonism between all the old art and our new art of comedy and understand why I hated at nineteen years Thackeray's novels and the new French painting. A big picture of *cocottes* sitting at little tables outside a café, by some followers of Manet, was exhibited at the Royal Hibernian Academy while I was a student at a life class there, and I was miserable for days. I found no desirable place, no man I could have wished to be, no woman I could have loved, no Golden Age, no lure for secret hope, no adventure with myself for theme out of that endless tale

[2] A play by Molière.

I told myself all day long. Years after, I saw the *Olympia* of Manet at the Luxembourg and watched it without hostility indeed, but as I might some incomparable talker whose precision of gesture gave me pleasure, though I did not understand his language. I returned to it again and again at intervals of years, saying to myself, "Some day I will understand"; and yet it was not until Sir Hugh Lane brought the *Eva Gonzales* to Dublin, and I had said to myself, "How perfectly that woman is realized as distinct from all other women that have lived or shall live," that I understood I was carrying on in my own mind that quarrel between a tragedian and a comedian which the Devil on Two Sticks in Le Sage[3] showed to the young man who had climbed through the window.

There is an art of the flood, the art of Titian when his *Ariosto*, and his *Bacchus and Ariadne*, give new images to the dreams of youth, and of Shakespeare when he shows us Hamlet broken away from life by the passionate hesitations of his reverie. And we call this art poetical, because we must bring more to it than our daily mood if we would take our pleasure; and because it takes delight in the moment of exaltation, of excitement, of dreaming (or in the capacity for it, as in that still face of Ariosto's that is like some vessel soon to be full of wine). And there is an art that we call real, because character can only express itself perfectly in a real world, being that world's creature, and because we understand it best through a delicate discrimination of the senses which is but entire wakefulness, the daily mood grown cold and crystalline.

We may not find either mood in its purity, but in mainly tragic art one distinguishes devices to exclude or lessen character, to diminish the power of that daily mood, to cheat or blind its too clear perception. If the real world is not altogether rejected, it is but touched here and there, and into the places we have left empty we summon rhythm, balance, pattern, images that remind us of vast passions, the vagueness of past times, all the chimeras that haunt the edge of trance; and if we are painters, we shall express personal emotion through ideal form, a symbolism handled by the generations, a mask from whose eyes the disembodied looks, a style that remembers many masters that it may escape contemporary suggestion; or we shall leave out some element of reality as in Byzantine painting, where there is no mass, nothing in

[3] Alain René LeSage (1668–1747).

relief; and so it is that in the supreme moment of tragic art there comes upon one that strange sensation as though the hair of one's head stood up. And when we love, if it be in the excitement of youth, do we not also, that the flood may find no stone to convulse, no wall to narrow it, exclude character or the signs of it by choosing that beauty which seems unearthly because the individual woman is lost amid the labyrinth of its lines as though life were trembling into stillness and silence, or at last folding itself away? Some little irrelevance of line, some promise of character to come, may indeed put us at our ease, "give more interest" as the humour of the old man with the basket does to Cleopatra's dying; but should it come, as we had dreamed in love's frenzy, to our dying for that woman's sake, we would find that the discord had its value from the tune. Nor have we chosen illusion in choosing the outward sign of that moral genius that lives among the subtlety of the passions, and can for her moment make her of the one mind with great artists and poets. In the studio we may indeed say to one another, "Character is the only beauty," but when we choose a wife, as when we go to the gymnasium to be shaped for woman's eyes, we remember academic form, even though we enlarge a little the point of interest and choose "a painter's beauty," finding it the more easy to believe in the fire because it has made ashes.

When we look at the faces of the old tragic paintings, whether it is in Titian or in some painter of mediaeval China, we find there sadness and gravity, a certain emptiness even, as of a mind that waited the supreme crisis (and indeed it seems at times as if the graphic art, unlike poetry which sings the crisis itself, were the celebration of waiting). Whereas in modern art, whether in Japan or Europe, "vitality" (is not that the great word of the studios?), the energy, that is to say, which is under the command of our common moments, sings, laughs, chatters or looks its busy thoughts.

Certainly we have here the Tree of Life and that of the Knowledge of Good and Evil which is rooted in our interests, and if we have forgotten their differing virtues it is surely because we have taken delight in a confusion of crossing branches. Tragic art, passionate art, the drowner of dykes, the confounder of understanding, moves us by setting us to reverie, by alluring us almost to the intensity of trance. The persons upon the stage, let us say, greaten till they are humanity itself. We feel our minds expand convulsively or spread out slowly like some moon-brightened image-crowded sea. That which is before our eyes perpetually vanishes and returns again in the midst of the excitement it creates, and the more enthralling it is, the more do we forget it.

August 1910

THE COUNTESS CATHLEEN

by WILLIAM BUTLER YEATS

1892

"The sorrowful are dumb for thee"
Lament of Morian Shehone
for Miss Mary Bourke

TO
MAUD GONNE

THE COUNTESS CATHLEEN[1]

CHARACTERS

SHEMUS RUA, *a Peasant*   ALEEL, *a Poet*

MARY, *his wife*   THE COUNTESS CATHLEEN

TEIGUE, *his son*   OONA, *her foster-mother*

TWO DEMONS DISGUISED AS MERCHANTS

PEASANTS, SERVANTS, ANGELICAL BEINGS

The Scene is laid in Ireland and in old times

[1] Reprinted with permission of The Macmillan Company from *The Collected Plays of W. B. Yeats* by William Butler Yeats. Copyright 1912 by The Macmillan Company, renewed 1940 by Bertha Georgie Yeats.

Scene 1

[*A room with lighted fire, and a door into the open air, through which one sees, perhaps, the trees of a wood, and these trees should be painted in flat colour upon a gold or diapered sky. The walls are of one colour. The scene should have the effect of missal painting.* MARY, *a woman of forty years or so, is grinding a quern.*]

MARY. What can have made the grey hen flutter so?

[TEIGUE, *a boy of fourteen, is coming in with turf, which he lays beside the hearth.*]

TEIGUE. They say that now the land is famine-struck
    The graves are walking.
MARY.   What can the hen have heard?
TEIGUE. And that is not the worst; at Tubber-vanach
    A woman met a man with ears spread out,
    And they moved up and down like a bat's wing.
MARY. What can have kept your father all this while?
TEIGUE. Two nights ago, at Carrick-orus churchyard,
    A herdsman met a man who had no mouth,
    Nor eyes, nor ears; his face a wall of flesh;
    He saw him plainly by the light of the moon.
MARY. Look out, and tell me if your father's coming.

[TEIGUE *goes to door.*]

TEIGUE. Mother!
MARY.   What is it?
TEIGUE.   In the bush beyond,
    There are two birds—if you can call them birds—
    I could not see them rightly for the leaves—
    But they've the shape and colour of horned owls,
    And I'm half certain they've a human face.
MARY. Mother of God, defend us!
TEIGUE.   They're looking at me.
    What is the good of praying? father says.
    God and the Mother of God have dropped asleep.
    What do they care, he says, though the whole land
    Squeal like a rabbit under a weasel's tooth?
MARY. You'll bring misfortune with your blasphemies

Upon your father, or yourself, or me.
Would God that he were home—ah, there he is.

[SHEMUS *comes in.*]

What was it kept you in the wood? You know
I cannot get all sorts of accidents
Out of my mind till you are home again.
SHEMUS. I'm in no mood to listen to your clatter.
　Although I tramped the woods for half a day,
　I've taken nothing, for the very rats,
　Badgers, and hedgehogs seem to have died of drought,
　And there was scarce a wind in the parched leaves.
TEIGUE. Then you have brought no dinner.
SHEMUS.　　　　　　　　　　　　After that
　I sat among the beggars at the cross-roads,
　And held a hollow hand among the others.
MARY. What, did you beg?
SHEMUS.　　　　　　　　　I had no chance to beg,
　For when the beggars saw me they cried out
　They would not have another share their alms,
　And hunted me away with sticks and stones.
TEIGUE. You said that you would bring us food or money.
SHEMUS. What's in the house?
TEIGUE.　　　　　　　　　　A bit of mouldy bread.
MARY. There's flour enough to make another loaf.
TEIGUE. And when that's gone?
MARY.　　　　　　　　　There is the hen in the coop.
SHEMUS. My curse upon the beggars, my curse upon them!
TEIGUE. And the last penny gone.
SHEMUS.　　　　　　　　When the hen's gone,
　What can we do but live on sorrel and dock,
　And dandelion, till our mouths are green?
MARY. God, that to this hour has found bit and sup,
　Will cater for us still.
SHEMUS.　　　　　His kitchen's bare.
　There were five doors that I looked through this day
　And saw the dead and not a soul to wake them.
MARY. Maybe He'd have us die because He knows,
　When the ear is stopped and when the eye is stopped,
　That every wicked sight is hid from the eye,
　And all fool talk from the ear!

[*A stringed instrument without.*]

SHEMUS.   Who's passing there?
  And mocking us with music?
TEIGUE.   A young man plays it.
  There's an old woman and a lady with him.
SHEMUS. What is the trouble of the poor to her?
  Nothing at all or a harsh radishy sauce
  For the day's meat.
MARY.   God's pity on the rich!
  Had we been through as many doors, and seen
  The dishes standing on the polished wood
  In the wax candle light, we'd be as hard,
  And there's the needle's eye at the end of all.
SHEMUS. My curse upon the rich!
TEIGUE.   They're coming here.
SHEMUS. Then down upon that stool, down quick, I say,
  And call up a whey face and a whining voice,
  And let your head be bowed upon your knees.
MARY. Had I but time to put the place to rights!

[CATHLEEN, OONA, *and* ALEEL *enter*.]

CATHLEEN. God save all here. There is a certain house,
  An old grey castle with a kitchen garden,
  A cider orchard and plot for flowers,
  Somewhere among these woods.
MARY.   We know it, lady.
  A place that's set among impassable walls
  As though world's trouble could not find it out.
CATHLEEN. It may be that we are that trouble, for we—
  Although we've wandered in the wood this hour—
  Have lost it too, yet I should know my way,
  For I lived all my childhood in that house.
MARY. Then you are Countess Cathleen?
CATHLEEN.   And this woman,
  Oona, my nurse, should have remembered it,
  For we were happy for a long time there.
OONA. The paths are overgrown with thickets now,
  Or else some change has come upon my sight.
CATHLEEN. And this young man, that should have known the
    woods—
  Because we met him on their border but now,
  Wandering and singing like a wave of the sea—
  Is so wrapped up in dreams of terrors to come
  That he can give no help.

MARY. You have still some way,
But I can put you on the trodden path
Your servants take when they are marketing.
But first sit down and rest yourself awhile,
For my old fathers served your fathers, lady,
Longer than books can tell—and it were strange
If you and yours should not be welcome here.

CATHLEEN. And it were stranger still were I ungrateful
For such kind welcome—but I must be gone,
For the night's gathering in.

SHEMUS. It is a long while
Since I've set eyes on bread or on what buys it.

CATHLEEN. So you are starving even in this wood,
Where I had thought I would find nothing changed.
But that's a dream, for the old worm o' the world
Can eat its way into what place it pleases.

[*She gives money.*]

TEIGUE. Beautiful lady, give me something too;
I fell but now, being weak with hunger and thirst,
And lay upon the threshold like a log.

CATHLEEN. I gave for all and that was all I had.
But look, my purse is empty. I have passed
But starving men and women all this day,
And they have had the rest; but take the purse,
The silver clasps on't may be worth a trifle.
And if you'll come to-morrow to my house
You shall have twice the sum.

[ALEEL *begins to play.*]

SHEMUS [*muttering*]. What, music, music!

CATHLEEN. Ah, do not blame the finger on the string;
The doctors bid me fly the unlucky times
And find distraction for my thoughts, or else
Pine to my grave.

SHEMUS. I have said nothing, lady.
Why should the like of us complain?

OONA. Have done.
Sorrows that she's but read of in a book
Weigh on her mind as if they had been her own.

[OONA, MARY, and CATHLEEN *go out.* ALEEL *looks defiantly at* SHEMUS.]

ALEEL [*singing*]. Were I but crazy for love's sake

I know who'd measure out his length,
I know the heads that I should break,
For crazy men have double strength.
I know—all's out to leave or take,
Who mocks at music mocks at love;
Were I but crazy for love's sake,
No need to pick and choose.
                    [*Snapping his fingers in* SHEMUS' *face.*]
                              Enough!
I know the heads that I should break.

[*He takes a step towards the door and then turns again.*]

Shut to the door before the night has fallen,
For who can say what walks, or in what shape
Some devilish creature flies in the air; but now
Two grey horned owls hooted above our heads.

[*He goes out, his singing dies away.* MARY *comes in.* SHEMUS
has been counting the money.]

SHEMUS. So that fool's gone.
TEIGUE.   He's seen the horned owls too.
  There's no good luck in owls, but it may be
  That the ill luck's to fall upon his head.
MARY. You never thanked her ladyship.
SHEMUS.   Thank her
  For seven halfpence and a silver bit?
TEIGUE. But for this empty purse?
SHEMUS.   What's that for thanks,
  Or what's the double of it that she promised,
  With bread and flesh and every sort of food
  Up to a price no man has heard the like of
  And rising every day?
MARY.   We have all she had;
  She emptied out the purse before our eyes.
SHEMUS [*to* MARY, *who has gone to close the door*]. Leave
  that door open.
MARY.   When those that have read books,
  And seen the seven wonders of the world,
  Fear what's above or what's below the ground,
  It's time that poverty should bolt the door.
SHEMUS. I'll have no bolts, for there is not a thing
  That walks above the ground or under it

I had not rather welcome to this house
Than any more of mankind, rich or poor.

TEIGUE. So that they brought us money.

SHEMUS.   I heard say
There's something that appears like a white bird,
A pigeon or a seagull or the like,
But if you hit it with a stone or a stick
It clangs as though it had been made of brass,
And that if you dig down where it was scratching
You'll find a crock of gold.

TEIGUE.   But dream of gold
For three nights running, and there's always gold.

SHEMUS. You might be starved before you've dug it out.

TEIGUE. But maybe if you called, something would come.
They have been seen of late.

MARY.   Is it call devils?
Call devils from the wood, call them in here?

SHEMUS. So you'd stand up against me, and you'd say
Who or what I am to welcome here.   [He hits her.]
That is to show who's master.

TEIGUE.   Call them in.

MARY. God help us all!

SHEMUS.   Pray, if you have a mind to.
It's little that the sleepy ears above
Care for your words; but I'll call what I please.

TEIGUE. There is many a one, they say, had money from them.

SHEMUS [at door]. Whatever you are that walk the woods at
    night,
So be it that you have not shouldered up
Out of a grave—for I'll have nothing human—
And have free hands, a friendly trick of speech,
I welcome you. Come, sit beside the fire.
What matter if your head's below your arms
Or you've a horse's tail to whip your flank,
Feathers instead of hair, that's all but nothing.
Come, share what bread and meat is in the house,
And stretch your heels and warm them in the ashes.
And after that, let's share and share alike
And curse all men and women. Come in, come in.
What, is there no one there?   [Turning from door.]
                              And yet they say
They are as common as the grass, and ride
Even upon the book in the priest's hand.

[TEIGUE *lifts one arm slowly and points towards the door and begins moving backward.* SHEMUS *turns, he also sees something and begins moving backward.* MARY *does the same. A man dressed as an Eastern merchant comes in carrying a small carpet. He unrolls it and sits crosslegged at one end of it. Another man dressed in the same way follows, and sits at the other end. This is done slowly and deliberately. When they are seated they take money out of embroidered purses at their girdles and begin arranging it on the carpet.*]

TEIGUE. You speak to them.

SHEMUS.   No, you.

TEIGUE.   'Twas you that called them.

SHEMUS [*coming nearer*]. I'd make so bold, if you would
        pardon it,
    To ask if there's a thing you'd have of us.
    Although we are but poor people, if there is,
    Why, if there is——

FIRST MERCHANT.   We've travelled a long road,
    For we are merchants that must tramp the world,
    And now we look for supper and a fire
    And a safe corner to count money in.

SHEMUS. I thought you were . . . but that's no matter now—
    There had been words between my wife and me
    Because I said I would be master here,
    And ask in what I pleased or who I pleased,
    And so . . . but that is nothing to the point,
    Because it's certain that you are but merchants.

FIRST MERCHANT. We travel for the Master of all merchants.

SHEMUS. Yet if you were that I had thought but now
    I'd welcome you no less. Be what you please
    And you'll have supper at the market rate.
    That means that what was sold for but a penny
    Is now worth fifty.

FIRST MERCHANT [*arranging money*]. Our Master bids us pay
    So good a price that all who deal with us
        Shall eat, drink, and be merry.

SHEMUS [*to* MARY].   Bestir yourself,
    Go kill and draw the fowl, while Teigue and I
    Lay out the plates and make a better fire.

MARY. I will not cook for you.

SHEMUS.   Not cook! not cook!
    Do not be angry. She wants to pay me back

Because I struck her in that argument.
But she'll get sense again. Since the dearth came
We rattle one on another as though we were
Knives thrown into a basket to be cleaned.

MARY. I will not cook for you, because I know
In what unlucky shape you sat but now
Outside this door.

TEIGUE.   It's this, your honours:
Because of some wild words my father said
She thinks you are not of those who cast a shadow.

SHEMUS. I said I'd make the devils of the wood
Welcome, if they'd a mind to eat and drink;
But it is certain that you are men like us.

FIRST MERCHANT. It's strange that she should think we cast
    no shadow,
For there is nothing on the ridge of the world
That's more substantial than the merchants are
That buy and sell you.

MARY.   If you are not demons,
And seeing what great wealth is spread out there,
Give food or money to the starving poor.

FIRST MERCHANT. If we knew how to find deserving poor
We'd do our share.

MARY.   But seek them patiently.

FIRST MERCHANT. We know the evils of mere charity.

MARY. Those scruples may befit a common time.
I had thought there was a pushing to and fro,
At times like this, that overset the scale
And trampled measure down.

FIRST MERCHANT.   But if already
We'd thought of a more prudent way than that?

SECOND MERCHANT. If each one brings a bit of merchandise,
We'll give him such a price he never dreamt of.

MARY. Where shall the starving come at merchandise?

FIRST MERCHANT. We will ask nothing but what all men have.

MARY. Their swine and cattle, fields and implements
Are sold and gone.

FIRST MERCHANT.   They have not sold all yet.
For there's a vaporous thing—that may be nothing,
But that's the buyer's risk—a second self,
They call immortal for a story's sake.

SHEMUS. They come to buy our souls?

TEIGUE.   I'll barter mine.

Why should we starve for what may be but nothing?

MARY. Teigue and Shemus——

SHEMUS.   What can it be but nothing?
   What has God poured out of His bag but famine?
   Satan gives money.

TEIGUE.   Yet no thunder stirs.

FIRST MERCHANT. There is a heap for each.

[SHEMUS *goes to take money*.]

                       But, no, not yet,
   For there's a work I have to set you to.

SHEMUS. So, then, you're as deceitful as the rest,
   And all that talk of buying what's but a vapour
   Is fancy bread. I might have known as much,
   Because that's how the trick-o'-the-loop man talks.

FIRST MERCHANT. That's for the work, each has its separate
     price;
   But neither price is paid till the work's done.

TEIGUE. The same for me.

MARY.   O God, why are You still?

FIRST MERCHANT. You've but to cry aloud at every crossroad,
   At every house door, that we buy men's souls
   And give so good a price that all may live
   In mirth and comfort till the famine's done,
   Because we are Christian men.

SHEMUS.   Come, let's away.

TEIGUE. I shall keep running till I've earned the price.

SECOND MERCHANT. [*who has risen and gone towards fire*].
   Stop; you must have proof behind the words,
   So here's your entertainment on the road.

        [*He throws a bag of money on the ground*.]

Live as you please; our Master's generous.

[TEIGUE *and* SHEMUS *have stopped.* TEIGUE *takes the money.
   They go out.*]

MARY. Destroyers of souls, God will destroy you quickly.
   You shall at last dry like dry leaves and hang
   Nailed like dead vermin to the doors of God.

SECOND MERCHANT. Curse to your fill, for saints will have
   their dreams.

FIRST MERCHANT. Though we're but vermin that our Master
   sent

To overrun the world, he at the end
Shall pull apart the pale ribs of the moon
And quench the stars in the ancestral night.
MARY. God is all-powerful.
SECOND MERCHANT.   Pray, you shall need Him.
You shall eat dock and grass, and dandelion,
Till that low threshold there becomes a wall,
And when your hands can scarcely drag your body
We shall be near you.

[MARY *faints. The* FIRST MERCHANT *takes up the carpet,
spreads it before the fire and stands in front of it warming
his hands.*]

FIRST MERCHANT.   Our faces go unscratched.
Wring the neck o' that fowl, scatter the flour,
And look if there is bread upon the shelves.
We'll turn the fowl upon the spit and roast it,
And eat the supper we were bidden to,
Now that the house is quiet, praise our Master,
And stretch and warm our heels among the ashes.

Scene 2

[FRONT SCENE.—*A wood with perhaps distant view of turreted
house at one side, but all in flat colour, without light and
shade and against a diapered or gold background.*]

[COUNTESS CATHLEEN *comes in leaning upon* ALEEL'S *arm.*
OONA *follows them.*]

CATHLEEN [*stopping*]. Surely this leafy corner, where one
    smells
The wild bee's honey, has a story too?
OONA. There is the house at last.
ALEEL.   A man, they say,
Loved Maeve the Queen of all the invisible host,
And died of his love nine centuries ago.
And now, when the moon's riding at the full,
She leaves her dancers lonely and lies there
Upon that level place, and for three days
Stretches and sighs and wets her long pale cheeks.
CATHLEEN. So she loves truly.

ALEEL.   No, but wets her cheeks,
  Lady, because she has forgot his name.
CATHLEEN. She'd sleep that trouble away—though it must be
  A heavy trouble to forget his name—
  If she had better sense.
OONA.   Your own house, lady.
ALEEL. She sleeps high up on wintry Knocknarea
  In an old cairn of stones; while her poor women
  Must lie and joy in the wave if they would sleep—
  Being water-born—yet if she cry their names
  They run up on the land and dance in the moon
  Till they are giddy and would love as men do,
  And be as patient and as pitiful.
  But there is nothing that will stop in their heads,
  They've such poor memories, though they weep for it.
  O yes, they weep; that's when the moon is full.
CATHLEEN. Is it because they have short memories
  They live so long?
ALEEL.   What's memory but the ash
  That chokes our fires that have begun to sink?
  And they've a dizzy, everlasting fire.
OONA. There is your own house, lady.
CATHLEEN.   Why, that's true,
  And we'd have passed it without noticing.
ALEEL. A curse upon it for a meddlesome house!
  Had it but stayed away I would have known
  What Queen Maeve thinks on when the moon is pinched;
  And whether now—as in the old days—the dancers
  Set their brief love on men.
OONA.   Rest on my arm.
  These are no thoughts for any Christian ear.
ALEEL. I am younger, she would be too heavy for you.

[*He begins taking his lute out of the bag.* CATHLEEN, *who has
  turned towards* OONA, *turns back to him.*]

  This hollow box remembers every foot
  That danced upon the level grass of the world,
  And will tell secrets if I whisper to it.

                     [*Sings*]

                 Lift up the white knee;
                 Hear what they sing,
                 Those young dancers

That in a ring
Raved but now
Of the hearts that broke
Long, long ago
For their sake.

OONA. New friends are sweet.

ALEEL. But the dance changes,
Lift up the gown,
All that sorrow
Is trodden down.

OONA. The empty rattle-pate! Lean on this arm,
That I can tell you is a christened arm,
And not like some, if we are to judge by speech.
But as you please. It is time I was forgot.
Maybe it is not on this arm you slumbered
When you were as helpless as a worm.

ALEEL. Stay with me till we come to your own house.

CATHLEEN [*sitting down*]. When I am rested I will need no
help.

ALEEL. I thought to have kept her from remembering
The evil of the times for full ten minutes;
But now when seven are out you come between.

OONA. Talk on; what does it matter what you say,
For you have not been christened?

ALEEL. Old woman, old woman,
You robbed her of three minutes' peace of mind,
And though you live unto a hundred years,
And wash the feet of beggars and give alms,
And climb Cro-Patrick, you shall not be pardoned.

OONA. How does a man who never was baptized
Know what Heaven pardons?

ALEEL. You are a sinful woman.

OONA. I care no more than if a pig had grunted.

[*Enter* CATHLEEN's *steward.*]

STEWARD. I am not to blame, for I had locked the gate.
The forester's to blame. The men climbed in
At the east corner where the elm-tree is.

CATHLEEN. I do not understand you. Who has climbed?

STEWARD. Then God be thanked, I am the first to tell you.
I was afraid some other of the servants—
Though I've been on the watch—had been the first,
And mixed up truth and lies, your ladyship.

CATHLEEN [*rising*]. Has some misfortune happened?

STEWARD.   Yes, indeed.
The forester that let the branches lie
Against the wall's to blame for everything,
For that is how the rogues got into the garden.

CATHLEEN. I thought to have escaped misfortune here.
Has any one been killed?

STEWARD.   O no, not killed.
They have stolen half a cart-load of green cabbage.

CATHLEEN. But maybe they were starving.

STEWARD.   That is certain.
To rob or starve, that was the choice they had.

CATHLEEN. A learned theologian has laid down
That starving men may take what's necessary,
And yet be sinless.

OONA.   Sinless and a thief!
There should be broken bottles on the wall.

CATHLEEN. And if it be a sin, while faith's unbroken
God cannot help but pardon. There is no soul
But it's unlike all others in the world,
Nor one but lifts a strangeness to God's love
Till that's grown infinite, and therefore none
Whose loss were less than irremediable
Although it were the wickedest in the world.

[*Enter* TEIGUE *and* SHEMUS.]

STEWARD. What are you running for? Pull off your cap.
Do you not see who's there?

SHEMUS.   I cannot wait.
I am running to the world with the best news
That has been brought it for a thousand years.

STEWARD. Then get your breath and speak.

SHEMUS.   If you'd my news
You'd run as fast and be as out of breath.

TEIGUE. Such news, we shall be carried on men's shoulders.

SHEMUS. There's something every man has carried with him
And thought no more of than if it were
A mouthful of the wind; and now it's grown
A marketable thing!

TEIGUE.   And yet it seemed
As useless as the paring of one's nails.

SHEMUS. What sets me laughing when I think of it,
Is that a rogue who's lain in lousy straw,

If he but sell it, may set up his coach.

TEIGUE [*laughing*]. There are two gentlemen who buy men's
souls.

CATHLEEN. O God!

TEIGUE.   And maybe there's no soul at all.

STEWARD. They're drunk or mad.

TEIGUE.   Look at the price they give. [*Showing money.*]

SHEMUS [*tossing up money*]. "Go cry it all about the world,"
they said.

" 'Money for souls, good money for a soul.' "

CATHLEEN. Give twice and thrice and twenty times their
money,

And get yours souls again. I will pay all.

SHEMUS. Not we! not we! For souls—if there are souls—

But keep the flesh out of its merriment.

I shall be drunk and merry.

TEIGUE.   Come, let's away.   [*He goes.*]

CATHLEEN. But there's a world to come.

SHEMUS.   And if there is,

I'd rather trust myself into the hands

That can pay money down than to the hands

That have but shaken famine from the bag.

[*He goes out R. lilting.*]

"There's money for a soul, sweet yellow money.

There's money for men's souls, good money, money."

CATHLEEN [*to ALEEL*]. Go call them here again, bring them
by force,

Beseech them, bribe, do anything you like;

[*ALEEL goes.*]

And you too follow, add your prayers to his.

[OONA, *who has been praying, goes out.*]

Steward, you know the secrets of my house.

How much have I?

STEWARD.   A hundred kegs of gold.

CATHLEEN. How much have I in castles?

STEWARD.   As much more.

CATHLEEN. How much have I in pasture?

STEWARD.   As much more.

CATHLEEN. How much have I in forests?

STEWARD.   As much more.

CATHLEEN. Keeping this house alone, sell all I have,

Go barter where you please, but come again

With herds of cattle and with ships of meal.
STEWARD. God's blessing light upon your ladyship.
    You will have saved the land.
CATHLEEN.   Make no delay.

[*He goes* L. ALEEL *and* OONA *return.*]

CATHLEEN. They have not come; speak quickly.
ALEEL.   One drew his knife
    And said that he would kill the man or woman
    That stopped his way; and when I would have stopped him
    He made this stroke at me; but it is nothing.
CATHLEEN. You shall be tended. From this day for ever
    I'll have no joy or sorrow of my own.
OONA. Their eyes shone like the eyes of birds of prey.
CATHLEEN. Come, follow me, for the earth burns my feet
    Till I have changed my house to such a refuge
    That the old and ailing, and all weak of heart,
    May escape from beak and claw; all, all, shall come
    Till the walls burst and the roof fall on us.
    From this day out I have nothing of my own.   [*She goes.*]
OONA [*taking* ALEEL *by the arm and as she speaks bandaging
    his wound.*]
    She has found something now to put her hand to,
    And you and I are of no more account
    Than flies upon a window-pane in the winter.
                     [*They go out.*]

Scene 3

[*Hall in the house of* COUNTESS CATHLEEN. *At the left an
oratory with steps leading up to it. At the right a tapestried
wall, more or less repeating the form of the oratory, and
a great chair with its back against the wall. In the centre
are two or more arches through which one can see dimly
the trees of the garden.* CATHLEEN *is kneeling in front of
the altar in the oratory; there is a hanging lighted lamp over
the altar.* ALEEL *enters.*]

ALEEL. I have come to bid you leave this castle and fly
    Out of these woods.

[CATHLEEN *rises from the altar and comes into the hall.*]

CATHLEEN.   What evil is there here
  That is not everywhere from this to the sea?
ALEEL. They who have sent me walk invisible.
CATHLEEN. So it is true that I have heard men say,
  That you have seen and heard what others cannot.
ALEEL. I was asleep in my bed, and while I slept
  My dream became a fire; and in the fire
  One walked and he had birds about his head.
CATHLEEN. I have heard that one of the old gods walked so.
ALEEL. It may be that he is angelical;
  And, lady, he bids me call you from these woods.
  And you must bring but your old foster-mother,
  And some few serving-men, and live in the hills,
  Among the sounds of music and the light
  Of waters, till the evil days are done.
  For here some terrible death is waiting you,
  Some unimagined evil, some great darkness
  That fable has not dreamt of, nor sun nor moon
  Scattered.
CATHLEEN.   No, not angelical.
ALEEL.   This house
  You are to leave with some old trusty man,
  And bid him shelter all that starve or wander
  While there is food and house-room.
CATHLEEN.   He bids me go
  Where none of mortal creatures but the swan
  Dabbles, and there you would pluck the harp, when the
    trees
  Had made a heavy shadow about our door,
  And talk among the rustling of the reeds,
  When night hunted the foolish sun away
  With stillness and pale tapers. No—no—no!
  I cannot. Although I weep, I do not weep
  Because that life would be most happy, and here
  I find no way, no end. Nor do I weep
  Because I had longed to look upon your face,
  But that a night of prayer has made me weary.
ALEEL [prostrating himself before her]. Let Him that made
    mankind,
  And dearth and plenty, mend what He has made,
  For when we labour in vain and eye still sees,
  Heart breaks in vain.
CATHLEEN.   How would that quiet end?

ALEEL. How but in healing?

CATHLEEN.   You have seen my tears,
  And I can see your hand shake on the floor.

ALEEL [*faltering*]. I thought but of healing. He was angelical.

CATHLEEN. [*turning away from him*]. No, not angelical, but
    of the old gods,
  Who wander about the world to waken the heart—
  The passionate, proud heart—that all the angels,
  Leaving nine heavens empty, would rock to sleep.

[*She goes to the oratory door;* ALEEL *holds his clasped hands
  towards her for a moment hesitatingly, and then lets them
  fall beside him.*]

CATHLEEN. Do not hold out to me beseeching hands.
  This heart shall never waken on earth. I have sworn,
  By her whose heart the seven sorrows have pierced,
  To pray before this altar until my heart
  Has grown to Heaven like a tree, and there
  Rustled its leaves, till Heaven has saved my people.

ALEEL [*who has risen*]. When one so great has spoken of love
    to one
  So little as I, though to deny him love,
  What can he but hold out beseeching hands,
  Then let them fall beside him, knowing how greatly
  They have overdared?

[*He goes towards the door of the hall. The* COUNTESS
  CATHLEEN *takes a few steps towards him.*]

CATHLEEN.   If the old tales are true,
  Queens have wed shepherds and kings beggar-maids;
  God's procreant waters flowing about your mind
  Have made you more than kings or queens; and not you
  But I am the empty pitcher.

ALEEL.   Being silent,
  I have said all, yet let me stay beside you.

CATHLEEN. No, no, not while my heart is shaken. No,
  But you shall hear wind cry and water cry,
  And curlew cry, and have the peace I longed for.

ALEEL. Give me your hand to kiss.

CATHLEEN.   I kiss your forehead.
  And yet I send you from me. Do not speak;
  There have been women that bid men to rob
  Crowns from the Country-under-Wave or apples

Upon a dragon-guarded hill, and all
That they might sift the hearts and wills of men,
And trembled as they bid it, as I tremble
That lay a hard task on you, that you go,
And silently, and do not turn your head.
Good-bye; but do not turn your head and look;
Above all else, I would not have you look.   [ALEEL *goes.*]
I never spoke to him of his wounded hand,
And now he is gone. [*She looks out.*]
I cannot see him, for all is dark outside.
Would my imagination and my heart
Were as little shaken as this holy flame!

[*She goes slowly into the oratory. The distant sound of an alarm bell. The two* MERCHANTS *enter hurriedly.*]

SECOND MERCHANT. They are ringing the alarm, and in a moment
They'll be upon us.

FIRST MERCHANT [*going to a door at the side*]. Here is the Treasury.
You'd my commands to put them all to sleep.

SECOND MERCHANT. Some angel or else her prayers protected them.

[*Goes into the Treasury and returns with bags of treasure.* FIRST MERCHANT *has been listening at the oratory door.*]

FIRST MERCHANT. She has fallen asleep.

[SECOND MERCHANT *goes out through one of the arches at the back and stands listening. The bags are at his feet.*]

SECOND MERCHANT.   We've all the treasure now,
So let's away before they've tracked us out.

FIRST MERCHANT. I have a plan to win her.

SECOND MERCHANT.   You have time enough
If you would kill her and bear off her soul
Before they are upon us with their prayers;
They search the Western Tower.

FIRST MERCHANT.   That may not be.
We cannot face the heavenly host in arms.
Her soul must come to us of its own will;
But being of the ninth and mightiest Hell,
Where all are kings, I have a plan to win it.
Lady, we've news that's crying out for speech.

[CATHLEEN *wakes and comes to door of oratory.*]

CATHLEEN. Who calls?

FIRST MERCHANT.   Lady, we have brought news.

CATHLEEN.   What are you?

FIRST MERCHANT. We are merchants, and we know the book
     of the world
  Because we have walked upon its leaves; and there
  Have read of late matters that much concern you;
  And noticing the castle door stand open,
  Come in to find an ear.

CATHLEEN.   The door stands open
  That no one who is famished or afraid
  Despair of help or of a welcome with it.
  But you have news, you say.

FIRST MERCHANT.   We saw a man
  Heavy with sickness in the bog of Allen,
  Whom you had bid buy cattle. Near Fair Head
  We saw your grain ships lying all becalmed
  In the dark night; and not less still than they,
  Burned all their mirrored lanthorns in the sea.

CATHLEEN. Thanks be to God there's money in the house
  That can buy grain from those who have stored it up
  To prosper on the hunger of the poor.
  But you've been far and know the signs of things,
  When will this famine end?

FIRST MERCHANT.   Day copies day,
  And there's no sign of change, nor can it change,
  With the wheat withered and the cattle dead.

CATHLEEN. And heard you of the demons who buy souls?

FIRST MERCHANT. There are some men who hold they have
     wolves' heads,
  And say their limbs—dried by the infinite flame—
  Have all the speed of storms; others, again,
  Say they are gross and little; while a few
  Will have it they seem much as mortals are
  But tall and brown and travelled—like us, lady—
  Yet all agree a power is in their looks
  That makes men bow, and flings a casting-net
  About their souls, and that all men would go
  And barter those poor vapours, were it not
  You bribe them with the safety of your gold.

CATHLEEN. Praise God that I am wealthy! Why do they sell?

FIRST MERCHANT. As we came in at the great door we saw
  Your porter sleeping in his niche—a soul
  Too little to be worth a hundred pence,
  And yet they buy it for a hundred crowns.
  But for a soul like yours, I heard them say,
  They would give five hundred thousand crowns and more.
CATHLEEN. How can a heap of crowns pay for a soul?
  Is the green grave so terrible a thing?
FIRST MERCHANT. Some sell because the money gleams, and
      some
  Because they are in terror of the grave,
  And some because their neighbours sold before,
  And some because there is a kind of joy
  In casting hope away, in losing joy,
  In ceasing all resistance, in at last
  Opening one's arms to the eternal flames,
  In casting all sails out upon the wind;
  To this—full of the gaiety of the lost—
  Would all folk hurry if your gold were gone.
CATHLEEN. There is a something, Merchant, in your voice
  That makes me fear. When you were telling how
  A man may lose his soul and lose his God
  Your eyes were lighted up, and when you told
  How my poor money serves the people, both—
  Merchants, forgive me—seemed to smile.
FIRST MERCHANT.   I laugh
  To think that all these people should be swung
  As on a lady's shoe-string,—under them
  The glowing leagues of never-ending flame.
CATHLEEN. There is a something in you that I fear;
  A something not of us; were you not born
  In some most distant corner of the world?

[*The* SECOND MERCHANT, *who has been listening at the door,
  comes forward, and as he comes a sound of voices and feet
  is heard.*]

SECOND MERCHANT. Away now—they are in the passage—
      hurry,
  For they will know us, and freeze up our hearts
  With Ave Marys, and burn all our skin
  With holy water.
FIRST MERCHANT.   Farewell; for we must ride

Many a mile before the morning come;
Our horses beat the ground impatiently.

[*They go out. A number of* PEASANTS *enter by other door.*]

FIRST PEASANT. Forgive us, lady, but we heard a noise.
SECOND PEASANT. We sat by the fireside telling vanities.
FIRST PEASANT. We heard a noise, but though we have searched
    the house
We have found nobody.
CATHLEEN.   You are too timid,
    For now you are safe from all the evil times,
    There is no evil that can find you here.
OONA [*entering hurriedly*]. Ochone! The treasure-room is
    broken in.
    The door stands open, and the gold is gone.

[PEASANTS *raise a lamentable cry.*]

CATHLEEN. Be silent. [*The cry ceases.*] Have you seen nobody?
OONA.   Ochone!
    That my good mistress should lose all this money!
CATHLEEN. Let those among you not too old to ride
    Get horses and search all the country round.
    I'll give a farm to him who finds the thieves.

[*A man with keys at his girdle has come in while she speaks.
There is a general murmur of* "The porter! the porter!"]

PORTER. Demons were here. I sat beside the door
    In my stone niche, and two owls passed me by,
    Whispering with human voices.
OLD PEASANT.   God forsakes us.
CATHLEEN. Old man, old man, He never closed a door
    Unless one opened. I am desolate
    Because of a strange thought that's in my heart;
    But I have still my faith; therefore be silent;
    For surely He does not forsake the world,
    But stands before it modelling in the clay
    And moulding there His image. Age by age
    The clay wars with His fingers and pleads hard
    For its old, heavy, dull and shapeless ease;
    But sometimes—though His hand is on it still—
    It moves awry and demon hordes are born.

[PEASANTS *cross themselves.*]

Yet leave me now, for I am desolate.
I hear a whisper from beyond the thunder.

[*She comes from the oratory door.*]

Yet stay an instant. When we meet again
I may have grown forgetful. Oona, take
These two—the larder and the dairy keys.

[*To the* PORTER.]

But take you this. It opens the small room
Of herbs for medicine, every kind of herb.
The book of cures is on the upper shelf.
PORTER. Why do you do this, lady; did you see
  Your coffin in a dream?
CATHLEEN.   Ah, no, not that.
But I have come to a strange thought. I have heard
A sound of wailing in unnumbered hovels,
And I must go down, down—I know not where—
Pray for all men and women mad from famine;
Pray, you good neighbours.

[*The* PEASANTS *all kneel.* COUNTESS CATHLEEN *ascends the
steps to the door of the oratory, and turning round stands
there motionless for a little, and then cries in a loud voice:*]

Mary, Queen of angels,
And all you clouds on clouds of saints, farewell!

Scene 4

[FRONT SCENE.—*A wood near the Castle, as in Scene 2.
A group of* PEASANTS *pass.*]

FIRST PEASANT. I have seen silver and copper, but not gold.
SECOND PEASANT. It's yellow and it shines.
FIRST PEASANT.   It's beautiful.
The most beautiful thing under the sun,
That's what I've heard.
THIRD PEASANT.   I have seen gold enough.
FOURTH PEASANT. I would not say that it's so beautiful.
FIRST PEASANT. But doesn't a gold piece glitter like the sun?
That's what my father, who'd seen better days,

Told me when I was but a little boy—
So high—so high, it's shining like the sun,
Round and shining, that is what he said.

SECOND PEASANT. There's nothing in the world it cannot buy.
FIRST PEASANT. They've bags and bags of it.

[*They go out. The two* MERCHANTS *follow silently. Then* ALEEL
passes over the stage singing.]

ALEEL.   Impetuous heart be still, be still,
            Your sorrowful love can never be told,
            Cover it up with a lonely tune.
            He who could bend all things to His Will
            Has covered the door of the infinite fold
            With the pale stars and the wandering moon.

Scene 5

[*The house of* SHEMUS RUA. *There is an alcove at the back
with curtains; in it a bed, and on the bed is the body of*
MARY *with candles round it. The two* MERCHANTS *while
they speak put a large book upon a table, arrange money,
and so on.*]

FIRST MERCHANT. Thanks to that lie I told about her ships
And that about the herdsman lying sick,
We shall be too much thronged with souls to-morrow.
SECOND MERCHANT. What has she in her coffers now but mice?
FIRST MERCHANT. When the night fell and I had shaped myself
Into the image of the man-headed owl,
I hurried to the cliffs of Donegal,
And saw with all their canvas full of wind
And rushing through the parti-coloured sea
Those ships that bring the woman grain and meal.
They're but three days from us.
SECOND MERCHANT.   When the dew rose
I hurried in like feathers to the east,
And saw nine hundred oxen driven through Meath
With goads of iron. They're but three days from us.
FIRST MERCHANT. Three days for traffic.

[PEASANTS *crowd in with* TEIGUE *and* SHEMUS.]

SHEMUS.   Come in, come in, you are welcome.
That is my wife. She mocked at my great masters,
And would not deal with them. Now there she is;
She does not even know she was a fool,
So great a fool she was.
TEIGUE.   She would not eat.
One crumb of bread bought with our masters' money,
But lived on nettles, dock, and dandelion.
SHEMUS. There's nobody could put into her head
That death is the worst thing can happen us,
Though that sounds simple, for her tongue grew rank
With all the lies that she had heard in chapel.
Draw to the curtain. [TEIGUE *draws it*.] You'll not play
the fool
While these good gentlemen are there to save you.
SECOND MERCHANT. Since the drought came they drift about
in a throng,
Like autumn leaves blown by the dreary winds.
Come, deal—come, deal.
FIRST MERCHANT.   Who will come deal with us?
SHEMUS. They are out of spirit, sir, with lack of food,
Save four or five. Here, sir, is one of these;
The others will gain courage in good time.
MIDDLE-AGED MAN. I come to deal—if you give honest price.
FIRST MERCHANT [*reading in a book*]. "John Maher, a man
of substance, with dull mind,
And quiet senses and unventurous heart.
The angels think him safe." Two hundred crowns,
All for a soul, a little breath of wind.
MIDDLE-AGED MAN. I ask three hundred crowns. You have
read there
That no mere lapse of days can make me yours.
FIRST MERCHANT. There is something more writ here—"Often
at night
He is wakeful from a dread of growing poor,
And thereon wonders if there's any man
That he could rob in safety."
A PEASANT.   Who'd have thought it?
And I was once alone with him at midnight.
ANOTHER PEASANT. I will not trust my mother after this.
FIRST MERCHANT. There is this crack in you—two hundred
crowns.
A PEASANT. That's plenty for a rogue.

ANOTHER PEASANT.   I'd give him nothing.
SHEMUS. You'll get no more—so take what's offered you.

[*A general murmur, during which the* MIDDLE-AGED MAN *takes
    money, and slips into background, where he sinks on to a
    seat.*]

FIRST MERCHANT. Has no one got a better soul than that?
    If only for the credit of your parishes,
    Traffic with us.
A WOMAN.   What will you give for mine?
FIRST MERCHANT [*reading in book*]. "Soft, handsome, and still
        young"—not much, I think.
    "It's certain that the man she's married to
    Knows nothing of what's hidden in the jar
    Between the hour-glass and the pepper pot."
THE WOMAN. The scandalous book!
FIRST MERCHANT.   "Nor how when he's away
    At the horse-fair the hand that wrote what's hid
    Will tap three times upon the window-pane."
THE WOMAN. And if there is a letter, that is no reason
    Why I should have less money than the others.
FIRST MERCHANT. You're almost safe. I give you fifty crowns.

[*She turns to go.*]

    A hundred, then.
SHEMUS.   Woman, have sense—come, come.
    Is this a time to haggle at the price?
    There, take it up. There, take it up. That's right.

[*She takes them and goes into the crowd.*]

FIRST MERCHANT. Come, deal, deal, deal. It is but for charity
    We buy such souls at all; a thousand sins
    Made them our Master's long before we came.

[ALEEL *enters.*]

ALEEL. Here, take my soul, for I am tired of it.
    I do not ask a price.
SHEMUS.   Not ask a price?
    How can you sell your soul without a price?
    I would not listen to his broken wits.
    His love for Countess Cathleen has so crazed him
    He hardly understands what he is saying.

ALEEL. The trouble that has come on Countess Cathleen,
　　The sorrow that is in her wasted face,
　　The burden in her eyes, have broke my wits,
　　And yet I know I'd have you take my soul.
FIRST MERCHANT. We cannot take your soul, for it is hers.
ALEEL. No, but you must. Seeing it cannot help her
　　I have grown tired of it.
FIRST MERCHANT. 　　　　　　Begone from me,
　　I may not touch it.
ALEEL. 　　　　　　Is your power so small?
　　And must I bear it with me all my days?
　　May you be scorned and mocked!
FIRST MERCHANT. 　　　　　　　　　Drag him away.
　　He troubles me.

[TEIGUE *and* SHEMUS *lead* ALEEL *into the crowd.*]

SECOND MERCHANT. 　His gaze has filled me, brother,
　　With shaking and a dreadful fear.
FIRST MERCHANT. 　　　　　　Lean forward
　　And kiss the circlet where my Master's lips
　　Were pressed upon it when he sent us hither;
　　You shall have peace once more.

[SECOND MERCHANT *kisses the gold circlet that is about the*
　　head of the FIRST MERCHANT.]

　　　　　　　　　　　　I, too, grow weary,
　　But there is something moving in my heart
　　Whereby I know that what we seek the most
　　Is drawing near—our labour will soon end.
　　Come, deal, deal, deal, deal, deal; are you all dumb?
　　What, will you keep me from our ancient home,
　　And from the eternal revelry?
SECOND MERCHANT. 　　　　　　Deal, deal.
SHEMUS. They say you beat the woman down too low.
FIRST MERCHANT. I offer this great price: a thousand crowns
　　For an old woman who was always ugly.

[*An old* PEASANT WOMAN *comes forward, and he takes up a*
　　book and reads:]

　　There is but little set down here against her.
　　"She has stolen eggs and fowl when times were bad,
　　But when the times grew better has confessed it;

She never missed her chapel of a Sunday
And when she could, paid dues." Take up your money.
OLD WOMAN. God bless you, sir. [*She screams.*] O, sir, a pain
    went through me!
FIRST MERCHANT. That name is like a fire to all damned souls.

[*Murmur among the* PEASANTS, *who shrink back from her as
she goes out.*]

A PEASANT. How she screamed out!
SECOND PEASANT.   And maybe we shall scream so.
THIRD PEASANT. I tell you there is no such place as Hell.
FIRST MERCHANT. Can such a trifle turn you from your profit?
    Come, deal; come, deal.
MIDDLE-AGED MAN.   Master, I am afraid.
FIRST MERCHANT. I bought your soul, and there's no sense in
    fear
    Now the soul's gone.
MIDDLE-AGED MAN.   Give me my soul again.
WOMAN [*going on her knees and clinging to* MERCHANT]. And
    take this money too, and give me mine.
SECOND MERCHANT. Bear bastards, drink or follow some wild
    fancy;
    For cryings out and sighs are the soul's work,
    And you have none.   [*Throws the* WOMAN *off.*]
PEASANT.   Come, let's away.
ANOTHER PEASANT.   Yes, yes.
ANOTHER PEASANT. Come quickly; if that woman had not
    screamed
    I would have lost my soul.
ANOTHER PEASANT.   Come, come away.

[*They turn to door, but are stopped by shouts of* "Countess
Cathleen! Countess Cathleen!"]

CATHLEEN [*entering*]. And so you trade once more?
FIRST MERCHANT.   In spite of you.
    What brings you here, saint with the sapphire eyes?
CATHLEEN. I come to barter a soul for a great price.
SECOND MERCHANT. What matter, if the soul be worth the
    price?
CATHLEEN. The people starve, therefore the people go
    Thronging to you. I hear a cry come from them
    And it is in my ears by night and day,

And I would have five hundred thousand crowns
That I may feed them till the dearth go by.

FIRST MERCHANT. It may be the soul's worth it.

CATHLEEN.   There is more:
The souls that you have bought must be set free.

FIRST MERCHANT. We know of but one soul that's worth the
    price.

CATHLEEN. Being my own it seems a priceless thing.

SECOND MERCHANT. You offer us——

CATHLEEN.   I offer my own soul.

A PEASANT. Do not, do not, for souls the like of ours
    Are not precious to God as your soul is.
    O, what would Heaven do without you, lady?

ANOTHER PEASANT. Look how their claws clutch in their
    leathern gloves.

FIRST MERCHANT. Five hundred thousand crowns; we give the
    price.
    The gold is here; the souls even while you speak
    Have slipped out of our bond, because your face
    Has shed a light on them and filled their hearts.
    But you must sign, for we omit no form
    In buying a soul like yours.

SECOND MERCHANT.   Sign with this quill.
    It was a feather growing on the cock
    That crowed when Peter dared deny his Master,
    And all who use it have great honour in Hell.

[CATHLEEN *leans forward to sign.*]

ALEEL [*rushing forward and snatching the pen from her*].
    Leave all things to the Builder of the Heavens.

CATHLEEN. I have no thoughts; I hear a cry—a cry.

ALEEL [*casting the pen on the ground*]. I have seen a vision
    under a green hedge,
    A hedge of hips and haws—men yet shall hear
    The archangels rolling Satan's empty skull
    Over the mountain-tops.

FIRST MERCHANT.   Take him away.

[TEIGUE *and* SHEMUS *drag him roughly away so that he falls
    upon the floor among the* PEASANTS. CATHLEEN *picks up
    the parchment and signs, then turns towards the* PEASANTS.]

CATHLEEN. Take up the money, and now come with me;

When we are far from this polluted place
I will give everybody money enough.

[*She goes out, the* PEASANTS *crowding round her and kissing
her dress.* ALEEL *and the two* MERCHANTS *are left alone.*]

SECOND MERCHANT. We must away and wait until she dies,
Sitting above her tower as two grey owls,
Waiting as many years as may be, guarding
Our precious jewel; waiting to seize her soul.
FIRST MERCHANT. We need but hover over her head in the air,
For she has only minutes. When she signed
Her heart began to break. Hush, hush, I hear
The brazen door of Hell move on its hinges,
And the eternal revelry float hither
To hearten us.
SECOND MERCHANT. Leap feathered on the air
And meet them with her soul caught in your claws.

[*They rush out.* ALEEL *crawls into the middle of the room.
The twilight has fallen and gradually darkens as the scene
goes on. There is a distant muttering of thunder and a
sound of rising storm.*]

ALEEL. The brazen door stands wide, and Balor comes
Borne in his heavy car, and demons have lifted
The age-weary eyelids from the eyes that of old
Turned gods to stone; Barach, the traitor, comes
And the lascivious race, Cailitin,
That cast a Druid weakness and decay
Over Sualtim's and old Dectora's child;
And that great king Hell first took hold upon
When he killed Naoise and broke Deirdre's heart;
And all their heads are twisted to one side,
For when they lived they warred on beauty and peace
With obstinate, crafty, sidelong bitterness.

[OONA *enters.*]

Crouch down, old heron, out of the blind storm.
OONA. Where is the Countess Cathleen? All this day
Her eyes were full of tears, and when for a moment
Her hand was laid upon my hand it trembled,
And now I do not know where she is gone.

ALEEL. Cathleen has chosen other friends than us,
And they are rising through the hollow world.
Demons are out, old heron.
OONA.   God guard her soul!
ALEEL. She's bartered it away this very hour,
As though we two were never in the world.
                              [*He points downward.*]
First, Orchil, her pale, beautiful head alive,
Her body shadowy as vapour drifting
Under the dawn, for she who awoke desire
Has but a heart of blood when others die;
About her in a vapoury multitude
Of women alluring devils with soft laughter;
Behind her a host heat of the blood made sin,
But all the little pink-white nails have grown
To be great talons.

[*He seizes* OONA *and drags her into the middle of the room
and points downward with vehement gestures. The wind
roars.*]

                    They begin a song
And there is still some music on their tongues.
OONA [*casting herself face downwards on the floor*]. O Maker
of all, protect her from the demons,
And if a soul must needs be lost, take mine.

[ALEEL *kneels beside her, but does not seem to hear her words.
The* PEASANTS *return. They carry the* COUNTESS CATHLEEN
and lay her upon the ground before OONA *and* ALEEL. *She
lies there as if dead.*]

OONA. O that so many pitchers of rough clay
Should prosper and the porcelain break in two!
                    [*She kisses the hands of* CATHLEEN.]
A PEASANT. We were under the tree where the path turns,
When she grew pale as death and fainted away.
And while we bore her hither cloudy gusts
Blackened the world and shook us on our feet.
Draw the great bolt, for no man has beheld
So black, bitter, blinding, and sudden a storm.

[*One who is near the door draws the bolt.*]

CATHLEEN. O, hold me, and hold me tightly, for the storm
Is dragging me away.

[OONA *takes her in her arms. A woman begins to wail.*]

PEASANTS.   Hush!
OTHER PEASANTS.   Hush!
PEASANT WOMEN.   Hush!
OTHER PEASANT WOMEN.   Hush!
CATHLEEN. [*half rising*]. Lay all the bags of money in a heap,
    And when I am gone, old Oona, share them out
    To every man and woman: judge, and give
    According to their needs.
A PEASANT WOMAN.   And will she give
    Enough to keep my children through the dearth?
ANOTHER PEASANT WOMAN. O Queen of Heaven, and all you
        blessed saints,
    Let us and ours be lost so she be shriven.
CATHLEEN. Bend down your faces, Oona and Aleel;
    I gaze upon them as the swallow gazes
    Upon the nest under the eave, before
    She wander the loud waters. Do not weep
    Too great a while, for there is many a candle
    On the High Altar though one fall. Aleel,
    Who sang about the dancers of the woods
    That know not the hard burden of the world,
    Having but breath in their kind bodies, farewell!
    And farewell, Oona, you who played with me,
    And bore me in your arms about the house
    When I was but a child and therefore happy,
    Therefore happy, even like those that dance.
    The storm is in my hair and I must go.   [*She dies.*]
OONA. Bring me the looking-glass.

[*A woman brings it to her out of the inner room.* OONA *holds
it over the lips of* CATHLEEN. *All is silent for a moment.
And then she speaks in a half scream;*]

                                        O, she is dead!
A PEASANT. She was the great white lily of the world.
ANOTHER PEASANT. She was more beautiful than the pale stars.
AN OLD PEASANT WOMAN. The little plant I loved is broken
    in two.

[ALEEL *takes looking-glass from* OONA *and flings it upon the
floor so that it is broken in many pieces.*]

ALEEL. I shatter you in fragments, for the face
    That brimmed you up with beauty is no more:
    And die, dull heart, for she whose mournful words

Made you a living spirit has passed away
And left you but a ball of passionate dust.
And you, proud earth and plumy sea, fade out!
For you may hear no more her faltering feet,
But are left lonely amid the clamorous war
Of angels upon devils.

[*He stands up; almost every one is kneeling, but it has grown so dark that only confused forms can be seen.*]

And I who weep
Call curses on you, Time and Fate and Change,
And have no excellent hope but the great hour
When you shall plunge headlong through bottomless space.

[*A flash of lightning followed immediately by thunder.*]

A PEASANT WOMAN. Pull him upon his knees before his curses
Have plucked thunder and lightning on our heads.
ALEEL. Angels and devils clash in the middle air,
And brazen swords clang upon brazen helms.

[*A flash of lightning followed immediately by thunder.*]

Yonder a bright spear, cast out of a sling,
Has torn through Balor's eye, and the dark clans
Fly screaming as they fled Moytura of old.

[*Everything is lost in darkness.*]

AN OLD MAN. The Almighty wrath at our great weakness and
sin
Has blotted out the world and we must die.

[*The darkness is broken by a visionary light. The PEASANTS seem to be kneeling upon the rocky slope of a mountain, and vapour full of storm and ever-changing light is sweeping above them and behind them. Half in the light, half in the shadow, stand armed angels. Their armour is old and worn, and their drawn swords dim and dinted. They stand as if upon the air in formation of battle and look downward with stern faces. The PEASANTS cast themselves on the ground.*]

ALEEL. Look no more on the half-closed gates of Hell,
But speak to me, whose mind is smitten of God,

That it may be no more with mortal things,
And tell of her who lies there.

> [*He seizes one of the angels.*]
>   Till you speak
You shall not drift into eternity.

THE ANGEL. The light beats down; the gates of pearl are wide;
And she is passing to the floor of peace,
And Mary of the seven times wounded heart
Has kissed her lips, and the long blessed hair
Has fallen on her face; The Light of Lights
Looks always on the motive, not the deed,
The Shadow of Shadows on the deed alone.

[ALEEL *releases the* ANGEL *and kneels.*]

OONA. Tell them who walk upon the floor of peace
That I would die and go to her I love;
The years like great black oxen tread the world,
And God the herdsman goads them on behind,
And I am broken by their passing feet.

[*A sound of far-off horns seems to come from the heart of the
light. The vision melts away, and the forms of the kneeling*
PEASANTS *appear faintly in the darkness.*]

THE END

JOHN MILLINGTON SYNGE

1871–1909

JOHN MILLINGTON SYNGE was the first significant playwright to emerge from the Irish theatrical renaissance that had been started by Yeats, the Fays, and Lady Gregory just before the turn of the century, but his involvement in all forms of Irish nationalism was so slight that he was accused of being an "alien of the spirit." His life and work are a study of extreme contrasts and nagging contradictions. In his plays he celebrated the primitive ways of life on the Aran Islands, and yet he was a wandering esthete who seemed to be more at home in a garret in Paris than in a cottage in Galway. He wrote realistically of the life of the peasants, and yet the rhythms of the Gaelic dialect that he used in his dialogue give his plays a poetic quality which tends to remove them from the simple realities of peasant life. His plays seem rooted in the life of the Irish countryside, yet each of them is derived from continental or classical models. His plays reflect great energy and an exuberant spirit, yet Synge himself was a shy and sickly young man who avoided all forms of public contact and died of cancer before he was forty.

But for all these contradictions—and many more—Synge must be ranked as one of the great masters of the modern drama. At Yeats' suggestion, Synge left Paris in 1898 to go to the Aran Islands "to express a life which has never found expression." He used the legends, language, and lore of these remote islands to fashion plays which had an element of magic to them and at the same time were both powerful and dramatically simple. The fusion of reality with fantasy is the dominant characteristic of all his work. He wrote in the preface to *The Playboy of the Western World* that "on the stage one must have reality, and one must have joy." His plays have these qualities, and they set the tone and the standard that all Irish dramatists of the twentieth century have tended to follow to this day.

PREFACE TO *THE PLAYBOY*
OF THE WESTERN WORLD[1]

IN WRITING *The Playboy of the Western World*, as in my other plays, I have used one or two words only that I have not heard among the country people of Ireland, or spoken in my own nursery before I could read the newspapers. A certain number of the phrases I employ I have heard also from herds and fishermen along the coast from Kerry to Mayo, or from beggarwomen and ballad singers near Dublin; and I am glad to acknowledge how much I owe to the folk imagination of these fine people. Anyone who has lived in real intimacy with the Irish peasantry will know that the wildest sayings and ideas in this play are tame indeed, compared with the fancies one may hear in any little hillside cabin in Geesala, or Carraroe, or Dingle Bay. All art is a collaboration! and there is little doubt that in the happy ages of literature, striking and beautiful phrases were as ready to the story-teller's or the playwright's hand, as the rich cloaks and dresses of his time. It is probable that when the Elizabethan dramatist took his inkhorn and sat down to his work he used many phrases that he had just heard, as he sat at dinner, from his mother or his children. In Ireland, those of us who know the people have the same privilege. When I was writing *The Shadow of the Glen*, some years ago, I got more aid than any learning could have given me from a chink in the floor of the old Wicklow house where I was staying, that let me hear what was being said by the servant girls in the kitchen. This matter, I think, is of importance, for in countries where the imagination of the people, and the language they use, is rich and living, it is possible for a writer to be rich and copious in his words, and

[1] Copyright 1907 and renewed 1934 by The Executors of the Estate of John M. Synge. Reprinted from *The Complete Works of John M. Synge*, by permission of Random House, Inc.

at the same time to give the reality, which is the root of all poetry, in a comprehensive and natural form. In the modern literature of towns, however, richness is found only in sonnets, or prose poems, or in one or two elaborate books that are far away from the profound and common interests of life. One has, on one side, Mallarmé and Huysmans[2] producing this literature; and on the other, Ibsen and Zola dealing with the reality of life in joyless and pallid words. On the stage one must have reality, and one must have joy; and that is why the intellectual modern drama has failed, and people have grown sick of the false joy of the musical comedy that has been given them in place of the rich joy found only in what is superb and wild in reality. In a good play every speech should be as fully flavored as a nut or apple, and such speeches cannot be written by anyone who works among people who have shut their lips on poetry. In Ireland, for a few years more, we have a popular imagination that is fiery and magnificent, and tender; so that those who wish to write start with a chance that is not given to writers in places where the springtime of the local life has been forgotten, and the harvest is a memory only, and the straw has been turned into bricks.

1907

PREFACE TO *THE TINKER'S WEDDING*[3]

The drama is made serious—in the French sense of the word—not by the degree in which it is taken up with problems that are serious in themselves, but by the degree in which it gives the nourishment, not very easy to define, on which our imaginations live. We should not go to the theatre as we go to a chemist's, or a dramshop, but as we go to a dinner, where the food we need is taken with pleasure and excitement. This was nearly always so in Spain and England and France when the drama was at its richest—the infancy and decay of the drama tend to be didactic—but in these days the playhouse is too often stocked with the drugs of many seedy problems, or with the absinthe or vermouth of the last musical comedy.

[2] Joris Karl Huysmans (1848–1907), French novelist and poet, most famous for *Against the Grain*.
[3] Copyright 1935 by The Modern Library, Inc. Reprinted from *The Complete Works of John M. Synge*, by permission of Random House, Inc.

The drama, like the symphony, does not teach or prove anything. Analysts with their problems, and teachers with their systems, are soon as old-fashioned as the pharmacopoeia of Galen,—look at Ibsen and the Germans—but the best plays of Ben Jonson and Molière can no more go out of fashion than the blackberries on the hedges.

Of the things which nourish the imagination humour is one of the most needful, and it is dangerous to limit or destroy it. Baudelaire calls laughter the greatest sign of the Satanic element in man; and where a country loses its humour, as some towns in Ireland are doing, there will be morbidity of mind, as Baudelaire's mind was morbid.

In the greater part of Ireland, however, the whole people, from the tinkers to the clergy, have still a life, and view of life, that are rich and genial and humorous. I do not think that these country people, who have so much humour themselves, will mind being laughed at without malice, as the people in every country have been laughed at in their own comedies.

December 2, 1907

THE PLAYBOY
OF THE WESTERN WORLD

by JOHN MILLINGTON SYNGE

1907

THE PLAYBOY
OF THE WESTERN WORLD[1]

CHARACTERS

CHRISTOPHER MAHON

OLD MAHON, *his father—a squatter*

MICHAEL JAMES FLAHERTY, *called* MICHAEL JAMES, *a publican*

MARGARET FLAHERTY, *called* PEGEEN MIKE, *his daughter*

WIDOW QUIN, *a woman of about thirty*

SHAWN KEOGH, *her cousin, a young farmer*

PHILLY CULLEN *and* JIMMY FARRELL, *small farmers*

SARA TANSEY, SUSAN BRADY, *and* HONOR BLAKE, *village girls*

A BELLMAN

SOME PEASANTS

The action takes place near a village, on a wild coast of Mayo. The first act passes on an evening of autumn, the other two acts on the following day.

ACT ONE

[SCENE—*Country public-house or shebeen, very rough and untidy. There is a sort of counter on the right with shelves, holding many bottles and jugs, just seen above it. Empty barrels stand near the counter. At back, a little to left of counter, there is a door into the open air, then, more to the left, there is a settle with shelves above it, with more jugs, and a table beneath a window. At the left there is a large open fire-place, with turf fire, and a small door into inner room.* PEGEEN, *a wild-looking but fine girl, of about twenty, is writing at table. She is dressed in the usual peasant dress.*]

PEGEEN [*slowly as she writes*]. Six yards of stuff for to make a yellow gown. A pair of lace boots with lengthy heels on them and brassy eyes. A hat is suited for a wedding day. A fine tooth comb. To be sent with three barrels of porter in Jimmy Farrell's creel cart on the evening of the coming Fair to Mister Michael James Flaherty. With the best compliments of this season. Margaret Flaherty.

SHAWN KEOGH [*a fat and fair young man comes in as she signs, looks round awkwardly, when he sees she is alone*]. Where's himself?

PEGEEN [*without looking at him*]. He's coming. [*She directs the letter.*] To Mister Sheamus Mulroy, Wine and Spirit Dealer, Castlebar.

SHAWN [*uneasily*]. I didn't see him on the road.

PEGEEN. How would you see him [*licks stamp and puts it on letter*] and it dark night this half hour gone by?

SHAWN [*turning towards the door again*]. I stood a while outside wondering would I have a right to pass on or to walk in and see you, Pegeen Mike [*comes to fire*], and I could hear the cows breathing, and sighing in the stillness of the air, and not a step moving any place from this gate to the bridge.

PEGEEN [*putting letter in envelope*]. It's above at the crossroads he is, meeting Philly Cullen; and a couple more are going along with him to Kate Cassidy's wake.

SHAWN [*looking at her blankly*]. And he's going that length in the dark night?

PEGEEN [*impatiently*]. He is surely, and leaving me lonesome on the scruff of the hill. [*She gets up and puts envelope on dresser, then winds clock.*] Isn't it long the nights are now, Shawn Keogh, to be leaving a poor girl with her own self counting the hours to the dawn of day?

SHAWN [*with awkward humour*]. If it is, when we're wedded in a short while you'll have no call to complain, for I've little will to be walking off to wakes or weddings in the darkness of the night.

PEGEEN [*with rather scornful good humour*]. You're making mighty certain, Shaneen, that I'll wed you now.

SHAWN. Aren't we after making a good bargain, the way we're only waiting these days on Father Reilly's dispensation from the bishops, or the Court of Rome.

PEGEEN [*looking at him teasingly, washing up at dresser*]. It's a wonder, Shaneen, the Holy Father'd be taking notice of the likes of you; for if I was him I wouldn't bother with this place where you'll meet none but Red Linahan, has a squint in his eye, and Patcheen is lame in his heel, or the mad Mulrannies were driven from California and they lost in their wits. We're a queer lot these times to go troubling the Holy Father on his sacred seat.

SHAWN [*scandalized*]. If we are, we're as good this place as another, maybe, and as good these times as we were for ever.

PEGEEN [*with scorn*]. As good, is it? Where now will you meet the like of Daneen Sullivan knocked the eye from a peeler, or Marcus Quin, God rest him, got six months for maiming ewes, and he a great warrant to tell stories of holy Ireland till he'd have the old women shedding down tears about their feet. Where will you find the like of them, I'm saying?

SHAWN [*timidly*]. If you don't, it's a good job, maybe; for [*with peculiar emphasis on the words*] Father Reilly has small conceit to have that kind walking around and talking to the girls.

PEGEEN [*impatiently, throwing water from basin out of the door*]. Stop tormenting me with Father Reilly [*imitating his voice*] when I'm asking only what way I'll pass these twelve hours of dark, and not take my death with the fear. [*Looking out of door.*]

SHAWN [*timidly*]. Would I fetch you the Widow Quin, maybe?

PEGEEN. Is it the like of that murderer? You'll not, surely.

SHAWN [*going to her, soothingly*]. Then I'm thinking himself will stop along with you when he sees you taking on, for it'll be a long night-time with great darkness, and I'm after feeling a kind of fellow above in the furzy ditch, groaning wicked like a maddening dog, the way it's good cause you have, maybe, to be fearing now.

PEGEEN [*turning on him sharply*]. What's that? Is it a man you seen?

SHAWN [*retreating*]. I couldn't see him at all; but I heard him groaning out, and breaking his heart. It should have been a young man from his words speaking.

PEGEEN [*going after him*]. And you never went near to see was he hurted or what ailed him at all?

SHAWN. I did not, Pegeen Mike. It was a dark, lonesome place to be hearing the like of him.

PEGEEN. Well, you're a daring fellow, and if they find his corpse stretched above in the dews of dawn, what'll you say then to the peelers, or the Justice of the Peace?

SHAWN [*thunderstruck*]. I wasn't thinking of that. For the love of God, Pegeen Mike, don't let on I was speaking of him. Don't tell your father and the men is coming above; for if they heard that story, they'd have great blabbing this night at the wake.

PEGEEN. I'll maybe tell them, and I'll maybe not.

SHAWN. They are coming at the door. Will you whisht, I'm saying?

PEGEEN. Whisht yourself.

[*She goes behind counter.* MICHAEL JAMES, *fat jovial publican, comes in followed by* PHILLY CULLEN, *who is thin and mistrusting, and* JIMMY FARRELL, *who is fat and amorous, about forty-five.*]

MEN [*together*]. God bless you. The blessing of God on this place.

PEGEEN. God bless you kindly.

MICHAEL [*to men who go to the counter*]. Sit down now, and take your rest. [*Crosses to* SHAWN *at the fire.*] And how is it you are, Shawn Keogh? Are you coming over the sands to Kate Cassidy's wake?

SHAWN. I am not, Michael James. I'm going home the short cut to my bed.

PEGEEN [*speaking across the counter*]. He's right too, and have you no shame, Michael James, to be quitting off for the whole night, and leaving myself lonesome in the shop?

MICHAEL [*good-humouredly*]. Isn't it the same whether I go for the whole night or a part only? and I'm thinking it's a queer daughter you are if you'd have me crossing backward through the Stooks of the Dead Women, with a drop taken.

PEGEEN. If I am a queer daughter, it's a queer father'd be leaving me lonesome these twelve hours of dark, and I piling the turf with the dogs barking, and the calves mooing, and my own teeth rattling with the fear.

JIMMY [*flatteringly*]. What is there to hurt you, and you a fine, hardy girl would knock the head of any two men in the place?

PEGEEN [*working herself up*]. Isn't there the harvest boys with their tongues red for drink, and the ten tinkers is camped in the east glen, and the thousand militia—bad cess to them!— walking idle through the land. There's lots surely to hurt me, and I won't stop alone in it, let himself do what he will.

MICHAEL. If you're that afeard, let Shawn Keogh stop along with you. It's the will of God, I'm thinking, himself should be seeing to you now.

[*They all turn on* SHAWN.]

SHAWN [*in horrified confusion*]. I would and welcome, Michael James, but I'm afeard of Father Reilly; and what at all would the Holy Father and the Cardinals of Rome be saying if they heard I did the like of that?

MICHAEL [*with contempt*]. God help you! Can't you sit in by the hearth with the light lit and herself beyond in the room? You'll do that surely, for I've heard tell there's a queer fellow above, going mad or getting his death, maybe, in the gripe of the ditch, so she'd be safer this night with a person here.

SHAWN [*with plaintive despair*]. I'm afeard of Father Reilly, I'm saying. Let you not be tempting me, and we near married itself.

PHILLY [*with cold contempt*]. Lock him in the west room. He'll stay then and have no sin to be telling to the priest.

MICHAEL [*to* SHAWN, *getting between him and the door*]. Go up now.

SHAWN [*at the top of his voice*]. Don't stop me, Michael James. Let me out of the door, I'm saying, for the love of the Almighty God. Let me out. [*Trying to dodge past him.*] Let me out of it, and may God grant you His indulgence in the hour of need.

MICHAEL [*loudly*]. Stop your noising, and sit down by the
hearth. [*Gives him a push and goes to counter laughing.*]

SHAWN [*turning back, wringing his hands*]. Oh, Father Reilly
and the saints of God, where will I hide myself to-day?
Oh, St. Joseph and St. Patrick and St. Brigid, and St.
James, have mercy on me now! [SHAWN *turns round, sees
door clear, and makes a rush for it.*]

MICHAEL [*catching him by the coat tail*]. You'd be going,
is it?

SHAWN [*screaming*]. Leave me go, Michael James, leave me
go, you old Pagan, leave me go, or I'll get the curse of the
priests on you, and of the scarlet-coated bishops of the
courts of Rome. [*With a sudden movement he pulls himself
out of his coat, and disappears out of the door, leaving his
coat in* MICHAEL'*s hands.*]

MICHAEL [*turning round, and holding up coat*]. Well, there's
the coat of a Christian man. Oh, there's sainted glory this
day in the lonesome west; and by the will of God I've got
you a decent man, Pegeen, you'll have no call to be spying
after if you've a score of young girls, maybe, weeding in
your fields.

PEGEEN [*taking up the defence of her property*]. What right
have you to be making game of a poor fellow for minding
the priest, when it's your own the fault is, not paying a
penny pot-boy to stand along with me and give me courage
in the doing of my work? [*She snaps the coat away from
him, and goes behind counter with it.*]

MICHAEL. [*taken aback*]. Where would I get a pot-boy? Would
you have me send the bellman screaming in the streets of
Castlebar?

SHAWN [*opening the door a chink and putting in his head, in a
small voice*]. Michael James!

MICHAEL [*imitating him*]. What ails you?

SHAWN. The queer dying fellow's beyond looking over the
ditch. He's come up, I'm thinking, stealing your hens.
[*Looks over his shoulder.*] God help me, he's following me
now [*he runs into room*], and if he's heard what I said,
he'll be having my life, and I going home lonesome in the
darkness of the night.

[*For a perceptible moment they watch the door with curiosity.
Some one coughs outside. Then* CHRISTY MAHON, *a slight
young man, comes in very tired and frightened and dirty.*]

CHRISTY [*in a small voice*]. God save all here!

MEN. God save you kindly.

CHRISTY [*going to the counter*]. I'd trouble you for a glass of porter, woman of the house. [*He puts down coin.*]

PEGEEN [*serving him*]. You're one of the tinkers, young fellow, is beyond camped in the glen?

CHRISTY. I am not; but I'm destroyed walking.

MICHAEL [*patronizingly*]. Let you come up then to the fire. You're looking famished with the cold.

CHRISTY. God reward you. [*He takes up his glass and goes a little way across to the left, then stops and looks about him.*] Is it often the police do be coming into this place, master of the house?

MICHAEL. If you'd come in better hours, you'd have seen "Licensed for the sale of Beer and Spirits, to be consumed on the premises," written in white letters above the door, and what would the polis want spying on me, and not a decent house within four miles, the way every living Christian is a bona fide, saving one widow alone?

CHRISTY [*with relief*]. It's a safe house, so. [*He goes over to the fire, sighing and moaning. Then he sits down, putting his glass beside him and begins gnawing a turnip, too miserable to feel the others staring at him with curiosity.*]

MICHAEL [*going after him*]. Is it yourself is fearing the polis? You're wanting, maybe?

CHRISTY. There's many wanting.

MICHAEL. Many surely, with the broken harvest and the ended wars. [*He picks up some stockings, etc., that are near the fire, and carries them away furtively.*] It should be larceny, I'm thinking?

CHRISTY [*dolefully*]. I had it in my mind it was a different word and a bigger.

PEGEEN. There's a queer lad. Were you never slapped in school, young fellow, that you don't know the name of your deed?

CHRISTY [*bashfully*]. I'm slow at learning, a middling scholar only.

MICHAEL. If you're a dunce itself, you'd have a right to know that larceny's robbing and stealing. Is it for the like of that you're wanting?

CHRISTY [*with a flash of family pride*]. And I the son of a strong farmer [*with a sudden qualm*], God rest his soul, could have bought up the whole of your old house a while

since, from the butt of his tailpocket, and not have missed
the weight of it gone.

MICHAEL [*impressed*]. If it's not stealing, it's maybe something big.

CHRISTY [*flattered*]. Aye; it's maybe something big.

JIMMY. He's a wicked-looking young fellow. Maybe he followed after a young woman on a lonesome night.

CHRISTY. [*shocked*]. Oh, the saints forbid, mister; I was all
times a decent lad.

PHILLY [*turning on* JIMMY]. You're a silly man, Jimmy
Farrell. He said his father was a farmer a while since, and
there's himself now in a poor state. Maybe the land was
grabbed from him, and he did what any decent man
would do.

MICHAEL [*to* CHRISTY, *mysteriously*]. Was it bailiffs?

CHRISTY. The divil a one.

MICHAEL. Agents?

CHRISTY. The divil a one.

MICHAEL. Landlords?

CHRISTY [*peevishly*]. Ah, not at all, I'm saying. You'd see the
like of them stories on any little paper of a Munster town.
But I'm not calling to mind any person, gentle, simple,
judge or jury, did the like of me.

[*They all draw nearer with delighted curiosity.*]

PHILLY. Well, that lad's a puzzle-the-world.

JIMMY. He'd beat Dan Davies' circus, or the holy missioners
making sermons on the villainy of man. Try him again,
Philly.

PHILLY. Did you strike golden guineas out of solder, young
fellow, or shilling coins itself?

CHRISTY. I did not, mister, not sixpence nor a farthing coin.

JIMMY. Did you marry three wives maybe? I'm told there's a
sprinkling have done that among the holy Luthers of the
preaching north.

CHRISTY [*shyly*]. I never married with one, let alone with a
couple or three.

PHILLY. Maybe he went fighting for the Boers, the like of the
man beyond, was judged to be hanged, quartered and
drawn. Were you off east, young fellow, fighting bloody
wars for Kruger and the freedom of the Boers?

CHRISTY. I never left my own parish till Tuesday was a week.

PEGEEN [*coming from counter*]. He's done nothing, so. [*To*

CHRISTY.] If you didn't commit murder or a bad, nasty
thing, or false coining, or robbery, or butchery, or the like
of them, there isn't anything that would be worth your
troubling for to run from now. You did nothing at all.

CHRISTY [*his feelings hurt*]. That's an unkindly thing to be
saying to a poor orphaned traveller, has a prison behind
him, and hanging before, and hell's gap gaping below.

PEGEEN [*with a sign to the men to be quiet*]. You're only
saying it. You did nothing at all. A soft lad the like of you
wouldn't slit the windpipe of a screeching sow.

CHRISTY [*offended*]. You're not speaking the truth.

PEGEEN [*in mock rage*]. Not speaking the truth, is it? Would
you have me knock the head of you with the butt of the
broom?

CHRISTY [*twisting round on her with a sharp cry of horror*].
Don't strike me. I killed my poor father, Tuesday was a
week, for doing the like of that.

PEGEEN [*with blank amazement*]. Is it killed your father?

CHRISTY [*subsiding*]. With the help of God I did surely, and
that the Holy Immaculate Mother may intercede for his
soul.

PHILLY [*retreating with* JIMMY]. There's a daring fellow.

JIMMY. Oh, glory be to God!

MICHAEL [*with great respect*]. That was a hanging crime,
mister honey. You should have had good reason for doing
the like of that.

CHRISTY [*in a very reasonable tone*]. He was a dirty man, God
forgive him, and he getting old and crusty, the way I
couldn't put up with him at all.

PEGEEN. And you shot him dead?

CHRISTY [*shaking his head*]. I never used weapons. I've no
license, and I'm a law-fearing man.

MICHAEL. It was with a hilted knife maybe? I'm told, in the
big world it's bloody knives they use.

CHRISTY [*loudly, scandalized*]. Do you take me for a slaughter-
boy?

PEGEEN. You never hanged him, the way Jimmy Farrell
hanged his dog from the license, and had it screeching and
wriggling three hours at the butt of a string, and himself
swearing it was a dead dog, and the peelers swearing it had
life?

CHRISTY. I did not then. I just riz the loy and let fall the
edge of it on the ridge of his skull, and he went down at

my feet like an empty sack, and never let a grunt or groan
from him at all.

MICHAEL [*making a sign to* PEGEEN *to fill* CHRISTY'S *glass*].
And what way weren't you hanged, mister? Did you bury
him then?

CHRISTY [*considering*]. Aye. I buried him then. Wasn't I
digging spuds in the field?

MICHAEL. And the peelers never followed after you the eleven
days that you're out?

CHRISTY [*shaking his head*]. Never a one of them, and I walking forward facing hog, dog, or divil on the highway of
the road.

PHILLY [*nodding wisely*]. It's only with a common week-day
kind of a murderer them lads would be trusting their carcase, and that man should be a great terror when his
temper's roused.

MICHAEL. He should then. [*To* CHRISTY.] And where was it,
mister honey, that you did the deed?

CHRISTY [*looking at him with suspicion*]. Oh, a distant place,
master of the house, a windy corner of high, distant hills.

PHILLY [*nodding with approval*]. He's a close man, and he's
right, surely.

PEGEEN. That'd be a lad with the sense of Solomon to have for
a pot-boy, Michael James, if it's the truth you're seeking
one at all.

PHILLY. The peelers is fearing him, and if you'd that lad in
the house there isn't one of them would come smelling
around if the dogs itself were lapping poteen from the
dung-pit of the yard.

JIMMY. Bravery's a treasure in a lonesome place, and a lad
would kill his father, I'm thinking, would face a foxy divil
with a pitch-pike on the flags of hell.

PEGEEN. It's the truth they're saying, and if I'd that lad in the
house, I wouldn't be fearing the loosèd kharki cut-throats,
or the walking dead.

CHRISTY [*swelling with surprise and triumph*]. Well, glory be to
God!

MICHAEL [*with deference*]. Would you think well to stop here
and be pot-boy, mister honey, if we gave you good wages,
and didn't destroy you with the weight of work?

SHAWN [*coming forward uneasily*]. That'd be a queer kind to
bring into a decent quiet household with the like of Pegeen
Mike.

PEGEEN [*very sharply*]. Will you whisht? Who's speaking to you?

SHAWN [*retreating*]. A bloody-handed murderer the like of . . .

PEGEEN [*snapping at him*]. Whisht I am saying; we'll take no fooling from your like at all. [*To* CHRISTY *with a honeyed voice.*] And you, young fellow, you'd have a right to stop, I'm thinking, for we'd do our all and utmost to content your needs.

CHRISTY [*overcome with wonder*]. And I'd be safe in this place from the searching law?

MICHAEL. You would, surely. If they're not fearing you, itself, the peelers in this place is decent droughty poor fellows, wouldn't touch a cur dog and not give warning in the dead of night.

PEGEEN [*very kindly and persuasively*]. Let you stop a short while anyhow. Aren't you destroyed walking with your feet in bleeding blisters, and your whole skin needing washing like a Wicklow sheep.

CHRISTY [*looking round with satisfaction*]. It's a nice room, and if it's not humbugging me you are, I'm thinking that I'll surely stay.

JIMMY [*jumps up*]. Now, by the grace of God, herself will be safe this night, with a man killed his father holding danger from the door, and let you come on, Michael James, or they'll have the best stuff drunk at the wake.

MICHAEL [*going to the door with men*]. And begging your pardon, mister, what name will we call you, for we'd like to know?

CHRISTY. Christopher Mahon.

MICHAEL. Well, God bless you, Christy, and a good rest till we meet again when the sun'll be rising to the noon of day.

CHRISTY. God bless you all.

MEN. God bless you.

[*They go out except* SHAWN, *who lingers at door.*]

SHAWN [*to* PEGEEN]. Are you wanting me to stop along with you to keep you from harm?

PEGEEN [*gruffly*]. Didn't you say you were fearing Father Reilly?

SHAWN. There'd be no harm staying now, I'm thinking, and himself in it too.

PEGEEN. You wouldn't stay when there was need for you, and let you step off nimble this time when there's none.

SHAWN. Didn't I say it was Father Reilly . . .

PEGEEN. Go on, then, to Father Reilly [*in a jeering tone*], and let him put you in the holy brotherhoods, and leave that lad to me.

SHAWN. If I meet the Widow Quin . . .

PEGEEN. Go on, I'm staying, and don't be waking this place with your noise. [*She hustles him out and bolts the door.*] That lad would wear the spirits from the saints of peace. [*Bustles about, then takes off her apron and pins it up in the window as a blind.* CHRISTY *watching her timidly. Then she comes to him and speaks with bland good humour.*] Let you stretch out now by the fire, young fellow. You should be destroyed travelling.

CHRISTY [*shyly again, drawing off his boots*]. I'm tired, surely, walking wild eleven days, and waking fearful in the night. [*He holds up one of his feet, feeling his blisters, and looking at them with compassion.*]

PEGEEN [*standing beside him, watching him with delight*]. You should have had great people in your family, I'm thinking, with the little, small feet you have, and you with a kind of a quality name, the like of what you'd find on the great powers and potentates of France and Spain.

CHRISTY [*with pride*]. We were great surely, with wide and windy acres of rich Munster land.

PEGEEN. Wasn't I telling you, and you a fine, handsome young fellow with a noble brow?

CHRISTY [*with a flash of delighted surprise*]. Is it me?

PEGEEN. Aye. Did you never hear that from the young girls where you come from in the west or south?

CHRISTY [*with venom*]. I did not then. Oh, they're bloody liars in the naked parish where I grew a man.

PEGEEN. If they are itself, you've heard it these days, I'm thinking, and you walking the world telling out your story to young girls or old.

CHRISTY. I've told my story no place till this night, Pegeen Mike, and it's foolish I was here, maybe, to be talking free, but you're decent people, I'm thinking, and yourself a kindly woman, the way I wasn't fearing you at all.

PEGEEN [*filling a sack with straw*]. You've said the like of that, maybe, in every cot and cabin where you've met a young girl on your way.

CHRISTY [*going over to her, gradually raising his voice*]. I've said it nowhere till this night, I'm telling you, for I've seen none the like of you the eleven long days I am walking the world, looking over a low ditch or a high ditch on my north or my south, into stony scattered fields, or scribes of bog, where you'd see young, limber girls, and fine prancing women making laughter with the men.

PEGEEN. If you weren't destroyed travelling, you'd have as much talk and streeleen, I'm thinking, as Owen Roe O'Sullivan or the poets of the Dingle Bay, and I've heard all times it's the poets are your like, fine fiery fellows with great rages when their temper's roused.

CHRISTY [drawing a little nearer to her]. You've a power of rings, God bless you, and would there be any offence if I was asking are you single now?

PEGEEN. What would I want wedding so young?

CHRISTY [with relief]. We're alike, so.

PEGEEN [she puts sack on settle and beats it up]. I never killed my father. I'd be afeard to do that, except I was the like of yourself with blind rages tearing me within, for I'm thinking you should have had great tussling when the end was come.

CHRISTY [expanding with delight at the first confidential talk he has ever had with a woman]. We had not then. It was a hard woman was come over the hill, and if he was always a crusty kind when he'd a hard woman setting him on, not the divil himself or his four fathers could put up with him at all.

PEGEEN [with curiosity]. And isn't it a great wonder that one wasn't fearing you?

CHRISTY [very confidentially]. Up to the day I killed my father, there wasn't a person in Ireland knew the kind I was, and I there drinking, waking, eating, sleeping, a quiet, simple poor fellow with no man giving me heed.

PEGEEN [getting a quilt out of the cupboard and putting it on the sack]. It was the girls were giving you heed maybe, and I'm thinking it's most conceit you'd have to be gaming with their like.

CHRISTY [shaking his head, with simplicity]. Not the girls itself, and I won't tell you a lie. There wasn't anyone heeding me in that place saving only the dumb beasts of the field. [He sits down at fire.]

PEGEEN [with disappointment]. And I thinking you should have been living the like of a king of Norway or the Eastern world. [She comes and sits beside him after placing bread and mug of milk on the table.]

CHRISTY [laughing piteously]. The like of a king, is it? And I

after toiling, moiling, digging, dodging from the dawn till
dusk with never a sight of joy or sport saving only when
I'd be abroad in the dark night poaching rabbits on hills, for
I was a divil to poach, God forgive me, [*very naïvely*] and I
near got six months for going with a dung fork and stabbing
a fish.

PEGEEN. And it's that you'd call sport, is it, to be abroad in
the darkness with yourself alone?

CHRISTY. I did, God help me, and there I'd be as happy as the
sunshine of St. Martin's Day, watching the light passing
the north or the patches of fog, till I'd hear a rabbit starting to screech and I'd go running in the furze. Then when
I'd my full share I'd come walking down where you'd see
the ducks and geese stretched sleeping on the highway of
the road, and before I'd pass the dunghill, I'd hear himself
snoring out, a loud lonesome snore he'd be making all times,
the while he was sleeping, and he a man'd be raging all
times, the while he was waking, like a gaudy officer you'd
hear cursing and damning and swearing oaths.

PEGEEN. Providence and Mercy, spare us all!

CHRISTY. It's that you'd say surely if you seen him and he
after drinking for weeks, rising up in the red dawn, or before it maybe, and going out into the yard as naked as an
ash tree in the moon of May, and shying clods against the
visage of the stars till he'd put the fear of death into the
banbhs and the screeching sows.

PEGEEN. I'd be well-nigh afeard of that lad myself, I'm thinking. And there was no one in it but the two of you alone?

CHRISTY. The divil a one, though he'd sons and daughters
walking all great states and territories of the world, and
not a one of them, to this day, but would say their seven
curses on him, and they rousing up to let a cough or sneeze,
maybe, in the deadness of the night.

PEGEEN [*nodding her head*]. Well, you should have been a
queer lot. I never cursed my father the like of that, though
I'm twenty and more years of age.

CHRISTY. Then you'd have cursed mine, I'm telling you, and
he a man never gave peace to any, saving when he'd get
two months or three, or be locked in the asylums for batter-
ing peelers or assaulting men [*with depression*] the way it
was a bitter life he led me till I did up a Tuesday and halve
his skull.

PEGEEN [*putting her hand on his shoulder*]. Well, you'll have

peace in this place, Christy Mahon, and none to trouble
you, and it's near time a fine lad like you should have your
good share of the earth.

CHRISTY. It's time surely, and I a seemly fellow with great
strength in me and bravery of . . .

[*Someone knocks.*]

CHRISTY [*clinging to* PEGEEN]. Oh, glory! it's late for knocking,
and this last while I'm in terror of the peelers, and the
walking dead.

[*Knocking again.*]

PEGEEN. Who's there?
VOICE [*outside*]. Me.
PEGEEN. Who's me?
VOICE. The Widow Quin.
PEGEEN [*jumping up and giving him the bread and milk*]. Go
on now with your supper, and let on to be sleepy, for if she
found you were such a warrant to talk, she'd be stringing
gabble till the dawn of day.

[*He takes bread and sits shyly with his back to the door.*]

PEGEEN [*opening door, with temper*]. What ails you, or what
is it you're wanting at this hour of the night?
WIDOW QUIN [*coming in a step and peering at* CHRISTY]. I'm
after meeting Shawn Keogh and Father Reilly below, who
told me of your curiosity man, and they fearing by this time
he was maybe roaring, romping on your hands with drink.
PEGEEN [*pointing to* CHRISTY]. Look now is he roaring, and
he stretched away drowsy with his supper and his mug of
milk. Walk down and tell that to Father Reilly and to
Shaneen Keogh.
WIDOW QUIN [*coming forward*]. I'll not see them again, for
I've their word to lead that lad forward for to lodge
with me.
PEGEEN [*in blank amazement*]. This night, is it?
WIDOW QUIN [*going over*]. This night. "It isn't fitting," says
the priesteen, "to have his likeness lodging with an orphaned
girl." [*To* CHRISTY.] God save you, mister!
CHRISTY [*shyly*]. God save you kindly.
WIDOW QUIN [*looking at him with half-amazed curiosity*].
Well, aren't you a little smiling fellow? It should have been

great and bitter torments did arouse your spirits to a deed
of blood.

CHRISTY [*doubtfully*]. It should, maybe.

WIDOW QUIN. It's more than "maybe" I'm saying, and it'd
soften my heart to see you sitting so simple with your cup
and cake, and you fitter to be saying your catechism than
slaying your da.

PEGEEN [*at counter, washing glasses*]. There's talking when
any'd see he's fit to be holding his head high with the wonders of the world. Walk on from this, for I'll not have him
tormented and he destroyed travelling since Tuesday was a
week.

WIDOW QUIN [*peaceably*]. We'll be walking surely when his
supper's done, and you'll find we're great company, young
fellow, when it's of the like of you and me you'd hear the
penny poets singing in an August Fair.

CHRISTY [*innocently*]. Did you kill your father?

PEGEEN [*contemptuously*]. She did not. She hit himself with a
worn pick, and the rusted poison did corrode his blood the
way he never overed it, and died after. That was a sneaky
kind of murder did win small glory with the boys itself.
[*She crosses to* CHRISTY's *left.*]

WIDOW QUIN [*with good humour*]. If it didn't, maybe all
knows a widow woman has buried her children and destroyed her man is a wiser comrade for a young lad than
a girl, the like of you, who'd go helter-skeltering after any
man would let you a wink upon the road.

PEGEEN [*breaking out into wild rage*]. And you'll say that,
Widow Quin, and you gasping with the rage you had racing
the hill beyond to look on his face.

WIDOW QUIN [*laughing derisively*]. Me, is it? Well, Father
Reilly has cuteness to divide you now. [*She pulls* CHRISTY
up.] There's great temptation in a man did slay his da,
and we'd best be going, young fellow; so rise up and come
with me.

PEGEEN [*seizing his arm*]. He'll not stir. He's pot-boy in this
place, and I'll not have him stolen off and kidnabbed while
himself's abroad.

WIDOW QUIN. It'd be a crazy pot-boy'd lodge him in the
shebeen where he works by day, so you'd have a right to
come on, young fellow, till you see my little houseen, a
perch off on the rising hill.

PEGEEN. Wait till morning, Christy Mahon. Wait till you lay

eyes on her leaky thatch is growing more pasture for her
buck goat than her square of fields, and she without a
tramp itself to keep in order her place at all.

WIDOW QUIN. When you see me contriving in my little gardens,
Christy Mahon, you'll swear the Lord God formed me to
be living lone, and that there isn't my match in Mayo for
thatching, or mowing, or shearing a sheep.

PEGEEN [*with noisy scorn*]. It's true the Lord God formed
you to contrive indeed. Doesn't the world know you reared
a black lamb at your own breast, so that the Lord Bishop
of Connaught felt the elements of a Christian, and he eating it after in a kidney stew? Doesn't the world know you've
been seen shaving the foxy skipper from France for a
threepenny bit and a sop of grass tobacco would wring the
liver from a mountain goat you'd meet leaping the hills?

WIDOW QUIN [*with amusement*]. Do you hear her now young
fellow? Do you hear the way she'll be rating at your own
self when a week is by?

PEGEEN [*to* CHRISTY]. Don't heed her. Tell her to go into her
pigsty and not plague us here.

WIDOW QUIN. I'm going; but he'll come with me.

PEGEEN [*shaking him*]. Are you dumb, young fellow?

CHRISTY [*timidly, to* WIDOW QUIN]. God increase you; but I'm
pot-boy in this place, and it's here I'd liefer stay.

PEGEEN [*triumphantly*]. Now you have heard him, and go on
from this.

WIDOW QUIN [*looking round the room*]. It's lonesome this
hour crossing the hill, and if he won't come along with me,
I'd have a right maybe to stop this night with yourselves.
Let me stretch out on the settle, Pegeen Mike; and himself
can lie by the hearth.

PEGEEN [*short and fiercely*]. Faith, I won't. Quit off or I will
send you now.

WIDOW QUIN [*gathering her shawl up*]. Well, it's a terror to be
aged a score. [*To* CHRISTY.] God bless you now, young
fellow, and let you be wary, or there's right torment will
await you here if you go romancing with her like, and she
waiting only, as they bade me say, on a sheepskin parch-
ment to be wed with Shawn Keogh of Killakeen.

CHRISTY [*going to* PEGEEN *as she bolts the door*]. What's that
she's after saying?

PEGEEN. Lies and blather, you've no call to mind. Well, isn't
Shawn Keogh an impudent fellow to send up spying on me?

Wait till I lay hands on him. Let him wait, I'm saying.

CHRISTY. And you're not wedding him at all?

PEGEEN. I wouldn't wed him if a bishop came walking for to join us here.

CHRISTY. That God in glory may be thanked for that.

PEGEEN. There's your bed now. I've put a quilt upon you I'm after quilting a while since with my own two hands, and you'd best stretch out now for your sleep, and may God give you a good rest till I call you in the morning when the cocks will crow.

CHRISTY [*as she goes to inner room*]. May God and Mary and St. Patrick bless you and reward you, for your kindly talk.

[*She shuts the door behind her. He settles his bed slowly, feeling the quilt with immense satisfaction.*]

Well, it's a clean bed and soft with it, and it's great luck and company I've won me in the end of time—two fine women fighting for the likes of me—till I'm thinking this night wasn't I a foolish fellow not to kill my father in the years gone by.

ACT TWO

[SCENE—*as before. Brilliant morning light.* CHRISTY, *looking bright and cheerful, is cleaning a girl's boots.*]

CHRISTY [*to himself, counting jugs on dresser*]. Half a hundred beyond. Ten there. A score that's above. Eighty jugs. Six cups and a broken one. Two plates. A power of glasses. Bottles, a school-master'd be hard set to count, and enough in them, I'm thinking, to drunken all the wealth and wisdom of the County Clare. [*He puts down the boot carefully.*] There's her boots now, nice and decent for her evening use, and isn't it grand brushes she has? [*He puts them down and goes by degrees to the looking-glass.*] Well, this'd be a fine place to be my whole life talking out with swearing Christians, in place of my old dogs and cat, and I stalking around, smoking my pipe and drinking my fill, and never a day's work but drawing a cork an odd time, or wiping a glass, or rinsing out a shiny tumbler for a decent man. [*He takes the looking-glass from the wall and puts it on the back of a chair; then sits down in front of it and begins washing his face.*] Didn't I know rightly I was handsome, though it was the divil's own mirror we had beyond, would twist a squint across an angel's brow; and I'll be growing fine from this day, the way I'll have a soft lovely skin on me and won't be the like of the clumsy young fellows do be ploughing all times in the earth and dung. [*He starts.*] Is she coming again? [*He looks out.*] Stranger girls. God help me, where'll I hide myself away and my long neck naked to the world? [*He looks out.*] I'd best go to the room maybe till I'm dressed again.

[*He gathers up his coat and the looking-glass, and runs into the inner room. The door is pushed open, and* SUSAN BRADY *looks in, and knocks on door.*]

SUSAN. There's nobody in it. [*Knocks again.*]
NELLY [*pushing her in and following her, with* HONOR BLAKE *and* SARA TANSEY]. It'd be early for them both to be out walking the hill.

SUSAN. I'm thinking Shawn Keogh was making game of us and there's no such man in it at all.

HONOR [*pointing to straw and quilt*]. Look at that. He's been sleeping there in the night. Well, it'll be a hard case if he's gone off now, the way we'll never set our eyes on a man killed his father, and we after rising early and destroying ourselves running fast on the hill.

NELLY. Are you thinking them's his boots?

SARA [*taking them up*]. If they are, there should be his father's track on them. Did you never read in the papers the way murdered men do bleed and drip?

SUSAN. Is that blood there, Sara Tansey?

SARA [*smelling it*]. That's bog water, I'm thinking, but it's his own they are surely, for I never seen the like of them for whity mud, and red mud, and turf on them, and the fine sands of the sea. That man's been walking, I'm telling you. [*She goes down right, putting on one of his boots.*]

SUSAN [*going to window*]. Maybe he's stolen off to Belmullet with the boots of Michael James, and you'd have a right so to follow after him, Sara Tansey, and you the one yoked the ass cart and drove ten miles to set your eyes on the man bit the yellow lady's nostril on the northern shore. [*She looks out.*]

SARA [*running to window with one boot on*]. Don't be talking, and we fooled today. [*Putting on other boot.*] There's a pair do fit me well, and I'll be keeping them for walking to the priest, when you'd be ashamed this place, going up winter and summer with nothing worth while to confess at all.

HONOR [*who has been listening at the door*]. Whisht! there's someone inside the room. [*She pushes door a chink open.*] It's a man.

[SARA *kicks off boots and puts them where they were. They all stand in a line looking through chink.*]

SARA. I'll call him. Mister! Mister! [*He puts in his head.*] Is Pegeen within?

CHRISTY [*coming in as meek as a mouse, with the looking-glass held behind his back*]. She's above on the cnuceen, seeking the nanny goats, the way she'd have a sup of goat's milk for to color my tea.

SARA. And asking your pardon, is it you's the man killed his father?

CHRISTY [*sidling toward the nail where the glass was hanging*].
I am, God help me!

SARA [*taking eggs she has brought*]. Then my thousand wel-
comes to you, and I've run up with a brace of duck's eggs
for your food today. Pegeen's ducks is no use, but these
are the real rich sort. Hold out your hand and you'll see it's
no lie I'm telling you.

CHRISTY [*coming forward shyly, and holding out his left
hand*]. They're a great and weighty size.

SUSAN. And I run up with a pat of butter, for it'd be a poor
thing to have you eating your spuds dry, and you after
running a great way since you did destroy your da.

CHRISTY. Thank you kindly.

HONOR. And I brought you a little cut of cake, for you should
have a thin stomach on you, and you that length walking
the world.

NELLY. And I brought you a little laying pullet—boiled and
all she is—was crushed at the fall of night by the curate's
car. Feel the fat of that breast, mister.

CHRISTY. It's bursting, surely. [*He feels it with the back of his
hand, in which he holds the presents.*]

SARA. Will you pinch it? Is your right hand too sacred for to
use at all? [*She slips round behind him.*] It's a glass he has.
Well, I never seen to this day a man with a looking-glass
held to his back. Them that kills their fathers is a vain lot
surely.

[*Girls giggle.*]

CHRISTY [*smiling innocently and piling presents on glass*]. I'm
very thankful to you all today . . .

WIDOW QUIN [*coming in quickly, at door*]. Sara Tansey, Susan
Brady, Honor Blake! What in glory has you here at this
hour of day?

GIRLS [*giggling*]. That's the man killed his father.

WIDOW QUIN [*coming to them*]. I know well it's the man; and
I'm after putting him down in the sports below for racing,
leaping, pitching, and the Lord knows what.

SARA [*exuberantly*]. That's right, Widow Quin. I'll bet my
dowry that he'll lick the world.

WIDOW QUIN. If you will, you'd have a right to have him fresh
and nourished in place of nursing a feast. [*Taking presents.*] Are you fasting or fed, young fellow?

CHRISTY. Fasting, if you please.

WIDOW QUIN [*loudly*]. Well, you're the lot. Stir up now and give him his breakfast. [*To* CHRISTY.] Come here to me [*She puts him on bench beside her while the girls make tea and get his breakfast*] and let you tell us your story before Pegeen will come, in place of grinning your ears off like the moon of May.

CHRISTY [*beginning to be pleased*]. It's a long story; you'd be destroyed listening.

WIDOW QUIN. Don't be letting on to be shy, a fine, gamey, treacherous lad the like of you. Was it in your house beyond you cracked his skull?

CHRISTY [*shy but flattered*]. It was not. We were digging spuds in his cold, sloping, stony, divil's patch of a field.

WIDOW QUIN. And you went asking money of him, or making talk of getting a wife would drive him from his farm?

CHRISTY. I did not, then; but there I was, digging and digging, and "You squinting idiot," says he, "let you walk down now and tell the priest you'll wed the Widow Casey in a score of days."

WIDOW QUIN. And what kind was she?

CHRISTY [*with horror*]. A walking terror from beyond the hills, and she two score and two hundredweights and five pounds in the weighing scales, with a limping leg on her, and a blinded eye, and she a woman of noted misbehavior with the old and young.

GIRLS [*clustering round him, serving him*]. Glory be.

WIDOW QUIN. And what did he want driving you to wed with her? [*She takes a bit of the chicken.*]

CHRISTY [*eating with growing satisfaction*]. He was letting on I was wanting a protector from the harshness of the world, and he without a thought the whole while but how he'd have her hut to live in and her gold to drink.

WIDOW QUIN. There's maybe worse than a dry hearth and a widow woman and your glass at night. So you hit him then?

CHRISTY [*getting almost excited*]. I did not. "I won't wed her," says I, "when all know she did suckle me for six weeks when I came into the world, and she a hag this day with a tongue on her has the crows and seabirds scattered, the way they wouldn't cast a shadow on her garden with the dread of her curse."

WIDOW QUIN [*teasingly*]. That one should be right company.

SARA [*eagerly*]. Don't mind her. Did you kill him then?

CHRISTY. "She's too good for the like of you," says he, "and

go on now or I'll flatten you out like a crawling beast has
passed under a dray." "You will not if I can help it," says I.
"Go on," says he, "or I'll have the divil making garters of
your limbs tonight." "You will not if I can help it," says I.
[*He sits up, brandishing his mug.*]

SARA. You were right surely.

CHRISTY [*impressively*]. With that the sun came out between
the cloud and the hill, and it shining green in my face. "God
have mercy on your soul," says he, lifting a scythe; "or on
your own," says I, raising the loy.

SUSAN. That's a grand story.

HONOR. He tells it lovely.

CHRISTY [*flattered and confident, waving bone*]. He gave a
drive with the scythe, and I gave a lep to the east. Then I
turned around with my back to the north, and I hit a blow
on the ridge of his skull, laid him stretched out, and he split
to the knob of his gullet. [*He raises the chicken bone to
his Adam's apple.*]

GIRLS [*together*]. Well, you're a marvel! Oh, God bless you!
You're the lad surely!

SUSAN. I'm thinking the Lord God sent him this road to make
a second husband to the Widow Quin, and she with a great
yearning to be wedded, though all dread her here. Lift him
on her knee, Sara Tansey.

WIDOW QUIN. Don't tease him.

SARA [*going over to dresser and counter very quickly, and
getting two glasses and porter*]. You're heroes surely, and let
you drink a supeen with your arms linked like the out-
landish lovers in the sailor's song. [*She links their arms and
gives them the glasses.*] There now. Drink a health to the
wonders of the western world, the pirates, preachers,
poteen-makers, with the jobbing jockies; parching peelers,
and the juries fill their stomachs selling judgments of the
English law. [*Brandishing the bottle.*]

WIDOW QUIN. That's a right toast, Sara Tansey. Now Christy.

[*They drink with their arms linked, he drinking with his left
hand, she with her right. As they are drinking, PEGEEN
MIKE comes in with a milk can and stands aghast. They
all spring away from CHRISTY. He goes down left. WIDOW
QUIN remains seated.*]

PEGEEN [*angrily, to SARA*]. What is it you're wanting?

SARA [*twisting her apron*]. A ounce of tobacco.

PEGEEN. Have you tuppence?

SARA. I've forgotten my purse.

PEGEEN. Then you'd best be getting it and not fooling us here. [*To the* WIDOW QUIN, *with more elaborate scorn.*] And what is it you're wanting, Widow Quin?

WIDOW QUIN [*insolently*]. A penn'orth of starch.

PEGEEN [*breaking out*]. And you without a white shift or a shirt in your whole family since the drying of the flood. I've no starch for the like of you, and let you walk on now to Killamuck.

WIDOW QUIN [*turning to* CHRISTY, *as she goes out with the girls*]. Well, you're mighty huffy this day, Pegeen Mike, and, you young fellow, let you not forget the sports and racing when the noon is by.

[*They go out.*]

PEGEEN [*imperiously*]. Fling out that rubbish and put them cups away.

[CHRISTY *tidies away in great haste.*]

Shove in the bench by the wall.

[*He does so.*]

And hang that glass on the nail. What disturbed it at all?

CHRISTY [*very meekly*]. I was making myself decent only, and this a fine country for young lovely girls.

PEGEEN [*sharply*]. Whisht your talking of girls. [*Goes to counter—right.*]

CHRISTY. Wouldn't any wish to be decent in a place . . .

PEGEEN. Whisht I'm saying.

CHRISTY [*looks at her face for a moment with great misgivings, then as a last effort, takes up a loy, and goes towards her, with feigned assurance*]. It was with a loy the like of that I killed my father.

PEGEEN [*still sharply*]. You've told me that story six times since the dawn of day.

CHRISTY [*reproachfully*]. It's a queer thing you wouldn't care to be hearing it and them girls after walking four miles to be listening to me now.

PEGEEN [*turning round astonished*]. Four miles.

CHRISTY [*apologetically*]. Didn't himself say there were only four bona fides living in this place?

PEGEEN. It's bona fides by the road they are, but that lot came over the river lepping the stones. It's not three perches when you go like that, and I was down this morning looking on the papers the post-boy does have in his bag. [*With meaning and emphasis.*] For there was great news this day, Christopher Mahon. [*She goes into room left.*]

CHRISTY [*suspiciously*]. Is it news of my murder?

PEGEEN [*inside*]. Murder, indeed.

CHRISTY [*loudly*]. A murdered da?

PEGEEN [*coming in again and crossing right*]. There was not, but a story filled half a page of the hanging of a man. Ah, that should be a fearful end, young fellow, and it worst of all for a man who destroyed his da, for the like of him would get small mercies, and when it's dead he is, they'd put him in a narrow grave, with cheap sacking wrapping him round, and pour down quicklime on his head, the way you'd see a woman pouring any frish-frash from a cup.

CHRISTY [*very miserably*]. Oh, God help me. Are you thinking I'm safe? You were saying at the fall of night, I was shut of jeopardy and I here with yourselves.

PEGEEN [*severely*]. You'll be shut of jeopardy no place if you go talking with a pack of wild girls the like of them to be walking abroad with the peelers, talking whispers at the fall of night.

CHRISTY [*with terror*]. And you're thinking they'd tell?

PEGEEN [*with mock sympathy*]. Who knows, God help you.

CHRISTY [*loudly*]. What joy would they have to bring hanging to the likes of me?

PEGEEN. It's queer joys they have, and who knows the thing they'd do, if it'd make the green stones cry itself to think of you swaying and swiggling at the butt of a rope, and you with a fine, stout neck, God bless you! the way you'd be a half an hour, in great anguish, getting your death.

CHRISTY [*getting his boots and putting them on*]. If there's that terror of them, it'd be best, maybe, I went on wandering like Esau or Cain and Abel on the sides of Neifin or the Erris plain.

PEGEEN [*beginning to play with him*]. It would, maybe, for I've heard the Circuit Judges this place is a heartless crew.

CHRISTY [*bitterly*]. It's more than Judges this place is a heartless crew. [*Looking up at her.*] And isn't it a poor thing to be starting again and I a lonesome fellow will be looking out on women and girls the way the needy fallen spirits do be looking on the Lord?

PEGEEN. What call have you to be that lonesome when there's poor girls walking Mayo in their thousands now?

CHRISTY [*grimly*]. It's well you know what call I have. It's well you know it's a lonesome thing to be passing small towns with the lights shining sideways when the night is down, or going in strange places with a dog noising before you and a dog noising behind, or drawn to the cities where you'd hear a voice kissing and talking deep love in every shadow of the ditch, and you passing on with an empty, hungry stomach failing from your heart.

PEGEEN. I'm thinking you're an odd man, Christy Mahon. The oddest walking fellow I ever set my eyes on to this hour today.

CHRISTY. What would any be but odd men and they living lonesome in the world?

PEGEEN. I'm not odd, and I'm my whole life with my father only.

CHRISTY [*with infinite admiration*]. How would a lovely handsome woman the like of you be lonesome when all men should be thronging around to hear the sweetness of your voice, and the little infant children should be pestering your steps I'm thinking, and you walking the roads.

PEGEEN. I'm hard set to know what way a coaxing fellow the like of yourself should be lonesome either.

CHRISTY. Coaxing?

PEGEEN. Would you have me think a man never talked with the girls would have the words you've spoken today? It's only letting on you are to be lonesome, the way you'd get around me now.

CHRISTY. I wish to God I was letting on; but I was lonesome all times, and born lonesome, I'm thinking, as the moon of dawn. [*Going to door.*]

PEGEEN [*puzzled by his talk*]. Well, it's a story I'm not understanding at all why you'd be worse than another, Christy Mahon, and you a fine lad with the great savagery to destroy your da.

CHRISTY. It's little I'm understanding myself, saving only that my heart's scalded this day, and I going off stretching out the earth between us, the way I'll not be waking near you another dawn of the year till the two of us do arise to hope or judgment with the saints of God, and now I'd best be going with my wattle in my hand, for hanging is a poor thing [*turning to go*], and it's little welcome only is left me in this house today.

PEGEEN [*sharply*]. Christy!

[*He goes towards her.*]

Come here to me.

[*He goes towards her.*]

Lay down that switch and throw some sods on the fire. You're pot-boy in this place, and I'll not have you mitch off from us now.

CHRISTY. You were saying I'd be hanged if I stay.

PEGEEN [*quite kindly at last*]. I'm after going down and reading the fearful crimes of Ireland for two weeks or three, and there wasn't a word of your murder. [*Getting up and going over to the counter.*] They've likely not found the body. You're safe so with ourselves.

CHRISTY [*astonished, slowly*]. It's making game of me you were [*following her with fearful joy*], and I can stay so, working at your side, and I not lonesome from this mortal day.

PEGEEN. What's to hinder you from staying, except the widow woman or the young girls would inveigle you off?

CHRISTY [*with rapture*]. And I'll have your words from this day filling my ears, and that look is come upon you meeting my two eyes, and I watching you loafing around in the warm sun, or rinsing your ankles when the night is come.

PEGEEN [*kindly, but a little embarassed*]. I'm thinking you'll be a loyal young lad to have working around, and if you vexed me a while since with your leaguing with the girls, I wouldn't give a thraneen for a lad hadn't a mighty spirit in him and a gamey heart.

[SHAWN KEOGH *runs in carrying a cleeve on his back, followed by the* WIDOW QUIN.]

SHAWN [*to* PEGEEN]. I was passing below, and I seen your mountainy sheep eating cabbages in Jimmy's field. Run up or they'll be bursting surely.

PEGEEN. Oh, God mend them! [*She puts a shawl over her head and runs out.*]

CHRISTY [*looking from one to the other. Still in high spirits*]. I'd best go to her aid maybe. I'm handy with ewes.

WIDOW QUIN [*closing the door*]. She can do that much, and there is Shaneen has long speeches for to tell you now. [*She sits down with an amused smile.*]

SHAWN [*taking something from his pocket and offering it to* CHRISTY]. Do you see that, mister?

CHRISTY [*looking at it*]. The half of a ticket to the Western States!

SHAWN [*trembling with anxiety*]. I'll give it to you and my new hat [*pulling it out of hamper*]; and my breeches with the double seat [*pulling it off*]; and my new coat is woven from the blackest shearings for three miles around [*giving him the coat*]; I'll give you the whole of them, and my blessing, and the blessing of Father Reilly itself, maybe, if you'll quit from this and leave us in the peace we had till last night at the fall of dark.

CHRISTY [*with a new arrogance*]. And for what is it you're wanting to get shut of me?

SHAWN [*looking to the* WIDOW *for help*]. I'm a poor scholar with middling faculties to coin a lie, so I'll tell you the truth, Christy Mahon. I'm wedding with Pegeen beyond, and I don't think well of having a clever fearless man the like of you dwelling in her house.

CHRISTY [*almost pugnaciously*]. And you'd be using bribery for to banish me?

SHAWN [*in an imploring voice*]. Let you not take it badly mister honey, isn't beyond the best place for you where you'll have golden chains and shiny coats and you riding upon hunters with the ladies of the land. [*He makes an eager sign to the* WIDOW QUIN *to come to help him.*]

WIDOW QUIN [*coming over*]. It's true for him, and you'd best quit off and not have that poor girl setting her mind on you, for there's Shaneen thinks she wouldn't suit you though all is saying that she'll wed you now.

[CHRISTY *beams with delight.*]

SHAWN [*in terrified earnest*]. She wouldn't suit you, and she with the divil's own temper the way you'd be strangling one another in a score of days. [*He makes the movement of strangling with his hands.*] It's the like of me only that she's fit for, a quiet simple fellow wouldn't raise a hand upon her if she scratched itself.

WIDOW QUIN [*putting* SHAWN's *hat on* CHRISTY]. Fit them clothes on you anyhow, young fellow, and he'd maybe loan them to you for the sports. [*Pushing him towards inner door.*] Fit them on and you can give your answer when you have them tried.

CHRISTY [*beaming, delighted with the clothes*]. I will then. I'd like herself to see me in them tweeds and hat. [*He goes into room and shuts the door.*]

SHAWN [*in great anxiety*]. He'd like herself to see them. He'll not leave us, Widow Quin. He's a score of divils in him the way it's well nigh certain he will wed Pegeen.

WIDOW QUIN [*jeeringly*]. It's true all girls are fond of courage and do hate the like of you.

SHAWN [*walking about in desperation*]. Oh, Widow Quin, what'll I be doing now? I'd inform again him, but he'd burst from Kilmainham and he'd be sure and certain to destroy me. If I wasn't so God-fearing, I'd near have courage to come behind him and run a pike into his side. Oh, it's a hard case to be an orphan and not to have your father that you're used to, and you'd easy kill and make yourself a hero in the sight of all. [*Coming up to her.*] Oh, Widow Quin, will you find me some contrivance when I've promised you a ewe?

WIDOW QUIN. A ewe's a small thing, but what would you give me if I did wed him and did save you so?

SHAWN [*with astonishment*]. You?

WIDOW QUIN. Aye. Would you give me the red cow you have and the mountainy ram, and the right of way across your rye path, and a load of dung at Michaelmas, and turbary upon the western hill?

SHAWN [*radiant with hope*]. I would surely, and I'd give you the wedding ring I have, and the loan of a new suit, the way you'd have him decent on the wedding day. I'd give you two kids for your dinner, and a gallon of poteen, and I'd call the piper on the long car to your wedding from Crossmolina or from Ballina. I'd give you . . .

WIDOW QUIN. That'll do so, and let you whisht, for he's coming now again.

[CHRISTY *comes in very natty in the new clothes.* WIDOW QUIN *goes to him admiringly.*]

WIDOW QUIN. If you seen yourself now, I'm thinking you'd be too proud to speak to us at all, and it'd be a pity surely to have your like sailing from Mayo to the Western World.

CHRISTY [*as proud as a peacock*]. I'm not going. If this is a poor place itself, I'll make myself contented to be lodging here.

[WIDOW QUIN *makes a sign to* SHAWN *to leave them.*]

SHAWN. Well, I'm going measuring the race-course while the
    tide is low, so I'll leave you the garments and my blessing
    for the sports today. God bless you! [*He wriggles out.*]

WIDOW QUIN [*admiring* CHRISTY]. Well, you're mighty spruce,
    young fellow. Sit down now while you're quiet till you talk
    with me.

CHRISTY [*swaggering*]. I'm going abroad on the hillside for to
    seek Pegeen.

WIDOW QUIN. You'll have time and plenty for to seek Pegeen,
    and you heard me saying at the fall of night the two of us
    should be great company.

CHRISTY. From this out I'll have no want of company when all
    sorts is bringing me their food and clothing [*he swaggers
    to the door, tightening his belt*], the way they'd set their
    eyes upon a gallant orphan cleft his father with one blow
    to the breeches belt. [*He opens door, then staggers back.*]
    Saints of glory! Holy angels from the throne of light!

WIDOW QUIN [*going over*]. What ails you?

CHRISTY. It's the walking spirit of my murdered da.

WIDOW QUIN [*looking out*]. Is it that tramper?

CHRISTY [*wildly*]. Where'll I hide my poor body from that
    ghost of hell?

[*The door is pushed open, and old* MAHON *appears on threshold.* CHRISTY *darts in behind door.*]

WIDOW QUIN [*in great amusement*]. God save you, my poor
    man.

MAHON [*gruffly*]. Did you see a young lad passing this way
    in the early morning or the fall of night?

WIDOW QUIN. You're a queer kind to walk in not saluting
    at all.

MAHON. Did you see the young lad?

WIDOW QUIN [*stiffly*]. What kind was he?

MAHON. An ugly young streeler with a murderous gob on him,
    and a little switch in his hand. I met a tramper seen him
    coming this way at the fall of night.

WIDOW QUIN. There's harvest hundreds do be passing these
    days for the Sligo boat. For what is it you're wanting him,
    my poor man?

MAHON. I want to destroy him for breaking the head on me
    with the clout of a loy. [*He takes off a big hat, and shows*

his head in a mass of bandages and plaster, with some pride.] It was he did that, and amn't I a great wonder to think I've traced him ten days with that rent in my crown?

WIDOW QUIN [*taking his head in both hands and examining it with extreme delight*]. That was a great blow. And who hit you? A robber maybe?

MAHON. It was my own son hit me, and he the divil a robber, or anything else, but a dirty, stuttering lout.

WIDOW QUIN [*letting go his skull and wiping her hands in her apron*]. You'd best be wary of a mortified scalp, I think they call it, lepping around with that wound in the splendor of the sun. It was a bad blow surely, and you should have vexed him fearful to make him strike that gash in his da.

MAHON. Is it me?

WIDOW QUIN [*amusing herself*]. Aye. And isn't it a great shame when the old and hardened do torment the young?

MAHON [*raging*]. Torment him is it? And I after holding out with the patience of a martyred saint till there's nothing but destruction on, and I'm driven out in my old age with none to aid me.

WIDOW QUIN [*greatly amused*]. It's a sacred wonder the way that wickedness will spoil a man.

MAHON. My wickedness, is it? Amn't I after saying it is himself has me destroyed, and he a liar on walls, a talker of folly, a man you'd see stretched the half of the day in the brown ferns with his belly to the sun.

WIDOW QUIN. Not working at all?

MAHON. The divil a work, or if he did itself, you'd see him raising up a haystack like the stalk of a rush, or driving our last cow till he broke her leg at the hip, and when he wasn't at that he'd be fooling over little birds he had— finches and felts—or making mugs at his own self in the bit of a glass we had hung on the wall.

WIDOW QUIN [*looking at* CHRISTY]. What way was he so foolish? It was running wild after the girls may be?

MAHON [*with a shout of derision*]. Running wild, is it? If he seen a red petticoat coming swinging over the hill, he'd be off to hide in the sticks, and you'd see him shooting out his sheep's eyes between the little twigs and the leaves, and his two ears rising like a hare looking out through a gap. Girls, indeed!

WIDOW QUIN. It was drink maybe?

MAHON. And he a poor fellow would get drunk on the smell

of a pint. He'd a queer rotten stomach, I'm telling you, and when I gave him three pulls from my pipe a while since, he was taken with contortions till I had to send him in the ass cart to the females' nurse.

WIDOW QUIN [*clasping her hands*]. Well, I never till this day heard tell of a man the like of that!

MAHON. I'd take a mighty oath you didn't surely, and wasn't he the laughing joke of every female woman where four baronies meet, the way the girls would stop their weeding if they seen him coming the road to let a roar at him, and call him the looney of Mahon's.

WIDOW QUIN. I'd give the world and all to see the like of him. What kind was he?

MAHON. A small low fellow.

WIDOW QUIN. And dark?

MAHON. Dark and dirty.

WIDOW QUIN [*considering*]. I'm thinking I seen him.

MAHON [*eagerly*]. An ugly young blackguard.

WIDOW QUIN. A hideous, fearful villain, and the spit of you.

MAHON. What way is he fled?

WIDOW QUIN. Gone over the hills to catch a coasting steamer to the north or south.

MAHON. Could I pull up on him now?

WIDOW QUIN. If you'll cross the sands below where the tide is out, you'll be in it as soon as himself, for he had to go round ten miles by the top of the bay. [*She points to the door.*] Strike down by the head beyond and then follow on the roadway to the north and east.

[MAHON *goes abruptly.*]

WIDOW QUIN [*shouting after him*]. Let you give him a good vengeance when you come up with him, but don't put yourself in the power of the law, for it'd be a poor thing to see a judge in his black cap reading out his sentence on a civil warrior the like of you. [*She swings the door to and looks at* CHRISTY, *who is cowering in terror, for a moment, then she bursts into a laugh.*]

WIDOW QUIN. Well, you're the walking Playboy of the Western World, and that's the poor man you had divided to his breeches belt.

CHRISTY [*looking out: then, to her*]. What'll Pegeen say when she hears that story? What'll she be saying to me now?

WIDOW QUIN. She'll knock the head of you, I'm thinking, and

drive you from the door. God help her to be taking you for a wonder, and you a little schemer making up the story you destroyed your da.

CHRISTY [*turning to the door, nearly speechless with rage, half to himself*]. To be letting on he was dead, and coming back to his life, and following after me like an old weasel tracing a rat, and coming in here laying desolation between my own self and the fine women of Ireland, and he a kind of carcase that you'd fling upon the sea . . .

WIDOW QUIN [*more soberly*]. There's talking for a man's one only son.

CHRISTY [*breaking out*]. His one son, is it? May I meet him with one tooth and it aching, and one eye to be seeing seven and seventy divils in the twists of the road, and one old timber leg on him to limp into the scalding grave. [*Looking out.*] There he is now crossing the strands, and that the Lord God would send a high wave to wash him from the world.

WIDOW QUIN [*scandalized*]. Have you no shame? [*Putting her hand on his shoulder and turning him round.*] What ails you? Near crying, is it?

CHRISTY [*in despair and grief*]. Amn't I after seeing the love-light of the star of knowledge shining from her brow, and hearing words would put you thinking on the holy Brigid speaking to the infant saints, and now she'll be turning again, and speaking hard words to me, like an old woman with a spavindy ass she'd have, urging on a hill.

WIDOW QUIN. There's poetry talk for a girl you'd see itching and scratching, and she with a stale stink of poteen on her from selling in the shop.

CHRISTY [*impatiently*]. It's her like is fitted to be handling merchandise in the heavens above, and what'll I be doing now, I ask you, and I a kind of wonder was jilted by the heavens when a day was by.

[*There is a distant noise of girls' voices.* WIDOW QUIN *looks from window and comes to him, hurriedly.*]

WIDOW QUIN. You'll be doing like myself, I'm thinking, when I did destroy my man, for I'm above many's the day, odd times in great spirits, abroad in the sunshine, darning a stocking or stitching a shift; and odd times again looking out on the schooners, hookers, trawlers is sailing the sea, and I thinking on the gallant hairy fellows are drifting beyond, and myself long years living alone.

CHRISTY [*interested*]. You're like me, so.

WIDOW QUIN. I am your like, and it's for that I'm taking a
fancy to you, and I with my little houseen above where
there'd be myself to tend you, and none to ask were you a
murderer or what at all.

CHRISTY. And what would I be doing if I left Pegeen?

WIDOW QUIN. I've nice jobs you could be doing, gathering
shells to make a whitewash for our hut within, building up
a little goosehouse, or stretching a new skin on an old
curragh I have, and if my hut is far from all sides, it's
there you'll meet the wisest old men, I tell you, at the corner
of my wheel, and it's there yourself and me will have great
times whispering and hugging. . . .

VOICES [*outside, calling far away*]. Christy! Christy Mahon!
Christy!

CHRISTY. Is it Pegeen Mike?

WIDOW QUIN. It's the young girls, I'm thinking, coming to
bring you to the sports below, and what is it you'll have me
to tell them now?

CHRISTY. Aid me for to win Pegeen. It's herself only that I'm
seeking now. [WIDOW QUIN *gets up and goes to window.*]
Aid me for to win her, and I'll be asking God to stretch
a hand to you in the hour of death, and lead you short cuts
through the Meadows of Ease, and up the floor of Heaven
to the Footstool of the Virgin's Son.

WIDOW QUIN. There's praying.

VOICES [*nearer*]. Christy! Christy Mahon!

CHRISTY [*with agitation*]. They're coming. Will you swear to
aid and save me for the love of Christ?

WIDOW QUIN [*Looks at him for a moment*]. If I aid you, will
you swear to give me a right of way I want, and a mountainy ram, and a load of dung at Michaelmas, the time that
you'll be master here?

CHRISTY. I will, by the elements and stars of night.

WIDOW QUIN. Then we'll not say a word of the old fellow,
the way Pegeen won't know your story till the end of time.

CHRISTY. And if he chances to return again?

WIDOW QUIN. We'll swear he's a maniac and not your da. I
could take an oath I seen him raving on the sands today.

[*Girls run in.*]

SUSAN. Come on to the sports below. Pegeen says you're to
come.

SARA TANSEY. The lepping's beginning, and we've a jockey's
suit to fit upon you for the mule race on the sands below.

HONOR. Come on, will you?

CHRISTY. I will then if Pegeen's beyond.

SARA TANSEY. She's in the boreen making game of Shaneen
Keogh.

CHRISTY. Then I'll be going to her now.

[*He runs out followed by the girls.*]

WIDOW QUIN. Well, if the worst comes in the end of all, it'll
be great game to see there's none to pity him but a widow
woman, the like of me, has buried her children and destroyed her man. [*She goes out.*]

ACT THREE

[SCENE—*as before. Later in the day.* JIMMY *comes in, slightly drunk.*]

JIMMY [*calls*]. Pegeen! [*Crosses to inner door.*] Pegeen Mike! [*Comes back again into the room.*] Pegeen!

[PHILLY *comes in in the same state.*]

[*To* PHILLY] Did you see herself?

PHILLY. I did not; but I sent Shawn Keogh with the ass cart for to bear him home. [*Trying cupboards which are locked.*] Well, isn't he a nasty man to get into such staggers at a morning wake? and isn't herself the divil's daughter for locking, and she so fussy after that young gaffer, you might take your death with drought and none to heed you?

JIMMY. It's little wonder she'd be fussy, and he after bringing bankrupt ruin on the roulette man, and the trick-o'-the-loop man, and breaking the nose of the cockshot-man, and winning all in the sports below, racing, lepping, dancing, and the Lord knows what! He's right luck, I'm telling you.

PHILLY. If he has, he'll be rightly hobbled yet, and he not able to say ten words without making a brag of the way he killed his father, and the great blow he hit with the loy.

JIMMY. A man can't hang by his own informing, and his father should be rotten by now.

[OLD MAHON *passes window slowly.*]

PHILLY. Supposing a man's digging spuds in that field with a long spade, and supposing he flings up the two halves of that skull, what'll be said then in the papers and the courts of law?

JIMMY. They'd say it was an old Dane, maybe, was drowned in the flood.

[OLD MAHON *comes in and sits down near door listening.*]

Did you never hear tell of the skulls they have in the city of Dublin, ranged out like blue jugs in a cabin of Connaught?

PHILLY. And you believe that?

JIMMY [*pugnaciously*]. Didn't a lad see them and he after

coming from harvesting in the Liverpool boat? "They have them there," says he, "making a show of the great people there was one time walking the world. White skulls and black skulls and yellow skulls, and some with full teeth, and some haven't only but one."

PHILLY. It was no lie, maybe, for when I was a young lad there was a graveyard beyond the house with the remnants of a man who had thighs as long as your arm. He was a horrid man, I'm telling you, and there was many a fine Sunday I'd put him together for fun, and he with shiny bones, you wouldn't meet the like of these days in the cities of the world.

MAHON [getting up]. You wouldn't, is it? Lay your eyes on that skull, and tell me where and when there was another the like of it, is splintered only from the blow of a loy.

PHILLY. Glory be to God! And who hit you at all?

MAHON [triumphantly]. It was my own son hit me. Would you believe that?

JIMMY. Well, there's wonders hidden in the heart of man!

PHILLY [suspiciously]. And what way was it done?

MAHON [wandering about the room]. I'm after walking hundreds and long scores of miles, winning clean beds and the fill of my belly four times in the day, and I doing nothing but telling stories of that naked truth. [He comes to them a little aggressively.] Give me a supeen and I'll tell you now.

[WIDOW QUIN comes in and stands aghast behind him. He is facing JIMMY and PHILLY, who are on the left.]

JIMMY. Ask herself beyond. She's the stuff hidden in her shawl.

WIDOW QUIN [coming to MAHON quickly]. You here, is it? You didn't go far at all?

MAHON. I seen the coasting steamer passing, and I got a drought upon me and a cramping leg, so I said, "The divil go along with him," and turned again. [Looking under her shawl.] And let you give me a supeen, for I'm destroyed travelling since Tuesday was a week.

WIDOW QUIN [getting a glass, in a cajoling tone]. Sit down then by the fire and take your ease for a space. You've a right to be destroyed indeed, with your walking, and fighting, and facing the sun. [Giving him poteen from a stone jar she has brought in.] There now is a drink for you, and may it be to your happiness and length of life.

MAHON [*taking glass greedily and sitting down by fire*]. God increase you!

WIDOW QUIN [*taking men to the right stealthily*]. Do you know what? That man's raving from his wound today, for I met him a while since telling a rambling tale of a tinker had him destroyed. Then he heard of Christy's deed, and he up and says it was his son had cracked his skull. O isn't madness a fright, for he'll go killing someone yet, and he thinking it's the man has struck him so?

JIMMY [*entirely convinced*]. It's a fright, surely. I knew a party was kicked in the head by a red mare, and he went killing horses a great while, till he eat the insides of a clock and died after.

PHILLY [*with suspicion*]. Did he see Christy?

WIDOW QUIN. He didn't. [*With a warning gesture.*] Let you not be putting him in mind of him, or you'll be likely summoned if there's murder done. [*Looking round at* MAHON.] Whisht! He's listening. Wait now till you hear me taking him easy and unravelling all. [*She goes to* MAHON.] And what way are you feeling, mister? Are you in contentment now?

MAHON [*slightly emotional from his drink*]. I'm poorly only, for it's a hard story the way I'm left today, when it was I did tend him from his hour of birth, and he a dunce never reached his second book, the way he'd come from school, many's the day, with his legs lamed under him, and he blackened with his beatings like a tinker's ass. It's a hard story, I'm saying, the way some do have their next and nighest raising up a hand of murder on them, and some is lonesome getting their death with lamentation in the dead of night.

WIDOW QUIN [*not knowing what to say*]. To hear you talking so quiet, who'd know you were the same fellow we seen pass today?

MAHON. I'm the same surely. The wrack and ruin of three score years; and it's a terror to live that length, I tell you, and to have your sons going to the dogs against you, and you wore out scolding them, and skelping them, and God knows what.

PHILLY [*to* JIMMY]. He's not raving. [*To* WIDOW QUIN.] Will you ask him what kind was his son?

WIDOW QUIN [*to* MAHON, *with a peculiar look*]. Was your son that hit you a lad of one year and a score maybe, a great hand at racing and lepping and licking the world?

MAHON [*turning on her with a roar of rage*]. Didn't you hear me say he was the fool of men, the way from this out he'll know the orphan's lot with old and young making game of him and they swearing, raging, kicking at him like a mangy cur.

[*A great burst of cheering outside, some way off.*]

MAHON [*putting his hands to his ears*]. What in the name of God do they want roaring below?

WIDOW QUIN [*with the shade of a smile*]. They're cheering a young lad, the champion Playboy of the Western World.

[*More cheering.*]

MAHON [*going to window*]. It'd split my heart to hear them, and I with pulses in my brain-pan for a week gone by. Is it racing they are?

JIMMY [*looking from door*]. It is then. They are mounting him for the mule race will be run upon the sands. That's the playboy on the winkered mule.

MAHON [*puzzled*]. That lad, is it? If you said it was a fool he was, I'd have laid a mighty oath he was the likeness of my wandering son. [*Uneasily, putting his hand to his head.*] Faith, I'm thinking I'll go walking for to view the race.

WIDOW QUIN [*stopping him, sharply*]. You will not. You'd best take the road to Belmullet, and not be dilly-dallying in this place where there isn't a spot you could sleep.

PHILLY [*coming forward*]. Don't mind her. Mount there on the bench and you'll have a view of the whole. They're hurrying before the tide will rise, and it'd be near over if you went down the pathway through the crags below.

MAHON [*mounts on bench, WIDOW QUIN beside him*]. That's a right view again the edge of the sea. They're coming now from the point. He'd leading. Who is he at all?

WIDOW QUIN. He's the champion of the world, I tell you, and there isn't a hop'orth isn't falling lucky to his hands today.

PHILLY [*looking out, interested in the race*]. Look at that. They're pressing him now.

JIMMY. He'll win it yet.

PHILLY. Take your time, Jimmy Farrell. It's too soon to say.

WIDOW QUIN [*shouting*]. Watch him taking the gate. There's riding.

JIMMY [*cheering*]. More power to the young lad!

MAHON. He's passing the third.

JIMMY. He'll lick them yet!

WIDOW QUIN. He'd lick them if he was running races with a score itself.

MAHON. Look at the mule he has, kicking the stars.

WIDOW QUIN. There was a lep! [*Catching hold of* MAHON *in her excitement.*] He's fallen! He's mounted again! Faith, he's passing them all!

JIMMY. Look at him skelping her!

PHILLY. And the mountain girls hooshing him on!

JIMMY. It's the last turn! The post's cleared for them now!

MAHON. Look at the narrow place. He'll be into the bogs! [*With a yell.*] Good rider! He's through it again!

JIMMY. He neck and neck!

MAHON. Good boy to him! Flames, but he's in!

[*Great cheering, in which all join.*]

MAHON [*with hesitation*]. What's that? They're raising him up. They're coming this way. [*With a roar of rage and astonishment.*] It's Christy! by the stars of God! I'd know his way of spitting and he astride the moon.

[*He jumps down and makes for the door, but* WIDOW QUIN *catches him and pulls him back.*]

WIDOW QUIN. Stay quiet, will you. That's not your son. [*To* JIMMY.] Stop him, or you'll get a month for the abetting of manslaughter and be fined as well.

JIMMY. I'll hold him.

MAHON [*struggling.*] Let me out! Let me out, the lot of you! till I have my vengeance on his head today.

WIDOW QUIN [*shaking him, vehemently*]. That's not your son. That's a man is going to make a marriage with the daughter of this house, a place with fine trade, with a license, and with poteen too.

MAHON [*amazed*]. That man marrying a decent and a moneyed girl! Is it mad yous are? Is it in a crazy house for females that I'm landed now?

WIDOW QUIN. It's mad yourself is with the blow upon your head. That lad is the wonder of the Western World.

MAHON. I seen it's my son.

WIDOW QUIN. You seen that you're mad. [*Cheering outside.*] Do you hear them cheering him in the zig-zags of the road? Aren't you after saying that your son's a fool, and how would they be cheering a true idiot born?

MAHON [*getting distressed*]. It's maybe out of reason that that man's himself. [*Cheering again.*] There's none surely will

go cheering him. Oh, I'm raving with a madness that would
fright the world! [*He sits down with his hand to his head.*]
There was one time I seen ten scarlet divils letting on they'd
cork my spirit in a gallon can; and one time I seen rats as
big as badgers sucking the life blood from the butt of my
lug; but I never till this day confused that dribbling idiot
with a likely man. I'm destroyed surely.

WIDOW QUIN. And who'd wonder when it's your brain-pan that
is gaping now?

MAHON. Then the blight of the sacred drought upon myself
and him, for I never went mad to this day, and I not three
weeks with the Limerick girls drinking myself silly, and
parlatic from the dusk to dawn. [*To* WIDOW QUIN, *suddenly.*] Is my visage astray?

WIDOW QUIN. It is then. You're sniggering maniac, a child
could see.

MAHON [*getting up more cheerfully*]. Then I'd best be going
to the union beyond, and there'll be a welcome before me,
I tell you [*with great pride*], and I a terrible and fearful
case, the way that there I was one time, screeching in a
straitened waistcoat, with seven doctors writing out my
sayings in a printed book. Would you believe that?

WIDOW QUIN. If you're a wonder itself, you'd best be hasty,
for them lads caught a maniac one time and pelted the poor
creature till he ran out, raving and foaming, and was
drowned in the sea.

MAHON [*with philosophy*]. It's true mankind is the divil when
your head's astray. Let me out now and I'll slip down the
boreen, and not see them so.

WIDOW QUIN [*showing him out*]. That's it. Run to the right,
and not a one will see.

[*He runs off.*]

PHILLY [*wisely*]. You're at some gaming, Widow Quin; but
I'll walk after him and give him his dinner and a time to
rest, and I'll see then if he's raving or as sane as you.

WIDOW QUIN [*annoyed*]. If you go near that lad, let you be
wary of your head, I'm saying. Didn't you hear him telling
he was crazed at times?

PHILLY. I heard him telling a power; and I'm thinking we'll
have right sport, before night will fall. [*He goes out.*]

JIMMY. Well, Philly's a conceited and foolish man. How could
that madman have his senses and his brain-pan slit? I'll go
after them and see him turn on Philly now.

[*He goes;* WIDOW QUIN *hides poteen behind counter. Then hubbub outside.*]

VOICES. There you are! Good jumper! Grand lepper! Darlint boy! He's the racer! Bear him on, will you!

[CHRISTY *comes in, in Jockey's dress, with* PEGEEN MIKE, SARA, *and other girls, and men.*]

PEGEEN [*to crowd*]. Go on now and don't destroy him and he drenching with sweat. Go along, I'm saying, and have your tug-of-warring till he's dried his skin.

CROWD. Here's his prizes! A bagpipes! A fiddle was played by a poet in the years gone by! A flat and three-thorned blackthorn would lick the scholars out of Dublin town!

CHRISTY [*taking prizes from the men*]. Thank you kindly, the lot of you. But you'd say it was little only I did this day if you'd seen me a while since striking my one single blow.

TOWN CRIER [*outside, ringing a bell*]. Take notice, last event of this day! Tug-of-warring on the green below! Come on, the lot of you! Great achievements for all Mayo men!

PEGEEN. Go on, and leave him for to rest and dry. Go on, I tell you, for he'll do no more.

[*She hustles crowd out;* WIDOW QUIN *following them.*]

MEN [*going*]. Come on then. Good luck for the while!

PEGEEN [*radiantly, wiping his face with her shawl*]. Well, you're the lad, and you'll have great times from this out when you could win that wealth of prizes, and you sweating in the heat of noon!

CHRISTY [*looking at her with delight*]. I'll have great times if I win the crowning prize I'm seeking now, and that's your promise that you'll wed me in a fortnight, when our banns is called.

PEGEEN [*backing away from him*]. You're right daring to go ask me that, when all knows you'll be starting to some girl in your own townland, when your father's rotten in four months, or five.

CHRISTY [*indignantly*]. Starting from you, is it? [*He follows her.*] I will not, then, and when the airs is warming in four months, or five, it's then yourself and me should be pacing Neifin in the dews of night, the times sweet smells do be rising, and you'd see a little shiny new moon, maybe, sinking on the hills.

PEGEEN [*looking at him playfully*]. And it's that kind of a poacher's love you'd make, Christy Mahon, on the sides of Neifin, when the night is down?

CHRISTY. It's little you'll think if my love's a poacher's, or an earl's itself, when you'll feel my two hands stretched around you, and I squeezing kisses on your puckered lips, till I'd feel a kind of pity for the Lord God is all ages sitting lonesome in his golden chair.

PEGEEN. That'll be right fun, Christy Mahon, and any girl would walk her heart out before she'd meet a young man was your like for eloquence, or talk, at all.

CHRISTY [*encouraged*]. Let you wait, to hear me talking, till we're astray in Erris, when Good Friday's by, drinking a sup from a well, and making mighty kisses with our wetted mouths, or gaming in a gap or sunshine, with yourself stretched back onto your necklace, in the flowers of the earth.

PEGEEN [*in a lower voice, moved by his tone*]. I'd be nice so, is it?

CHRISTY [*with rapture*]. If the mitred bishops seen you that time, they'd be the like of the holy prophets, I'm thinking, do be straining the bars of Paradise to lay eyes on the Lady Helen of Troy, and she abroad, pacing back and forward, with a nosegay in her golden shawl.

PEGEEN [*with real tenderness*]. And what is it I have, Christy Mahon, to make me fitting entertainment for the like of you, that has such poet's talking, and such bravery of heart?

CHRISTY [*in a low voice*]. Isn't there the light of seven heavens in your heart alone, the way you'll be an angel's lamp to me from this out, and I abroad in the darkness, spearing salmons in the Owen, or the Carrowmore?

PEGEEN. If I was your wife, I'd be along with you those nights, Christy Mahon, the way you'd see I was a great hand at coaxing bailiffs, or coining funny nick-names for the stars of night.

CHRISTY. You, is it? Taking your death in the hailstones, or in the fogs of dawn.

PEGEEN. Yourself and me would shelter easy in a narrow bush [*with a qualm of dread*], but we're only talking, maybe, for this would be a poor, thatched place to hold a fine lad is the like of you.

CHRISTY [*putting his arm around her*]. If I wasn't a good Christian, it's on my naked knees I'd be saying my prayers

and paters to every jackstraw you have roofing your head,
and every stony pebble is paving the laneway to your door.

PEGEEN [*radiantly*]. If that's the truth, I'll be burning candles
from this out to the miracles of God that have brought you
from the south today, and I, with my gowns bought ready,
the way that I can wed you, and not wait at all.

CHRISTY. It's miracles, and that's the truth. Me there toiling a
long while, and walking a long while, not knowing at all
I was drawing all times nearer to this holy day.

PEGEEN. And myself, a girl, was tempted often to go sailing
the seas till I'd marry a Jew-man, with ten kegs of gold, and
I not knowing at all there was the like of you drawing
nearer, like the stars of God.

CHRISTY. And to think I'm long years hearing women talking
that talk, to all bloody fools, and this the first time I've
heard the like of your voice talking sweetly for my own
delight.

PEGEEN. And to think it's me is talking sweetly, Christy
Mahon, and I the fright of seven townlands for my biting
tongue. Well, the heart's a wonder; and, I'm thinking, there
won't be our like in Mayo, for gallant lovers, from this
hour, today.

[*Drunken singing is heard outside.*]

There's my father coming from the wake, and when he's
had his sleep we'll tell him, for he's peaceful then.

[*They separate.*]

MICHAEL [*singing outside*].
    The jailor and the turnkey
    They quickly ran us down,
    And brought us back as prisoners
    Once more to Cavan town.

[*He comes in supported by* SHAWN.]

    There we lay bewailing
    All in a prison bound. . . .

[*He sees* CHRISTY. *Goes and shakes him drunkenly by the
hand, while* PEGEEN *and* SHAWN *talk on the left.*]

MICHAEL [*to* CHRISTY]. The blessing of God and the holy
angels on your head, young fellow. I hear tell you're after
winning all in the sports below; and wasn't it a shame I

didn't bear you along with me to Kate Cassidy's wake, a fine, stout lad, the like of you, for you'd never see the match of it for flows of drink, the way when we sunk her bones at noonday in her narrow grave, there were five men, aye, and six men, stretched out retching speechless on the holy stones.

CHRISTY [*uneasily, watching* PEGEEN]. Is that the truth?

MICHAEL. It is then, and aren't you a louty schemer to go burying your poor father unbeknownst when you'd a right to throw him on the crupper of a Kerry mule and drive him westwards, like holy Joseph in the days gone by, the way we could have given him a decent burial, and not have him rotting beyond, and not a Christian drinking a smart drop to the glory of his soul?

CHRISTY [*gruffly*]. It's well enough he's lying, for the likes of him.

MICHAEL [*slapping him on the back*]. Well, aren't you a hardened slayer? It'll be a poor thing for the household man where you go sniffing for a female wife; and [*pointing to* SHAWN] look beyond at that shy and decent Christian I have chosen for my daughter's hand, and I after getting the gilded dispensation this day for to wed them now.

CHRISTY. And you'll be wedding them this day, is it?

MICHAEL [*drawing himself up*]. Aye. Are you thinking, if I'm drunk itself, I'd leave my daughter living single with a little frisky rascal is the like of you?

PEGEEN [*breaking away from* SHAWN]. Is it the truth the dispensation's come?

MICHAEL [*triumphantly*]. Father Reilly's after reading it in gallous Latin, and "It's come in the nick of time," says he; "so I'll wed them in a hurry, dreading that young gaffer who'd capsize the stars."

PEGEEN [*fiercely*]. He's missed his nick of time, for it's that lad, Christy Mahon, that I'm wedding now.

MICHAEL [*loudly with horror*]. You'd be making him a son to me, and he wet and crusted with his father's blood?

PEGEEN. Aye. Wouldn't it be a bitter thing for a girl to go marrying the like of Shaneen, and he a middling kind of a scarecrow, with no savagery or fine words in him at all?

MICHAEL [*gasping and sinking on a chair*]. Oh, aren't you a heathen daughter to go shaking the fat of my heart, and I swamped and drownded with the weight of drink? Would you have them turning on me the way that I'd be roaring

to the dawn of day with the wind upon my heart? Have you
not a word to aid me, Shaneen? Are you not jealous at all?

SHAWN [*in great misery*]. I'd be afeard to be jealous of a man
did slay his da.

PEGEEN. Well, it'd be a poor thing to go marrying your like.
I'm seeing there's a world of peril for an orphan girl, and
isn't it a great blessing I didn't wed you, before himself
came walking from the west or south?

SHAWN. It's a queer story you'd go picking a dirty tramp up
from the highways of the world.

PEGEEN [*playfully*]. And you think you're a likely beau to go
straying along with, the shiny Sundays of the opening year,
when it's sooner on a bullock's liver you'd put a poor girl
thinking than on the lily or the rose?

SHAWN. And have you no mind of my weight of passion, and
the holy dispensation, and the drift of heifers I am giving,
and the golden ring?

PEGEEN. I'm thinking you're too fine for the like of me,
Shawn Keogh of Killakeen, and let you go off till you'd find
a radiant lady with droves of bullocks on the plains of
Meath, and herself bedizened in the diamond jewelleries
of Pharaoh's ma. That'd be your match, Shaneen. So God
save you now! [*She retreats behind* CHRISTY.]

SHAWN. Won't you hear me telling you . . . ?

CHRISTY [*with ferocity*]. Take yourself from this, young fellow,
or I'll maybe add a murder to my deeds today.

MICHAEL [*springing up with a shriek*]. Murder is it? Is it mad
yous are? Would you go making murder in this place, and
it piled with poteen for our drink tonight? Go on to the
foreshore if it's fighting you want, where the rising tide will
wash all traces from the memory of man. [*Pushing* SHAWN
towards CHRISTY.]

SHAWN [*shaking himself free, and getting behind* MICHAEL].
I'll not fight him, Michael James. I'd liefer live a bachelor,
simmering in passions to the end of time, than face a lepping
savage the like of him has descended from the Lord knows
where. Strike him yourself, Michael James, or you'll lose
my drift of heifers and my blue bull from Sneem.

MICHAEL. Is it me fight him, when it's father-slaying he's
bred to now? [*Pushing* SHAWN.] Go on you fool and fight
him now.

SHAWN [*coming forward a little*]. Will I strike him with my
hand?

MICHAEL. Take the loy is on your western side.

SHAWN. I'd be afeard of the gallows if I struck him with that.

CHRISTY [*taking up the loy*]. Then I'll make you face the gallows or quit off from this.

[SHAWN *flies out of the door.*]

CHRISTY. Well, fine weather be after him, [*going to* MICHAEL, *coaxingly*] and I'm thinking you wouldn't wish to have that quaking blackguard in your house at all. Let you give us your blessing and hear her swear her faith to me, for I'm mounted on the springtide of the stars of luck, the way it'll be good for any to have me in the house.

PEGEEN [*at the other side of* MICHAEL]. Bless us now, for I swear to God I'll wed him, and I'll not renege.

MICHAEL [*standing up in the center, holding on to both of them*]. It's the will of God, I'm thinking, that all should win an easy or a cruel end, and it's the will of God that all should rear up lengthy families for the nurture of the earth. What's a single man, I ask you, eating a bit in one house and drinking a sup in another, and he with no place of his own, like an old braying jackass strayed upon the rocks? [*To* CHRISTY.] It's many would be in dread to bring your like into their house for to end them, maybe, with a sudden end; but I'm a decent man of Ireland, and I liefer face the grave untimely and I seeing a score of grandsons growing up little gallant swearers by the name of God, than go peopling my bedside with puny weeds the like of what you'd breed, I'm thinking, out of Shaneen Keogh. [*He joins their hands.*] A daring fellow is the jewel of the world, and a man did split his father's middle with a single clout, should have the bravery of ten, so may God and Mary and St. Patrick bless you, and increase you from this mortal day.

CHRISTY *and* PEGEEN. Amen, O Lord!

[*Hubbub outside.* OLD MAHON *rushes in, followed by all the crowd, and* WIDOW QUIN. *He makes a rush at* CHRISTY, *knocks him down, and begins to beat him.*]

PEGEEN [*dragging back his arm*]. Stop that, will you. Who are you at all?

MAHON. His father, God forgive me!

PEGEEN [*drawing back*]. Is it rose from the dead?

MAHON. Do you think I look so easy quenched with the tap of a loy? [*Beats* CHRISTY *again.*]

PEGEEN [*glaring at* CHRISTY]. And it's lies you told, letting on you had him slitted, and you nothing at all.

CHRISTY [*catching* MAHON'S *stick*]. He's not my father. He's a raving maniac would scare the world. [*Pointing to* WIDOW QUIN.] Herself knows it is true.

CROWD. You're fooling Pegeen! The Widow Quin seen him this day, and you likely knew! You're a liar!

CHRISTY [*dumbfounded*]. It's himself was a liar, lying stretched out with an open head on him, letting on he was dead.

MAHON. Weren't you off racing the hills before I got my breath with the start I had seeing you turn on me at all?

PEGEEN. And to think of the coaxing glory we had given him, and he after doing nothing but hitting a soft blow and chasing northward in a sweat of fear. Quit off from this.

CHRISTY [*piteously*]. You've seen my doings this day, and let you save me from the old man; for why would you be in such a scorch of haste to spur me to destruction now?

PEGEEN. It's there your treachery is spurring me, till I'm hard set to think you're the one I'm after lacing in my heart-strings half-an-hour gone by. [*To* MAHON.] Take him on from this, for I think bad the world should see me raging for a Munster liar, and the fool of men.

MAHON. Rise up now to retribution, and come on with me.

CROWD [*jeeringly*]. There's the playboy! There's the lad thought he'd rule the roost in Mayo. Slate him now, mister.

CHRISTY [*getting up in shy terror*]. What is it drives you to torment me here, when I'd asked the thunders of the might of God to blast me if I ever did hurt to any saving only that one single blow.

MAHON [*loudly*]. If you didn't, you're a poor good-for-nothing, and isn't it by the like of you the sins of the whole world are committed?

CHRISTY [*raising his hands*]. In the name of the Almighty God. . . .

MAHON. Leave troubling the Lord God. Would you have him sending down droughts, and fevers, and the old hen and the cholera morbus?

CHRISTY [*to* WIDOW QUIN]. Will you come between us and protect me now?

WIDOW QUIN. I've tried a lot, God help me, and my share is done.

CHRISTY [*looking round in desperation*]. And I must go back into my torment is it, or run off like a vagabond straying through the Unions with the dusts of August making mud-stains in the gullet of my throat, or the winds of March blowing on me till I'd take an oath I felt them making whistles of my ribs within?

SARA. Ask Pegeen to aid you. Her like does often change.

CHRISTY. I will not then, for there's torment in the splendor of her like, and she a girl any moon of midnight would take pride to meet, facing southwards on the heaths of Keel. But what did I want crawling forward to scorch my understanding at her flaming brow?

PEGEEN [to MAHON, vehemently, fearing she will break into tears]. Take him on from this or I'll set the young lads to destroy him here.

MAHON [going to him, shaking his stick]. Come on now if you wouldn't have the company to see you skelped.

PEGEEN [half laughing, through her tears]. That's it, now the world will see him pandied, and he an ugly liar was playing off the hero, and the fright of men.

CHRISTY [to MAHON, very sharply]. Leave me go!

CROWD. That's it. Now Christy. If them two set fighting, it will lick the world.

MAHON [making a grab at CHRISTY]. Come here to me.

CHRISTY [more threateningly]. Leave me go, I'm saying.

MAHON. I will maybe, when your legs is limping, and your back is blue.

CROWD. Keep it up, the two of you. I'll back the old one. Now the playboy.

CHRISTY [in low and intense voice]. Shut your yelling, for if you're after making a mighty man of me this day by the power of a lie, you're setting me now to think if it's a poor thing to be lonesome, it's worse maybe to go mixing with the fools of earth.

[MAHON makes a movement towards him.]

CHRISTY [almost shouting]. Keep off . . . lest I do show a blow unto the lot of you would set the guardian angels winking in the clouds above. [He swings round with a sudden rapid movement and picks up a loy.]

CROWD [half frightened, half amused]. He's going mad! Mind yourselves! Run from the idiot!

CHRISTY. If I am an idiot, I'm after hearing my voice this day saying words would raise the topknot on a poet in a mer-chant's town. I've won your racing, and your lepping, and . . .

MAHON. Shut your gullet and come on with me.

CHRISTY. I'm going, but I'll stretch you first.

[*He runs at old* MAHON *with the loy, chases him out of the door, followed by* CROWD *and* WIDOW QUIN. *There is a great noise outside, then a yell, and dead silence for a moment.* CHRISTY *comes in, half dazed, and goes to fire.*]

WIDOW QUIN [*coming in, hurriedly, and going to him*]. They're turning again you. Come on, or you'll be hanged, indeed.

CHRISTY. I'm thinking, from this out, Pegeen'll be giving me praises the same as in the hours gone by.

WIDOW QUIN [*impatiently*]. Come by the back door. I'd think bad to have you stifled on the gallows tree.

CHRISTY [*indignantly*]. I will not, then. What good'd be my life-time, if I left Pegeen?

WIDOW QUIN. Come on, and you'll be no worse than you were last night; and you with a double murder this time to be telling to the girls.

CHRISTY. I'll not leave Pegeen Mike.

WIDOW QUIN [*impatiently*]. Isn't there the match of her in every parish public, from Binghamstown unto the plain of Meath? Come on, I tell you, and I'll find you finer sweethearts at each waning moon.

CHRISTY. It's Pegeen I'm seeking only, and what'd I care if you brought me a drift of chosen females, standing in their shifts itself, maybe, from this place to the Eastern World?

SARA [*runs in, pulling off one of her petticoats*]. They're going to hang him. [*Holding out petticoat and shawl.*] Fit these upon him, and let him run off to the east.

WIDOW QUIN. He's raving now; but we'll fit them on him, and I'll take him, in the ferry, to the Achill boat.

CHRISTY [*struggling feebly*]. Leave me go, will you? When I'm thinking of my luck today, for she will wed me surely, and I a proven hero in the end of all.

[*They try to fasten petticoat round him.*]

WIDOW QUIN. Take his left hand, and we'll pull him now. Come on, young fellow.

CHRISTY [*suddenly starting up*]. You'll be taking me from her? You're jealous, is it, of her wedding me? Go on from this. [*He snatches up a stool, and threatens them with it.*]

WIDOW QUIN [*going*]. It's in the mad-house they should put him, not in jail, at all. We'll go by the back door, to call the doctor, and we'll save him so.

[*She goes out, with* SARA, *through inner room. Men crowd in the doorway.* CHRISTY *sits down again by the fire.*]

MICHAEL [*in a terrified whisper*]. Is the old lad killed surely?

PHILLY. I'm after feeling the last gasps quitting his heart.

[*They peer in at* CHRISTY.]

MICHAEL [*with a rope*]. Look at the way he is. Twist a hangman's knot on it, and slip it over his head, while he's not minding at all.

PHILLY. Let you take it, Shaneen. You're the soberest of all that's here.

SHAWN. Is it me to go near him, and he the wickedest and worst with me? Let you take it, Pegeen Mike.

PEGEEN. Come on, so.

[*She goes forward with the others, and they drop the double hitch over his head.*]

CHRISTY. What ails you?

SHAWN [*triumphantly, as they pull the rope tight on his arms*]. Come on to the peelers, till they stretch you now.

CHRISTY. Me!

MICHAEL. If we took pity on you, the Lord God would, maybe, bring us ruin from the law today, so you'd best come easy, for hanging is an easy and a speedy end.

CHRISTY. I'll not stir. [*To* PEGEEN.] And what is it you'll say to me, and I after doing it this time in the face of all?

PEGEEN. I'll say, a strange man is a marvel, with his mighty talk; but what's a squabble in your back yard, and the blow of a loy, have taught me that there's a great gap between a gallous story and a dirty deed. [*To* MEN.] Take him on from this, or the lot of us will be likely put on trial for his deed today.

CHRISTY [*with horror in his voice*]. And it's yourself will send me off, to have a horny-fingered hangman hitching his bloody slip-knots at the butt of my ear.

MEN [*pulling rope*]. Come on, will you?

[*He is pulled down on the floor.*]

CHRISTY [*twisting his legs round the table*]. Cut the rope, Pegeen, and I'll quit the lot of you, and live from this out, like the madmen of Keel, eating muck and green weeds, on the faces of the cliffs.

PEGEEN. And leave us to hang, is it, for a saucy liar, the like of you? [*To* MEN.] Take him on, out from this.

SHAWN. Pull a twist on his neck, and squeeze him so.

PHILLY. Twist yourself. Sure he cannot hurt you, if you keep your distance from his teeth alone.

SHAWN. I'm afeard of him. [*To* PEGEEN.] Lift a lighted sod, will you, and scorch his leg.

PEGEEN [*blowing the fire, with a bellows*]. Leave go now, young fellow, or I'll scorch your shins.

CHRISTY. You're blowing for to torture me. [*His voice rising and growing stronger.*] That's your kind, is it? Then let the lot of you be wary, for, if I've to face the gallows, I'll have a gay march down, I tell you, and shed the blood of some of you before I die.

SHAWN [*in terror*]. Keep a good hold, Philly. Be wary, for the love of God. For I'm thinking he would liefest wreak his pains on me.

CHRISTY [*almost gaily*]. If I do lay my hands on you, it's the way you'll be at the fall of night, hanging as a scarecrow for the fowls of hell. Ah, you'll have a gallous jaunt I'm saying, coaching out through Limbo with my father's ghost.

SHAWN [*to* PEGEEN]. Make haste, will you? Oh, isn't he a holy terror, and isn't it true for Father Reilly, that all drink's a curse that has the lot of you so shaky and uncertain now?

CHRISTY. If I can wring a neck among you, I'll have a royal judgment looking on the trembling jury in the courts of law. And won't there be crying out in Mayo the day I'm stretched upon the rope with ladies in their silks and satins snivelling in their lacy kerchiefs, and they rhyming songs and ballads on the terror of my fate? [*He squirms round on the floor and bites* SHAWN's *leg.*]

SHAWN [*shrieking*]. My leg's bit on me. He's the like of a mad dog, I'm thinking, the way that I will surely die.

CHRISTY [*delighted with himself*]. You will then, the way you can shake out hell's flags of welcome for my coming in two weeks or three, for I'm thinking Satan hasn't many have killed their da in Kerry, and in Mayo too.

[OLD MAHON *comes in behind on all fours and looks on unnoticed.*]

MEN [*to* PEGEEN]. Bring the sod, will you?

PEGEEN [*coming over*]. God help him so. [*Burns his leg.*]

CHRISTY [*kicking and screaming*]. O, glory be to God! [*He kicks loose from the table, and they all drag him towards the door.]*

JIMMY [*seeing old* MAHON]. Will you look what's come in?

[*They all drop* CHRISTY *and run left.*]

CHRISTY [*scrambling on his knees face to face with old* MAHON]. Are you coming to be killed a third time, or what ails you now?

MAHON. For what is it they have you tied?

CHRISTY. They're taking me to the peelers to have me hanged for slaying you.

MICHAEL [*apologetically*]. It is the will of God that all should guard their little cabins from the treachery of law, and what would my daughter be doing if I was ruined or was hanged itself?

MAHON [*grimly, loosening* CHRISTY]. It's little I care if you put a bag on her back, and went picking cockles till the hour of death; but my son and myself will be going our own way, and we'll have great times from this out telling stories of the villainy of Mayo, and the fools is here. [*To* CHRISTY, *who is freed.*] Come on now.

CHRISTY. Go with you, is it? I will then, like a gallant captain with his heathen slave. Go on now and I'll see you from this day stewing my oatmeal and washing my spuds, for I'm master of all fights from now. [*Pushing* MAHON.] Go on, I'm saying.

MAHON. Is it me?

CHRISTY. Not a word out of you. Go on from this.

MAHON [*walking out and looking back at* CHRISTY *over his shoulder*]. Glory be to God! [*With a broad smile.*] I am crazy again! [*Goes.*]

CHRISTY. Ten thousand blessings upon all that's here, for you've turned me a likely gaffer in the end of all, the way I'll go romancing through a romping lifetime from this hour to the drawing of the judgment day. [*He goes out.*]

MICHAEL. By the will of God, we'll have peace now for our drinks. Will you draw the porter, Pegeen?

SHAWN [*going up to her*]. It's a miracle Father Reilly can wed us in the end of all, and we'll have none to trouble us when his vicious bite is healed.

PEGEEN [*hitting him a box on the ear*]. Quit my sight. [*Putting her shawl over her head and breaking out into wild lamentations.*] Oh my grief, I've lost him surely. I've lost the only Playboy of the Western World.

RIDERS TO THE SEA

by JOHN MILLINGTON SYNGE

1904

RIDERS TO THE SEA[1]

CHARACTERS

MAURYA, *an old woman* NORA, *a younger daughter*
BARTLEY, *her son* MEN AND WOMEN
CATHLEEN, *her daughter*

SCENE

An Island off the West of Ireland

[1] Riders to the Sea appears in *The Complete Works of John M. Synge*, published 1935 by Random House.

[*Cottage kitchen, with nets, oil-skins, spinningwheel, some new boards standing by the wall, etc.* CATHLEEN, *a girl of about twenty, finishes kneading cake, and puts it down in the pot oven by the fire; then wipes her hands, and begins to spin at the wheel.* NORA, *a young girl, puts her head in at the door.*]

NORA [*in a low voice*]. Where is she?

CATHLEEN. She's lying down, God help her, and may be sleeping, if she's able.

[NORA *comes in softly, and takes a bundle from under her shawl.*]

CATHLEEN [*spinning the wheel rapidly*]. What is it you have?

NORA. The young priest is after bringing them. It's a shirt and a plain stocking were got off a drowned man in Donegal.

[CATHLEEN *stops her wheel with a sudden movement, and leans out to listen.*]

NORA. We're to find out if it's Michael's they are, some time herself will be down looking by the sea.

CATHLEEN. How would they be Michael's, Nora? How would he go the length of that way to the far north?

NORA. The young priest says he's known the like of it. "If it's Michael's they are," says he, "you can tell herself he's got a clean burial by the grace of God, and if they're not his, let no one say a word about them, for she'll be getting her death," says he, "with crying and lamenting."

[*The door which* NORA *half closed is blown open by a gust of wind.*]

CATHLEEN [*looking out anxiously*]. Did you ask him would he stop Bartley going this day with the horses to the Galway fair?

NORA. "I won't stop him," says he, "but let you not be afraid. Herself does be saying prayers half through the night, and the Almighty God won't leave her destitute," says he, "with no son living."

[137]

CATHLEEN. Is the sea bad by the white rocks, Nora?

NORA. Middling bad, God help us. There's a great roaring in the west, and it's worse it'll be getting when the tide's turned to the wind. [*She goes over to the table with the bundle.*] Shall I open it now?

CATHLEEN. Maybe she'd wake up on us, and come in before we'd done. [*Coming to the table.*] It's a long time we'll be, and the two of us crying.

NORA [*goes to the inner door and listens*]. She's moving about on the bed. She'll be coming in a minute.

CATHLEEN. Give me the ladder, and I'll put them up in the turf-loft, the way she won't know of them at all, and maybe when the tide turns she'll be going down to see would he be floating from the east.

[*They put the ladder against the gable of the chimney;* CATHLEEN *goes up a few steps and hides the bundle in the turf-loft.* MAURYA *comes from the inner room.*]

MAURYA [*looking up at* CATHLEEN *and speaking querulously*]. Isn't it turf enough you have for this day and evening?

CATHLEEN. There's a cake baking at the fire for a short space [*throwing down the turf*] and Bartley will want it when the tide turns if he goes to Connemara.

[NORA *picks up the turf and puts it round the pot-oven.*]

MAURYA [*sitting down on a stool at the fire*]. He won't go this day with the wind rising from the south and west. He won't go this day, for the young priest will stop him surely.

NORA. He'll not stop him, mother, and I heard Eamon Simon and Stephen Pheety and Colum Shawn saying he would go.

MAURYA. Where is he itself?

NORA. He went down to see would there be another boat sailing in the week, and I'm thinking it won't be long till he's here now, for the tide's turning at the green head, and the hooker's tacking from the east.

CATHLEEN. I hear some one passing the big stones.

NORA [*looking out*]. He's coming now, and he in a hurry.

BARTLEY [*comes in and looks round the room. Speaking sadly and quietly*]. Where is the bit of new rope, Cathleen, was bought in Connemara?

CATHLEEN [*coming down*]. Give it to him, Nora; it's on a nail by the white boards. I hung it up this morning, for the pig with the black feet was eating it.

NORA [*giving him a rope*]. Is that it, Bartley?

MAURYA. You'd do right to leave that rope, Bartley, hanging by the board. [BARTLEY *takes the rope.*] It will be wanting in this place, I'm telling you, if Michael is washed up tomorrow morning, or the next morning, or any morning in the week, for it's a deep grave we'll make him by the grace of God.

BARTLEY [*beginning to work with the rope*]. I've no halter the way I can ride down on the mare, and I must go now quickly. This is the one boat going for two weeks or beyond it, and the fair will be a good fair for horses I heard them saying below.

MAURYA. It's a hard thing they'll be saying below if the body is washed up and there's no man in it to make the coffin, and I after giving a big price for the finest white boards you'd find in Connemara. [*She looks round at the boards.*]

BARTLEY. How would it be washed up, and we after looking each day for nine days, and a strong wind blowing a while back from the west and south?

MAURYA. If it wasn't found itself, that wind is raising the sea, and there was a star up against the moon, and it rising in the night. If it was a hundred horses, or a thousand horses you had itself, what is the price of a thousand horses against a son where there is one son only?

BARTLEY [*working at the halter, to* CATHLEEN]. Let you go down each day, and see the sheep aren't jumping in on the rye, and if the jobber comes you can sell the pig with the black feet if there is a good price going.

MAURYA. How would the like of her get a good price for a pig?

BARTLEY [*to* CATHLEEN]. If the west wind holds with the last bit of the moon let you and Nora get up weed enough for another cock for the kelp. It's hard set we'll be from this day with no one in it but one man to work.

MAURYA. It's hard set we'll be surely the day you're drownd'd with the rest. What way will I live and the girls with me, and I an old woman looking for the grave?

[BARTLEY *lays down the halter, takes off his old coat, and puts on a newer one of the same flannel.*]

BARTLEY [*to* NORA]. Is she coming to the pier?

NORA [*looking out*]. She's passing the green head and letting fall her sails.

BARTLEY [*getting his purse and tobacco*]. I'll have half an hour to go down, and you'll see me coming again in two days, or in three days, or maybe in four days if the wind is bad.

MAURYA [*turning round to the fire, and putting her shawl over her head*]. Isn't it a hard and cruel man won't hear a word from an old woman, and she holding him from the sea?

CATHLEEN. It's the life of a young man to be going on the sea, and who would listen to an old woman with one thing and she saying it over?

BARTLEY [*taking the halter*]. I must go now quickly. I'll ride down on the red mare, and the gray pony'll run behind me. . . . The blessing of God on you. [*He goes out.*]

MAURYA [*crying out as he is in the door*]. He's gone now, God spare us, and we'll not see him again. He's gone now, and when the black night is falling I'll have no son left me in the world.

CATHLEEN. Why wouldn't you give him your blessing and he looking round in the door? Isn't it sorrow enough is on every one in this house without your sending him out with an unlucky word behind him, and a hard word in his ear?

[MAURYA *takes up the tongs and begins raking the fire aimlessly without looking round.*]

NORA [*turning towards her*]. You're taking away the turf from the cake.

CATHLEEN [*crying out*]. The Son of God forgive us, Nora, we're after forgetting his bit of bread. [*She comes over to the fire.*]

NORA. And it's destroyed he'll be going till dark night, and he after eating nothing since the sun went up.

CATHLEEN [*turning the cake out of the oven*]. It's destroyed he'll be, surely. There's no sense left on any person in a house where an old woman will be talking forever.

[MAURYA *sways herself on her stool.*]

CATHLEEN [*cutting off some of the bread and rolling it in a cloth; to* MAURYA]. Let you go down now to the spring well and give him this and he passing. You'll see him then and the dark word will be broken, and you can say "God speed you," the way he'll be easy in his mind.

MAURYA [*taking the bread*]. Will I be in it as soon as himself?

CATHLEEN. If you go now quickly.

MAURYA [*standing up unsteadily*]. It's hard set I am to walk.

CATHLEEN [*looking at her anxiously*]. Give her the stick, Nora, or maybe she'll slip on the big stones.

NORA. What stick?

CATHLEEN. The stick Michael brought from Connemara.

MAURYA [*taking a stick* NORA *gives her*]. In the big world the old people do be leaving things after them for their sons and children, but in this place it is the young men do be leaving things behind for them that do be old.

[*She goes out slowly.* NORA *goes over to the ladder.*]

CATHLEEN. Wait, Nora, maybe she'd turn back quickly. She's that sorry, God help her, you wouldn't know the thing she'd do.

NORA. Is she gone round by the bush?

CATHLEEN [*looking out*]. She's gone now. Throw it down quickly, for the Lord knows when she'll be out of it again.

NORA [*getting the bundle from the loft*]. The young priest said he'd be passing tomorrow, and we might go down and speak to him below if it's Michael's they are surely.

CATHLEEN [*taking the bundle*]. Did he say what way they were found?

NORA [*coming down*]. "There were two men," says he, "and they rowing round with poteen before the cocks crowed, and the oar of one of them caught the body, and they passing the black cliffs of the north."

CATHLEEN [*trying to open the bundle*]. Give me a knife, Nora, the string's perished with the salt water, and there's a black knot on it you wouldn't loosen in a week.

NORA [*giving her a knife*]. I've heard tell it was a long way to Donegal.

CATHLEEN [*cutting the string*]. It is surely. There was a man in here a while ago—the man sold us that knife—and he said if you set off walking from the rocks beyond, it would be seven days you'd be in Donegal.

NORA. And what time would a man take, and he floating?

[CATHLEEN *opens the bundle and takes out a shirt and a bit of a stocking. They look at them eagerly.*]

CATHLEEN [*in a low voice*]. The Lord spare us, Nora! isn't it a queer hard thing to say if it's his they are surely?

NORA. I'll get his shirt off the hook the way we can put the one flannel on the other. [*She looks through some clothes hanging in the corner.*] It's not with them, Cathleen, and where will it be?

CATHLEEN. I'm thinking Bartley put it on him in the morning, for his own shirt was heavy with the salt in it. [*Pointing to the corner.*] There's a bit of a sleeve was of the same stuff. Give me that and it will do.

[NORA *brings it to her and they compare the flannel.*]

CATHLEEN. It's the same stuff, Nora; but if it is itself aren't there great rolls of it in the shops of Galway, and isn't it many another man may have a shirt of it as well as Michael himself?

NORA [*who has taken up the stocking and counted the stitches, crying out*]. It's Michael, Cathleen, it's Michael; God spare his soul, and what will herself say when she hears this story, and Bartley on the sea?

CATHLEEN [*taking the stocking*]. It's a plain stocking.

NORA. It's the second one of the third pair I knitted, and I put up three score stitches, and I dropped four of them.

CATHLEEN [*counts the stitches*]. It's that number is in it. [*Crying out.*] Ah, Nora, isn't it a bitter thing to think of him floating that way to the far north, and no one to keen him but the black hags that do be flying on the sea?

NORA [*swinging herself round, and throwing out her arms on the clothes*]. And isn't it a pitiful thing when there is nothing left of a man who was a great rower and fisher, but a bit of an old shirt and a plain stocking?

CATHLEEN [*after an instant*]. Tell me is herself coming, Nora? I hear a little sound on the path.

NORA [*looking out*]. She is, Cathleen. She's coming up to the door.

CATHLEEN. Put these things away before she'll come in. Maybe it's easier she'll be after giving her blessing to Bartley, and we won't let on we've heard anything the time he's on the sea.

NORA [*helping* CATHLEEN *to close the bundle*]. We'll put them here in the corner.

[*They put them into a hole in the chimney corner.* CATHLEEN *goes back to the spinning-wheel.*]

NORA. Will she see it was crying I was?

CATHLEEN. Keep your back to the door the way the light'll not be on you.

[NORA *sits down at the chimney corner, with her back to the door.* MAURYA *comes in very slowly, without looking at the girls, and goes over to her stool at the other side of the fire. The cloth with the bread is still in her hand. The girls look at each other, and* NORA *points to the bundle of bread.*]

CATHLEEN [*after spinning for a moment*]. You didn't give him his bit of bread?

[MAURYA *begins to keen softly, without turning round.*]

CATHLEEN. Did you see him riding down?

[MAURYA *goes on keening.*]

CATHLEEN [*a little impatiently*]. God forgive you; isn't it a better thing to raise your voice and tell what you seen, than to be making lamentation for a thing that's done? Did you see Bartley, I'm saying to you.

MAURYA [*with a weak voice*]. My heart's broken from this day.

CATHLEEN [*as before*]. Did you see Bartley?

MAURYA. I seen the fearfulest thing.

CATHLEEN [*leaves her wheel and looks out*]. God forgive you; he's riding the mare now over the green head, and the gray pony behind him.

MAURYA [*starts, so that her shawl falls back from her head and shows her white tossed hair. With a frightened voice*]. The gray pony behind him.

CATHLEEN [*coming to the fire*]. What is it ails you, at all?

MAURYA [*speaking very slowly*]. I've seen the fearfulest thing any person has seen, since the day Bride Dara seen the dead man with the child in his arms.

CATHLEEN *and* NORA. Uah. [*They crouch down in front of the old woman at the fire.*]

NORA. Tell us what it is you seen.

MAURYA. I went down to the spring well, and I stood there saying a prayer to myself. Then Bartley came along, and he riding on the red mare with the gray pony behind him. [*She puts up her hands, as if to hide something from her eyes.*] The Son of God spare us, Nora!

CATHLEEN. What is it you seen?

MAURYA. I seen Michael himself.

CATHLEEN [*speaking softly*]. You did not, mother; it wasn't

Michael you seen, for his body is after being found in the far north, and he's got a clean burial by the grace of God.

MAURYA [*a little defiantly*]. I'm after seeing him this day, and he riding and galloping. Bartley came first on the red mare; and I tried to say "God speed you," but something choked the words in my throat. He went by quickly; and "the blessing of God on you," says he, and I could say nothing. I looked up then, and I crying, at the gray pony, and there was Michael upon it—with fine clothes on him, and new shoes on his feet.

CATHLEEN [*begins to keen*]. It's destroyed we are from this day. It's destroyed, surely.

NORA. Didn't the young priest say the Almighty God wouldn't leave her destitute with no son living?

MAURYA [*in a low voice, but clearly*]. It's little the like of him knows of the sea. . . . Bartley will be lost now, and let you call in Eamon and make me a good coffin out of the white boards, for I won't live after them. I've had a husband, and a husband's father, and six sons in this house—six fine men, though it was a hard birth I had with every one of them and they coming to the world—and some of them were found and some of them were not found, but they're gone now the lot of them. . . . There were Stephen, and Shawn, were lost in the great wind, and found after in the Bay of Gregory of the Golden Mouth, and carried up the two of them on the one plank, and in by that door. [*She pauses for a moment, the girls start as if they heard something through the door that is half open behind them.*]

NORA [*in a whisper*]. Did you hear that, Cathleen? Did you hear a noise in the northeast?

CATHLEEN [*in a whisper*]. There's some one after crying out by the seashore.

MAURYA [*continues without hearing anything*]. There was Sheamus and his father, and his own father again, were lost in a dark night, and not a stick or sign was seen of them when the sun went up. There was Patch after was drowned out of a curragh that turned over. I was sitting here with Bartley, and he a baby, lying on my two knees, and I seen two women, and three women, and four women coming in, and they crossing themselves, and not saying a word. I looked out then, and there were men coming after them, and they holding a thing in the half of a red sail, and water dripping out of it—it was a dry day, Nora—and leaving a track to the door.

[*She pauses again with her hand stretched out towards the door. It opens softly and old women begin to come in, crossing themselves on the threshold, and kneeling down in front of the stage with red petticoats over their heads.*]

MAURYA [*half in a dream, to* CATHLEEN]. Is it Patch, or Michael, or what is it at all?

CATHLEEN. Michael is after being found in the far north, and when he is found there how could he be here in this place?

MAURYA. There does be a power of young men floating round in the sea, and what way would they know if it was Michael they had, or another man like him, for when a man is nine days in the sea, and the wind blowing, it's hard set his own mother would be to say what man was it.

CATHLEEN. It's Michael, God spare him, for they're after sending us a bit of his clothes from the far north.

[*She reaches out and hands* MAURYA *the clothes that belonged to Michael.* MAURYA *stands up slowly and takes them in her hands.* NORA *looks out.*]

NORA. They're carrying a thing among them and there's water dripping out of it and leaving a track by the big stones.

CATHLEEN [*in a whisper to the women who have come in*]. Is it Bartley it is?

ONE OF THE WOMEN. It is surely, God rest his soul.

[*Two younger women come in and pull out the table. Then men carry in the body of* BARTLEY, *laid on a plank, with a bit of a sail over it, and lay it on the table.*]

CATHLEEN [*to the women, as they are doing so*]. What way was he drowned?

ONE OF THE WOMEN. The gray pony knocked him into the sea, and he was washed out where there is a great surf on the white rocks.

[MAURYA *has gone over and knelt down at the head of the table. The women are keening softly and swaying themselves with a slow movement.* CATHLEEN *and* NORA *kneel at the other end of the table. The men kneel near the door.*]

MAURYA [*raising her head and speaking as if she did not see the people around her*]. They're all gone now, and there isn't anything more the sea can do to me. . . . I'll have no call now to be up crying and praying when the wind breaks from the south, and you can hear the surf is in the east, and the surf is in the west, making a great stir with the two noises, and they hitting one on the other. I'll have no call now to be going down and getting Holy Water in the dark nights after Samhain, and I won't care what way the sea is when the other women will be keening. [*To* NORA.] Give me the Holy Water, Nora, there's a small sup still on the dresser.

[NORA *gives it to her.*]

MAURYA [*drops Michael's clothes across Bartley's feet, and sprinkles the Holy Water over him*]. It isn't that I haven't prayed for you, Bartley, to the Almighty God. It isn't that I haven't said prayers in the dark night till you wouldn't know what I'd be saying; but it's a great rest I'll have now, and it's time surely. It's a great rest I'll have now, and great sleeping in the long nights after Samhain, if it's only a bit of wet flour we do have to eat, and maybe a fish that would be stinking. [*She kneels down again, crossing herself, and saying prayers under her breath.*]

CATHLEEN [*to* AN OLD MAN]. Maybe yourself and Eamon would make a coffin when the sun rises. We have fine white boards herself bought, God help her, thinking Michael would be found, and I have a new cake you can eat while you'll be working.

THE OLD MAN [*looking at the boards*]. Are there nails with them?

CATHLEEN. There are not, Colum; we didn't think of the nails.

ANOTHER MAN. It's a great wonder she wouldn't think of the nails, and all the coffins she's seen made already.

CATHLEEN. It's getting old she is, and broken.

[MAURYA *stands up again very slowly and spreads out the pieces of Michael's clothes beside the body, sprinkling them with the last of the Holy Water.*]

NORA [*in a whisper to* CATHLEEN]. She's quiet now and easy; but the day Michael was drowned you could hear her crying out from this to the spring well. It's fonder she was of Michael, and would any one have thought that?

CATHLEEN [*slowly and clearly*]. An old woman will be soon tired with anything she will do, and isn't it nine days herself is after crying and keening, and making great sorrow in the house?

MAURYA [*puts the empty cup mouth downwards on the table,*

and lays her hands together on Bartley's feet]. They're all together this time, and the end is come. May the Almighty God have mercy on Bartley's soul, and on Michael's soul, and on the souls of Sheamus and Patch, and Stephen and Shawn; [*bending her head*] and may He have mercy on my soul, Nora, and on the soul of every one is left living in the world.

[*She pauses, and the keen rises a little more loudly from the women, then sinks away.*]

MAURYA [*continuing*]. Michael has a clean burial in the far north, by the grace of the Almighty God. Bartley will have a fine coffin out of the white boards, and a deep grave surely. What more can we want than that? No man at all can be living forever, and we must be satisfied. [*She kneels down again and the curtain falls slowly.*]

SEAN O'CASEY

1884-1964

SEAN O'CASEY described himself as a "Green Crow," a fighting man who would be better fed if he would only keep his mouth shut. The modern theatre can be thankful that O'Casey was more interested in having his say than in filling his stomach or his pocket book. O'Casey always had something to say on stage and off, and no writer better exemplified the eclecticism and fascinating experimentation that characterizes the modern theatre than did this lovable, waspish man who lived in England in self-imposed exile from his native Ireland from 1927 until his death.

In all his plays, O'Casey was vigorously on the side of life, and, for him, to be alive was to be in conflict. From his childhood struggles for survival, through the riots of 1927 at the opening of *The Plough and the Stars* at the Abbey, to his most recent struggles with critics, censors, and producers, O'Casey's life was one of constant turmoil, and this quality pervades everything he ever wrote. It is possible, however, to divide his work into two main periods: those plays written before he left Ireland and those written after he settled in England. The first group spring, root and branch, out of O'Casey's deep involvement in Irish history and the politics of the first quarter of the century. They are blaringly nationalistic and are written with great vitality according to the more-or-less standard conventions of naturalism in the realistic idiom of the Dublin streets. In each of them O'Casey dramatizes the inevitable disenchantment and disillusionment of the romantic rebel idealist who is either insufficiently endowed to serve a noble cause or, as is more likely, who fights for a cause unworthy of the struggle and the sacrifice. The plays of the second group, written after O'Casey had escaped from the confusing limits of Irish parochialism, also deal with Irish life, but there is a universality about them which his earlier plays lacked. The brilliant language of the first plays is still there, but the form is allegorical and far more open. The influence of the expressionists on his style and his themes is clearly evident.

But no matter how many differences we can find between these two periods, there are certain constants in all of

O'Casey's work: his tendency to bring tragic and comic scenes into head-on collision; his great compassion for the sufferings of all men; the lilting music of his language; his pixie sense of humor; his anti-heroic stance; and, above all, his constant belief that all art must celebrate the joy of life. In a century of increasing international tension and individual despair, the cawings of this Green Crow consistently urge audiences to live life more consciously, fully, and joyously.

THE GREEN GODDESS OF REALISM[1]

IN THE THEATRE of today, realism is the totem pole of the dramatic critics.

Matter-of-fact plays, true true-to-life arrangement, and real, live characters are the three gods the critics adore and saturate with the incense of their commonplace praise once a day and twice on Sundays in their trimly-dressed little articles. What the dramatic critics mean by the various terms they use for Realism is the yearly ton of rubbish that falls on the English stage and is swiftly swept away into the dust-bins. The critics give a cordial welcome to the trivial plays because, in my opinion, they are, oh, so easy to understand, and gorge the critics with the ease of an easy explanation. It is very dangerous for a dramatist to be superior to the critics, to be a greater dramatist than the critic is a critic. They don't like it, and so most of them do all they can to discourage any attempt in the theatre towards an imagination fancy-free, or an attempt to look on life and mold it into a form fit for the higher feeling and intelligence of the stage. They are those who compare Beaumont and Fletcher's *Philaster* with *Charley's Aunt*, and in their heart of hearts vote for the farce and shove the poetic play out of their way (a few spit the preference in our face, as Archer did). Charley's Aunt is loved by Charley's uncles. They have grown fat and lazy on triviality, so fat and so lazy that they are hardly able to move. The curse is that these critics do their best to prevent anyone else from moving either. They will have simply to be roughly shunted out of the way, and these few words are one of the first sharp prods to get them to buzz off and do their sleeping somewhere else. Realism, or what the critics childishly believe to be Realism, has had its day, and has earned a rest. It began on a sunny

[1] GEORGE BRAZILLER, INC.—"The Green Goddess of Realism" from *The Green Crow* by Sean O'Casey, reprinted with the permission of the publisher. Copyright © 1956 by Sean O'Casey.

autumn evening in 1886, or thereabouts, as the lawyers say, at the first production of *Ours* by Robertson, when the miracle took place. "In reading the play today," says William Archer, the world-famous dramatic critic, "we recognize in Robertson —just what the stage wanted in its progress towards veri-similitude—the genius of the commonplace. The first act of *Ours* was, in intention at any rate, steeped in an atmosphere quite new to the theater. The scene was an avenue in Shendryn Park which Robertson describes in the abhorrent prompt-book jargon of the time. But one line had, I venture to say, as yet appeared in no prompt-book in the world: *'Throughout the act the autumn leaves fall from the trees.'* How this effect was produced and whether it was successful, I cannot say. Nor can I discuss the question whether it was a desirable effect, or a mere trick of mechanical realism which the true artist would despise." Now the falling of the leaves from the trees was and could have been nothing but "a mere trick of mechanical realism," because the trees couldn't have been true-to-life trees, and, even if they were, the autumnal leaves couldn't have fallen with the regularity and rhythm required to create the desirable effect. And no true artist of the theater would despise "a mere trick of mechanical realism" by which to get a scenic or an emotional effect out of his play and over to his audience. We remember the fine effect that the first sound of the first fall of rain had as it fell in the first act of Obey's *Noah*; and this fall of rain was a mere trick of mechanical realism as it was also the opening of the floodgates of Heaven, swelling into a flood that destroyed all life that was in the world save only those who found safe shelter in the faith of Noah; or the sudden change in the wind in *Saint Joan* that set the pennon streaming eastward, and sent Dunois and Saint Joan hurrying out to make for the flash of the guns, and drive the English out of France. You see the artist in the theatre never despises a mere trick of mechanical realism; but he knows how to keep it in its proper place. Let Archer open his mouth again: "Then as the act proceeds, *The patter of rain is heard upon the leaves,* and again, *The rain comes down more heavily and the stage darkens.*" The stage darkens, mind you, not the sky. "This effect of the rain falling and the stage darkening would," Archer tells us, "have been absolutely impossible in a candle-lit scene." Well, we have our floodlights, our spotlights, our baby-spots, our amber, blue, and pink foot-lights, but rarely do we get in our great progress towards verisimilitude the thunder, the lightning, and the rain that flashed and roared and fell on the heath scene in Shakespeare's *Macbeth*. Archer speaks again: "Then enter the sentimental hero and heroine, caught in the rain; and—conceive the daring novelty!—*Blanche carries the skirt of her dress over her head*. In the center of the stage was a large tree with a bench around it, and to get the best shelter possible, the hero and the heroine stand on the bench. Meanwhile Sir Alexander and Lady Shendryn, a middle-aged couple, hop in and sit down on the stump of a tree under another shelter. Unaware of each other's presence, the two couples talk in a sort of counterpoint, the romantic dialogue of the youthful pair contrasting with the weary snappiness of the elderly couple." And this is called an exact imitation of real life. Two couples, unknown to each other, carry on a counterpoint conversation on the same stage in the same scene at the same time, and Archer calls this "an exact imitation at any rate of the surfaces of life." Here's a bit of the dialogue:

ANGUS. What was the song you sang at the Sylvesters'?
BLANCHE. Oh!
ANGUS. I wish you'd hum it now.
BLANCHE. Without music?
ANGUS. It won't be without music.

—and Blanche croons over Offenbach's exquisite *Chanson de Fortunio*, and then we are told that we may search the Restoration and eighteenth-century comedy in vain for a piece of subtle truth like this. Where the subtle truth is in a girl under the rain holding her skirt over her head, standing on a bench, crooning Offenbach's *Chanson de Fortunio* or murmuring to her young man, "Cousin, do you know, I rather like to see you getting wet," only Archer or some other present-day critic–guardian angel of the theatre could tell us. This archcritical prate about verisimilitude, exact imitation of real life, and the unmistakable originality of the conception of this scene in Robertson's *Ours*, is an example of the commonplace genius of dramatic criticism. The incident of two couples taking their set times to say their say on the same stage in the same scene at the same time in full view of the audience is as true to life, is about as exact an imitation of real life, as the incident of Malvolio's soliloquy in full view of his tormentors and his audience. But the autumn leaves falling one by one and two by two, the sound of the rain pattering on the leaves, and the stage getting darker and darker and the rain getting heavier and heavier as the act proceeds, is all so sweet and all so simple to see and feel and follow that Archer and his fellow-follows-on hail this exact imitation of real life on the stage as a great and glorious godsend to them and their wives and children. They are so easy to manage in a weekly article; no beating about the bush, no humiliating strain on the mind or the emotions, no danger of giving a stupid judgment, for autumn leaves are autumn leaves, rain is rain, and the darkening night means the end of the day. And so we find that stuff like *Call It a Day* gets a rosy welcome from our regimental sergeant-major critics, while a work like *Strange Interlude* is pooh-bahed off the stage. And how quietly and clever and exact this realism, or naturalism, or exact imitation of life has made the critics! Commenting on *Espionage*, Mr. Agate tells us that "the First Act is a corker, and readers will note my wideawakeness in the perception that whereas the draught in the railway carriage fritters the blinds, the passengers are able to put their heads out of window without a hair stirring." I'm sure all the readers felt an exaltation in the conscientiousness of criticism when they got sufficiently soaked in that wonderful bit of information. It gave them something to look forward to when they went to see the play. Not a hair stirring! Fancy that now. Strange that the same wideawakeness which saw a corker in *Espionage*, saw nothing, or very little, in O'Neill's *Strange Interlude*. But then O'Neill's great plays are "morbid masterpieces which have to be seen under the penalty of remaining mum in Bloomsbury," or, if the truth be told, of remaining mum in any civilized place where the drama is honored more in the observance than in the breach. And Mr. Ivor Brown, commenting on O'Neill's *Ah, Wilderness!* tells us that "The producers introduced the music of *The Merry Widow* to a Connecticut small town of 1906. In that case New England was well ahead of Old, for that operetta did not reach Daly's till a year later." Well, that is something worth knowing anyway, but it wouldn't have the faintest effect on the play or production even if the music hadn't yet reached the small town in Connecticut, or even if the music given in the play had been the first composition made on the first psaltery or sackbut, if the music fitted the theme. Is it a waste of time to hint in the ear of the critics that it is much harder for a dramatist to stir the heart than to stir the hair, and much harder to make music apt for the theme and the trend of a play than it is to bring the music in to the correct tick of the clock? These critics are like the tailors who visit an exhibition to see if the buttons are put in their proper places on the coats in the pictures that are hanging on the walls.

This headlong search or quiet scrutiny for realism, exact imitation of life in the drama, has outwitted the critics into being puzzled over everything in a play that doesn't fit calmly into their poor spirit level and timid thumb rule. The dramatist is told that he must see life steadily and see it whole; and a critic-at-arms (there are barons, knights, esquires, men-at-arms, and grooms among the critics) writing in the *Evening Standard* complained that a play he saw wasn't "a study of the whole seething brew of life!" He wasn't asking for much. The whole world, parallels of longitude and meridians of latitude and all, popped on to the stage in a flood of limelight, and the critics tossing it about like kids playing with a balloon. This critic-at-arms didn't (and doesn't still, I'm sure) realize that no one can view or understand the brew of life encased in an acorn cup; or holding this little miracle in the palm of the hand, no human pair of eyes can at any time see it steadily and see it whole. So the complaint about a play failing to show the whole seething brew of life is the complaint of a dodo critic.

Although the bone of realism in the theatre has been picked pretty clean, the critics keep gnawing away at it, so that if a playwright as much as gets a character to blow his nose (preferably when "the autumn leaves are falling from the trees"), the critics delightedly nod to each other, and murmur, "An exact imitation of life, brothers." Commenting on *Call It a Day*, a play in which everything is attempted and nothing done, Mr. Agate tells us that "Miss Dodie Smith is never concerned whether 'it' is a play or not, but whether she has assembled on her stage characters so real that she might have gone into the street and compelled them into the theater," though these characters that might have been pulled in off the street are as tender and delicate and true as the tenderest and most delicate characters wistfully wandering about in the most wistful Barrie play. J.G.B., commenting on *Love from a Stranger*, tells us that "it is written with brilliant matter-of-factness, and is a real play about real people." Here our noses are shoved up against the image of realism in the theatre. A real play about real people: here's a sentence that apparently punches home; but look well into it, and you'll find it empty of any real meaning. Week in and week out these commonplace plays are reducing the poor critics into more and more vague and vapid expressions that would give a

sparkle to the mouth of a politician trying to cod his con-
stituents—and very often succeeding. A real play about real
people—what does it mean? This is something of a triumph—
a real play with real people in a real theater before a real
audience. But every play is a real play whether it be good or
bad, just as a real lion is a real lion and a real mouse is
a real mouse, and both are animals. But the real mouse isn't a
real lion, nor is the real lion a real mouse, though both are
animals. I wonder do the critics get this? There is a big difference between a lion and a mouse, though both are animals,
and there is a bigger difference between a good and a bad
play, though both are plays just the same. What is a "real
play?" Answer, according to J.G.B., *Love from a Stranger*
is a real play, therefore the nearer we get to this praised play,
the nearer we get to a real play. Now is *The Dream Play* by
Strindberg a real play? It certainly bears no resemblance to
Love from a Stranger, but the imagination can handle *The
Dream Play* just as well and with far fuller satisfaction.
Apparently the critics think that a play to be a real play must
have real people in it, though they never take breath to tell us
what they mean by real people. Take people off the street or
carry them out of a drawing-room, plonk them on the stage
and make them speak as they speak in real, real life, and
you will have the dullest thing imaginable. I suppose the critics
will be shocked to hear that no real character can be put in a
play unless some of the reality is taken out of him through the
heightening, widening, and deepening of the character by the
dramatist who creates him. Would the dramatic critics call
the characters in *Hamlet* real people, or only the creations out
of the mind of a poet, and isn't *Hamlet* all the better for its
want of reality? Isn't it more of a play, and what has the
word "play" got to do with reality? Is Caliban a real person,
found in the street and compelled into the theatre? If he isn't,
then, isn't the character just as powerful as if he were? What
peculiar quality does this term of "real people in a real play"
give to a play, seeing that many plays, some of them in step
with the greatest, have in them characters far removed from
this critic-quality of matter-of-factness? Isn't Caliban as real
a character as Gustav Bergmann in *Close Quarters*, or the
ladies and gents in *Fallen Angels*, or *Night Must Fall*, or *Call
It a Day*, the author of which, as Mr. Agate tells us, assembles
on her stage characters so real (again this word "real"—the
spyhole through which the critics view the stage) that she
might have gone into the street and compelled them into the

theater. (Though how a critic couples a play dealing with sex almost from the word "go" to the last lap, a play in which an accountant goes to the flat of an actress-client and nothing happens; in which the accountant's wife is entertained by a friend, and then entertains the friend alone in her house, and nothing happens; in which their daughter flings herself at an artist, and nothing happens; in which her brother falls for a young lassie that climbs over the garden wall to him, and nothing happens; in which the maid falls for the manservant of the family a few doors down, and nothing happens; and the bitch brought out for a walk by the manservant rubs noses with the dog taken out by the maid, and nothing happens— how a critic couples all this sort of thing with characters hustled in off the streets, only a critic could know, and only a critic can tell.) If all that is in this play be life, then life is a mass of sentimentally holy hokum.

As a matter-of-factness no one, least of all a playwright, can go out into the streets and lanes of the city and compel the people to come on to the stage, for the people on the stage must be of the stage and not of the streets and lanes of the city or of the highways and hedges of the country. The most realistic characters in the most realistic play cannot be true to life. Perhaps the most real character in any play we know of is the character of Falstaff done by Shakespeare. Here is realism as large as life; but it is realism larger, and a lot larger, than life. Falstaff was never pulled off the streets into the theatre by Shakespeare. God never created Falstaff— he sprang from Shakespeare's brain. God, if you like, created Shakespeare, but Shakespeare created Falstaff. Falstaff is no more real, there is no more matter-of-factness in the character of Falstaff, than there is in Caliban or Puck or Ariel. He is a bigger creation than any of these three, and that is all. A play, says Dryden, ought to be a just image of human nature, and this is true of *Hamlet*, of *John Bull's Other Island*, of *Strange Interlude*, of *Six Characters in Search of an Author*, of *Peer Gynt*, of *The Dream Play*; but it is not true of the trivial tomtit-realism in the thousand and one entertainment plays patted and praised by the dramatic critics. Why, even the sawdust characters of the Moor, Petroushka, and the Ballerina are a more just image of human nature than the characters in the matter-of-fact, exact-imitation-of-life plays that flit about on the English stage.

As it is with the play, so it is with the dressed-up stage— the critics want to be doped into the belief that the scene on

the stage is as real as life itself. The stirring of the hair is
more to them than the stirring of the heart. But things as real
as life itself on the stage they can never have; a room can
never be a room, a tree a tree, or a death a death. These must
take the nature of a child's toys and a child's play. Let me
quote from Allardyce Nicoll's *British Drama:*

> Illusion for the ordinary spectator is only partial at the best,
> and nearly all of us are aware, even at the moment of highest
> tension or most hilarious laughter, that the battlements are not
> of Elsinore and the trees are not of Arden forest. The scene-
> painter's art allied to that of the electrician can now obtain
> effects undreamt of before. Our drawing-rooms can look like
> drawing-rooms now, our woods can look like woods, and our
> seas like seas. Those, too, who have witnessed some recent
> productions in which the new German lighting effects were
> employed will agree that it would be hard to tell the fictional
> clouds that flit over the painted sky from real clouds, or the
> fictional sunrise from real sunrise. The question is, however,
> not whether the semblance of actuality can be obtained, but
> whether it is precisely that which we desire. Would we not
> rather have the real drawing-room of Mrs. So-and-so, the real
> Epping Forest, the real Atlantic, rather than these feigned
> copies of them? Would we not choose to watch those beautiful
> clouds from an open moorland rather than from our seats in
> gallery or in stalls? It is precisely the same problem that arises
> in the consideration of drama itself. We do not want merely an
> excerpt from reality; it is the imaginative transformation of
> reality, as it is seen through the eyes of the poet, that we desire.
> The great art of the theatre is to suggest, not to tell openly; to
> dilate the mind by symbols, not by actual things; to express in
> Lear a world's sorrow, and in Hamlet the grief of humanity.
> Many of our modern producers are striving in this direction,
> although it must be confessed that England here is well in the
> background.

And what is the greatest obstacle the progressive producers
have to face? In my opinion, the dramatic critics who prefer
the stirring of the hair to the stirring of the heart; the death-
or-drivel boys gunning with their gab from their pill-boxes in
the theatre and make it more of a temple and less of a den
of thieves.

This rage for real, real life on the stage has taken all the
life out of the drama. If everything on the stage is to be a
fake exact imitation (for fake realism it can only be), where
is the chance for the original and imaginative artist? Less
chance for him than there was for Jonah in the whale's belly.

The beauty, fire, and poetry of drama have perished in the storm of fake realism. Let real birds fly through the air (not like Basil Dean's butterflies in *Midsummer Night's Dream*, fluttering over the stage and pinning themselves to trees), real animals roam through the jungle, real fish swim in the sea, but let us have the make-believe of the artist and the child in the theatre. Less of what the critics call "life," and more of symbolism; for even in the most commonplace of realistic plays the symbol can never be absent. A house on a stage can never be a house, and that which represents it must always be a symbol. A room in a realistic play must always be a symbol for a room. There can never be any important actuality on the stage, except an actuality that is unnecessary and out of place. An actor representing a cavalier may come on the stage mounted on a real horse, but the horse will always look only a little less ridiculous than the "cavalier." The horse can have nothing to do with the drama. I remember a play written round Mr. Pepys, and in this play was used "the identical snuff-box used by him when he was head of the Admiralty in the reign of Charles the Second." So much was said about the snuff-box that I expected it to be carried in on a cushion preceded by a brass band, and hawked around for all to admire before the play began. Now this snuff-box added nothing to the play, and because of this commonplace spirit in the play, the play added nothing to the drama. It seems that the closer we move to actual life, the further we move away from the drama. Drama purely imitative of life isn't drama at all. Now the critics are beginning to use the word "theatre" when they find themselves in a bit of a tangle over what they should say about a play that has a bad whiff of staleness in its theme, character, and form. For instance, Mr. Ivor Brown, writing of a recent play, said that "the play is not life, it is theatre and might be allowed to wear its flamboyant colors"; "might be allowed," mind you—he, too, isn't sure. He doesn't tell us to what theatre the play belonged. He left his readers to find that out for themselves. Was it what theatre of Shakespeare, of Shaw, of Strindberg, of Ibsen, of Goldsmith, of O'Neill, of Pirandello, of Toller? Or the theatre of Dan Leno, Marie Lloyd, George Robey, Charlie Chaplin, Sidney Howard, or Will Hay? These are all good theatre and so they are all good life. But it is not the life that they imitate in their plays or in their actions that makes them good theatre, but the unique and original life that is in themselves. They have the life that the present dramatic critics lack, for the critics cannot, or are

afraid to, be lively. They wouldn't venture to give the plays
they call "theatre" their baptismal name of rubbish. Where
would we see a criticism like unto the meet criticisms for such
plays given by George Jean Nathan:

THE FIRST APPLE.   Lynn Starling.   Oh!
THE LAKE.   A play that got a lot of praise in England. By
   Dorothy Massingham and Murray MacDonald. Badly confused
   effort to mix a little Chekhov with a lot of boiled-over Henry
   Arthur Jones, the result being even worse Massingham-
   MacDonald.
THE LOCKED ROOM.   Junk.
THE GODS WE MAKE.   Terrible!

The Government would probably go out of office if even
one of the sharp sentences just quoted came out of the mouth
of a London dramatic critic. We haven't a critic like Nathan
in the English Theatre, and it is time we had. We have only to
read some of his works—*Testament of a Critic, Art of the
Night, The House of Satan, Since Ibsen, The Critic and the
Drama, Another Book on the Theater, The Theater of the
Moment*—to realize that in the Theatre of Nathan the curtain
is always going up, while in the Theatre of the critics here the
curtain is always coming down. The critics here are afraid
to be alive or alert. They take their timid thoughts out of a
pouncet box. Every bare expression they use is carefully
covered with a frill. They take the moaning echo of a shell
to be the thunder of the sea. Their criticisms come to us on a
pseudo-silver salver. Instead of knocking a bad play over the
head with a stick, they flick it over the cheek with a kid glove.
They are pew-openers in the temple of drama, nicely showing
the people to their places. They are the modern groundlings
in the theatre—always waiting to be entertained. Shakespeare,
of course, they are certain about, for tradition shoves them on
to their knees the minute Shakespeare turns the corner. They
often take a patch of flame-colored taffeta to be the burning
sun. "Critics," says George Jean Nathan, "are artist–partners
with the artist himself. The former creates, the latter recreates.
Without criticism art would, of course, still be art, and so, with
its windows walled in and its lights out, the Louvre would
still be the Louvre." Quite right; but the weekly and daily purr
of praise given by our critics to commonplace plays, packed
with "matter-of-factness" and "exact imitation of life," like
stuffed geese, is just unwalling the windows, opening wide the
doors, and lighting a great gathering of lamps in a hen-house.

THE SILVER TASSIE

A Tragi-Comedy in Four Acts

by SEAN O'CASEY

1928

TO

EILEEN

WITH THE YELLOW DAFFODILS

IN THE GREEN VASE

THE SILVER TASSIE[1]

NOTES

THE Croucher's make-up should come as close as possible to a death's head, a skull; and his hands should show like those of a skeleton's. He should sit somewhere *above* the group of Soldiers; preferably to one side, on the left, from view-point of audience, so as to overlook the Soldiers. He should look languid, as if very tired of life.

The group of Soldiers—Act Two—should enter in a close mass, as if each was keeping the other from falling, utterly weary and tired out. They should appear as if they were almost locked together.

The Soldiers' last response to the Staff-Wallah's declaration, namely, "To the Guns!" should have in these three words the last high notes of "The Last Post."

The song sung at the end of the play should be given to the best two (or one) singers in the cast. If, on the other hand, there be no passable singer among the players, the song should be omitted.

Perhaps a more suitable Spiritual than "Sweet Chariot" would be chosen for Harry to sing. For instance, "Keep Inchin' Along," or "Keep Me from Sinkin' Down."

The Chants in the play are simple Plain Song. The first chant is given in full as an example of the way in which they are sung. In the others, the dots . . . indicate that the note preceding them should be sustained till the music indicates a change. There are three parts in each chant: the Intonation; the Meditation; and the Ending. After a little practice, they will be found to be easy to sing. The Soldiers having the better voices should be selected to intone the chants, irrespective of

[1] Reprinted by permission of St. Martin's Press, Inc. and Macmillan & Company, Ltd. of London. Copyright 1928 by Macmillan & Company, Ltd., renewed 1955 by Sean O'Casey.

the numbers allotted to them as characters in the book of the play.

CHARACTERS

SYLVESTER HEEGAN
MRS. HEEGAN, *his wife*
SIMON NORTON
SUSIE MONICAN
MRS. FORAN
TEDDY FORAN, *her husband*
HARRY HEEGAN, D.C.M.,
  Heegan's son
JESSIE TAITE
BARNEY BAGNAL
THE CROUCHER
1ST SOLDIER

2ND SOLDIER
3RD SOLDIER
4TH SOLDIER
THE CORPORAL
THE VISITOR
THE STAFF-WALLAH
1ST STRETCHER-BEARER
2ND STRETCHER-BEARER
1ST CASUALTY
2ND CASUALTY
SURGEON FORBY MAXWELL
THE SISTER OF THE WARD

ACT ONE—*Room in Heegan's home.*
ACT TWO—*Somewhere in France* [later on].
ACT THREE—*Ward in a Hospital* [a little later on].
ACT FOUR—*Room in Premises of Avondale Football Club*
      [later on still].

ACT ONE

[*The eating, sitting, and part sleeping room of the Heegan family. A large window at back looks on to a quay, from which can be seen the centre mast of a steamer, at the top of which gleams a white light. Another window at right looks down on a side street. Under the window at back, plumb in the centre, is a stand, the legs gilded silver and the top gilded gold; on the stand is a purple velvet shield on which are pinned a number of silver medals surrounding a few gold ones. On each side of the shield is a small vase holding a bunch of artificial flowers. The shield is draped with red and yellow ribbons. To the left of the stand is a bed covered with a bedspread of black striped with vivid green. To the right of the stand is a dresser and chest of drawers combined. The fireplace is to the left. Beside the fireplace is a door leading to a bedroom, another door which gives access to the rest of the house and the street, on the right. At the corner left is a red-coloured stand resembling an easel, having on it a silver-gilt framed picture photograph of Harry Heegan in football dress, crimson jersey with yellow collar and cuffs and a broad yellow belt, black stockings, and yellow football boots. A table on which are a half-pint bottle of whisky, a large parcel of bread and meat sandwiches, and some copies of English illustrated magazines.*

SYLVESTER HEEGAN *and* SIMON NORTON *are sitting by the fire.* SYLVESTER HEEGAN *is a stockily built man of sixty-five; he has been a docker all his life since first the muscles of his arms could safely grip a truck, and even at sixty-five the steel in them is only beginning to stiffen.*

SIMON NORTON *is a tall man, originally a docker too, but by a little additional steadiness, a minor effort towards self-education, a natural, but very slight superior nimbleness of mind, has risen in the Company's estimation and has been given the position of checker, a job entailing as many hours of work as a docker, almost as much danger, twice as much responsibility, and a corresponding reduction in his earning powers. He is not so warmly, but a little more circumspectly*

[167]

dressed than SYLVESTER, *and in his manner of conduct and
speech there is a hesitant suggestion of greater refinement
than in those of* SYLVESTER, *and a still more vague indica-
tion that he is aware of it. This timid semi-conscious sense
of superiority, which Simon sometimes forgets, is shown
frequently by a complacent stroking of a dark beard which
years are beginning to humiliate. The night is cold, and*
SIMON *and* SYLVESTER *occasionally stretch longingly towards
the fire. They are fully dressed and each has his topcoat and
hat beside him, as if ready to go out at a moment's notice.*
SUSIE MONICAN *is standing at the table polishing a Lee–
Enfield rifle with a chamois cloth; the butt of the rifle is
resting on the table. She is a girl of twenty-two, well-shaped
limbs, challenging breasts, all of which are defiantly hidden
by a rather long dark blue skirt and bodice buttoning up to
the throat, relieved by a crimson scarf around her neck,
knotted in front and falling down her bosom like a man's
tie. She is undeniably pretty, but her charms are almost
completely hidden by her sombre, ill-fitting dress, and the
rigid manner in which she has made her hair up declares
her unflinching and uncompromising modesty. Just now she
is standing motionless, listening intently, looking towards
the door on right.*

MRS. HEEGAN *is standing at the window at right, listening
too, one hand pulling back the curtain, but her attention,
taken from the window, is attracted to the door. She is older
than* SYLVESTER, *stiffened with age and rheumatism; the end
of her life is unknowingly lumbering towards a rest: the
impetus necessity has given to continual toil and striving is
beginning to slow down, and everything she has to do is
done with a quiet mechanical persistence. Her inner ear
cannot hear even a faint echo of a younger day. Neither*
SYLVESTER *nor* SIMON *has noticed the attentive attitude of*
MRS. HEEGAN *or* SUSIE, *for* SYLVESTER, *with one arm outstretched crooked at the elbow, is talking with subdued
intensity to* SIMON.]

SYLVESTER. I seen him do it, mind you. I seen him do it.
SIMON. I quite believe you, Sylvester.
SYLVESTER. Break a chain across his bisseps! [*With panto-
mime action.*] Fixes it over his arm . . . bends it up . . . a
little strain . . . snaps in two . . . right across his bisseps!
SUSIE. Shush you, there!

[MRS. HEEGAN *goes out with troubled steps by door. The rest remain still for a few moments.*]

SYLVESTER. A false alarm.

SIMON. No cause for undue anxiety; there's plenty of time yet.

SUSIE [*chanting as she resumes the polishing of rifle*]:
> Man walketh in a vain shadow, and disquieteth himself
> in vain:
> He heapeth up riches, and cannot tell who shall gather
> them.

[*She sends the chant in the direction of* SYLVESTER *and* SIMON, SUSIE *coming close to the two men and sticking an angry face in between them.*]

SUSIE. When the two of yous stand quiverin' together on the dhread day of the Last Judgement, how will the two of yous feel if yous have nothin' to say but "he broke a chain across his bisseps"? Then the two of you'll know that the wicked go down into hell, an' all the people who forget God! [*She listens a moment, and leaving down the rifle, goes out by door left.*]

SYLVESTER. It's persecutin', that tambourine theology of Susie's. I always get a curious, sickenin' feelin', Simon, when I hear the Name of the Supreme Bein' tossed into the quietness of a sensible conversation.

SIMON. The day he won the Cross Country Championship of County Dublin, Syl, was a day to be chronicled.

SYLVESTER. In a minor way, yes, Simon. But the day that caps the chronicle was the one when he punched the fear of God into the heart of Police Constable 63 C under the stars of a frosty night on the way home from Terenure.

SIMON. Without any exaggeration, without any exaggeration, mind you, Sylvester, that could be called a memorable experience.

SYLVESTER. I can see him yet [*he gets up, slides from side to side, dodging and parrying imaginary blows*] glidin' round the dazzled Bobby, cross-ey'd tryin' to watch him.

SIMON [*tapping his pipe resolutely on the hob*]. Unperturbed, mind you, all the time.

SYLVESTER. An' the hedges by the road-side standin' stiff in the silent cold of the air, the frost beads on the branches glistenin' like toss'd-down diamonds from the breasts of the stars, the quietness of the night stimulated to a fuller stillness by the mockin' breathin' of Harry, an' the heavy, ragin' pantin' of the Bobby, an' the quickenin' beats of our own hearts afraid, of hopin' too little or hopin' too much.

[*During the last speech by* SYLVESTER, SUSIE *has come in with a bayonet, and has commenced to polish it.*]

SUSIE. We don't go down on our knees often enough; that's why we're not able to stand up to the Evil One: we don't go down on our knees enough. . . . I can hear some persons fallin' with a splash of sparks into the lake of everlastin' fire. . . . An account of every idle word shall be given at the last day. [*She goes out again with rifle.*]

SUSIE [*bending towards* SIMON *and* SYLVESTER *as she goes*]. God is listenin' to yous; God is listenin' to yous!

SYLVESTER. Dtch, dtch, dtch. People ought to be forcibly restrained from constantly cannonadin' you with the name of the Deity.

SIMON. Dubiety never brush'd a thought into my mind, Syl, while I was waitin' for the moment when Harry would stretch the Bobby hors dee combaa on the ground.

SYLVESTER [*resuming his pantomime actions*]. There he was staggerin', beatin' out blindly, every spark of energy panted out of him, while Harry feinted, dodg'd, side-stepp'd, then suddenly sail'd in an' put him asleep with . . .

SIMON. A right-handed hook to the jaw! ⎫
SYLVESTER. A left-handed hook to the jaw! ⎬ [*Together.*]

SYLVESTER [*after a pause*]. A left-handed hook to the jaw, Simon.

SIMON. No, no, Syl, a right-handed hook to the jaw.

[MRS. FORAN *runs quickly in by the door with a frying-pan in her hand, on which is a steak. She comes to the fire, pushing, so as to disturb the two men. She is one of the many gay, careworn women of the working-class.*]

MRS. FORAN [*rapidly*]. A pot of clothes is boilin' on the fire above, an' I knew yous wouldn't mind me slappin' a bit of a steak on here for a second to show him, when he comes in before he goes away, that we're mindful of his needs, an' I'm hopeful of a dream to-night that the sea's between us, not lookin' very haggard in the mornin' to find the dream a true one. [*With satisfied anticipation*]:

For I'll be single again, yes, I'll be single again;
An' I eats what I likes, . . . an' I drinks what I likes,

An' I likes what I likes, when I'm——

[*Stopping suddenly.*] What's the silence for?

SYLVESTER [*slowly and decidedly*]. I was at the fight, Simon, an' I seen him givin' a left-handed hook to the jaw.

MRS. FORAN. What fight?

SIMON [*slowly and decidedly*]. I was there too, an' I saw him down the Bobby with a right-handed hook to the jaw.

MRS. FORAN. What Bobby?

[*A pause.*]

SYLVESTER. It was a close up, an' I don't know who'd know better if it wasn't the boy's own father.

MRS. FORAN. What boy . . . what father?

SYLVESTER. Oh, shut up, woman, an' don't be smotherin' us with a shower of questions.

SUSIE [*who has entered on the last speech, and has started to polish a soldier's steel helmet*]. Oh, the miserableness of them that don't know the things that belong unto their peace. They try one thing after another, they try everything, but they never think of trying God. [*Coming nearer to them.*] Oh, the happiness of knowing that God's hand has pick'd you out for heaven. [*To Mrs. Foran.*] What's the honey-pot kiss of a lover to the kiss of righteousness and peace?

[MRS. FORAN, *embarrassed, goes over to window.*]

SUSIE [*turning to Simon*]. Simon, will you not close the dandy door of the public-house and let the angels open the pearly gates of heaven for you?

SYLVESTER. We feel very comfortable where we are, Susie.

SUSIE. Don't mock, Sylvester, don't mock. You'd run before a great wind, tremble in an earthquake, and flee from a fire; so don't treat lightly the still, small voice calling you to repentance and faith.

SYLVESTER [*with appeal and irritation*]. Oh, do give over worryin' a man, Susie.

SUSIE. God shows His love by worrying, and worrying, and worrying the sinner. The day will come when you will call on the mountains to cover you, and then you'll weep and gnash your teeth that you did not hearken to Susie's warning. [*Putting her hands appealingly on his shoulders.*] Sylvester, if you pray long enough, and hard enough, and deep enough, you'll get the power to fight and conquer Beelzebub.

MRS. FORAN. I'll be in a doxological mood to-night, not because the kingdom of heaven'll be near me, but because my
husband'll be far away, and to-morrow

[*singing*]:

> I'll be single again, yes, single again;
> An' I goes where I likes, an' I does what I likes,
> An' I likes what I likes now I'm single again!

SIMON. Go on getting Harry's things ready, Susie, and defer
the dosing of your friends with canticles till the time is ripe
with rest for them to listen quietly.

[SIMON *and* SYLVESTER *are very self-conscious during* SUSIE'S
talk to them. SIMON *empties his pipe by tapping the head
on the hob of the grate. He then blows through it. As he is
blowing through it,* SYLVESTER *is emptying his by tapping
it on the hob; as he is blowing it* SIMON *taps his again; as*
SIMON *taps* SYLVESTER *taps with him, and then they look
into the heads of the pipes and blow together.*]

SUSIE. It must be mercy or it must be judgement: if not mercy
to-day it may be judgement to-morrow. He is never tired of
waiting and waiting and waiting; and watching and watching and watching; and knocking and knocking and knocking
for the sinner—you, Sylvester, and you, Simon—to turn
from his wickedness and live. Oh, if the two of you only
knew what it was to live! Not to live leg-staggering an'
belly-creeping among the pain-spotted and sin-splashed
desires of the flesh; but to live, oh, to live swift-flying from
a holy peace to a holy strength, and from holy strength to a
holy joy, like the flashing flights of a swallow in the deep
beauty of a summer sky.

[SIMON *and* SYLVESTER *shift about, self-conscious and uneasy.*]

SUSIE [*placing her hand first on* SIMON'S *shoulder and then on*
SYLVESTER'S]. The two of you God's elegant swallows; a
saved pair; a loving pair strong-wing'd, freed from the gin
of the snarer, tip of wing to tip of wing, flying fast or
darting swift together to the kingdom of heaven.

SIMON [*expressing a protecting thought to Sylvester*]. One of
the two of us should go out and hunt back the old woman
from the perishing cold of watching for the return of Harry.

SYLVESTER. She'll be as cold as a naked corpse, an' unstinted
watchin' won't bring Harry back a minute sooner. I'll go an'

drive her back. [*He rises to go.*] I'll be back in a minute, Susie.

SIMON [*hurriedly*]. Don't bother, Syl, I'll go; she won't be farther than the corner of the street; you go on toasting yourself where you are. [*He rises.*] I'll be back in a minute, Susie.

MRS. FORAN [*running to the door*]. Rest easy the two of you, an' I'll go, so as to give Susie full time to take the sin out of your bones an' put you both in first-class form for the kingdom of heaven. [*She goes out.*]

SUSIE. Sinners that jeer often add to the glory of God: going out, she gives you, Sylvester, and you, Simon, another few moments, precious moments—oh, how precious, for once gone, they are gone for ever—to listen to the warning from heaven.

SIMON [*suddenly*]. Whisht, here's somebody coming, I think?

SYLVESTER. I'll back this is Harry comin' at last.

[*A pause as the three listen.*]

SYLVESTER. No, it's nobody.

SIMON. Whoever it was 's gone by.

SUSIE. Oh, Syl, oh, Simon, don't try to veil the face of God with an evasion. You can't, you can't cod God. This may be your last chance before the pains of hell encompass the two of you. Hope is passing by; salvation is passing by, and glory arm-in-arm with her. In the quietness left to you go down on your knees and pray that they come into your hearts and abide with you for ever. . . . [*With fervour, placing her left hand on* SIMON'S *shoulder and her right hand on* SYLVESTER'S, *and shaking them.*] Get down on your knees, get down on your knees, get down on your knees and pray for conviction of sin, lest your portion in David become as the portion of the Canaanites, the Amorites, the Perizzites and the Jebusites!

SYLVESTER. Eh, eh, Susie; cautious now—you seem to be forgettin' yourself.

SIMON. Desist, Susie, desist. Violence won't gather people to God. It only ingenders hostility to what you're trying to do.

SYLVESTER. You can't batter religion into a man like that.

SIMON. Religion is love, but that sort of thing is simply a nulli-fication of religion.

SUSIE. Bitterness and wrath in exhortation is the only hope

of rousing the pair of yous into a sense of coming and
everlasting penalties.

SYLVESTER. Well, give it a miss, give it a miss to me now.
Don't try to claw me into the kingdom of heaven. An' you
only succeed in distempering piety when you try to mangle
it into a man's emotions.

SIMON. Heaven is all the better, Susie, for being a long way
off.

SYLVESTER. If I want to pray I do it voluntarily, but I'm not
going to be goaded an' goaded into it.

SUSIE. I go away in a few days to help to nurse the wounded,
an' God's merciful warnings may depart along with me,
then sin'll usher the two of you into Gehenna for all
eternity. Oh, if the two of you could only grasp the meaning of the word eternity! [*Bending down and looking up
into their faces.*] Time that had no beginning and never can
have an end—an' there you'll be—two cockatrices creeping
together, a desolation, an astonishment, a curse and a hissing
from everlasting to everlasting. [*She goes into room.*]

SYLVESTER. Cheerful, what! Cockatrices—be-God, that's a
good one, Simon!

SIMON. Always a trying thing to have to listen to one that's
trying to push the kingdom of God into a reservation of a
few yards.

SYLVESTER. A cockatrice! Now where did she manage to pick
up that term of approbation, I wonder?

SIMON. From the Bible. An animal somewhere mentioned in
the Bible, I think, that a serpent hatched out of a cock's
egg.

SYLVESTER. A cock's egg! It couldn't have been the egg of an
ordinary cock. Not the male of what we call a hen?

SIMON. I think so.

SYLVESTER. Well, be-God, that's a good one! You know
Susie'll have to be told to disintensify her soul-huntin', for
religion even isn't an excuse for saying that a man'll become a cockatrice.

SIMON. In a church, somehow or other, it seems natural
enough, and even in the street it's all right, for one thing is
as good as another in the wide-open ear of the air, but in
the delicate quietness of your own home it, it——

SYLVESTER. Jars on you!

SIMON. Exactly!

SYLVESTER. If she'd only confine her glory-to-God business to

the festivals, Christmas, now, or even Easter, Simon, it
would be recommendable; for a few days before Christmas,
like the quiet raisin' of a curtain, an' a few days after,
like the gentle lowerin' of one, there's nothing more . . .
more——

SIMON. Appropriate. . . .

SYLVESTER. Exhilaratin' than the singin' of the Adestay
Fidellis.

SIMON. She's damned pretty, an' if she dressed herself justly,
she'd lift some man's heart up, an' toss down many another.
It's a mystery now, what affliction causes the disablement,
for most women of that kind are plain, an' when a woman's
born plain she's born good. I wonder what caused the
peculiar bend in Susie's nature? Narrow your imagination
to the limit and you couldn't call it an avocation.

SYLVESTER [giving the head of his pipe a sharp, quick blow
on the palm of his hand to clear it]. Adoration.

SIMON. What?

SYLVESTER. Adoration, Simon, accordin' to the flesh. . . . She
fancied Harry and Harry fancied Jessie, so she hides her
rage an' loss in the love of a scorchin' Gospel.

SIMON. Strange, strange.

SYLVESTER. Oh, very curious, Simon.

SIMON. It's a problem, I suppose.

SYLVESTER. An inconsolable problem, Simon.

[MRS. FORAN enters by door, helping in MRS. HEEGAN, who is
pale and shivering with cold.]

MRS. HEEGAN [shivering and shuddering]. U-u-uh, I feel the
stream of blood that's still trickling through me old veins
icifyin' fast; u-uh.

MRS. FORAN. Madwoman, dear, to be waitin' out there on the
quay an' a wind risin' as cold as a stepmother's breath,
piercin' through your old bones, mockin' any effort a body
would make to keep warm, an' [suddenly rushing over to
the fireplace in an agony of dismay, scattering SIMON and
SYLVESTER, and whipping the frying-pan off the fire]—The
steak, the steak; I forgot the blasted steak an' onions fryin'
on the fire! God Almighty, there's not as much as a bead
of juice left in either of them. The scent of the burnin'
would penetrate to the street, an' not one of you'd stir a
hand to lift them out of danger. Oh, look at the condition
they're in. Even the gospel-gunner couldn't do a little target

practice by helpin' the necessity of a neighbour. [*As she goes out.*] I can hear the love for your neighbours almost fizzlin' in your hearts.

MRS. HEEGAN [*pushing in to the fire, to* SIMON *and* SYLVESTER]. Push to the right and push to the left till I get to the fosterin' fire. Time eatin' his heart out, an' no sign of him yet. The two of them, the two of my legs is numb . . . an' the wind's risin' that'll make the sea heave an' sink under the boat to-night, under shaded lights an' the submarines about. [SUSIE *comes in, goes over to window, and looks out.*] Hours ago the football match must have been over, an' no word of him yet, an' all drinkin' if they won, an' all drinkin' if they lost; with Jessie hitchin' on after him, an' no one thinkin' of me an' the maintenance money.

SYLVESTER. He'll come back in time; he'll have to come back; he must come back.

SIMON. He got the goals, Mrs. Heegan, that won the last two finals, and it's only fair he'd want to win this, which'll mean that the Cup before two——

SYLVESTER [*butting in*]. Times hand runnin'.

SIMON. Two times consecutively before, makin' the Cup the property of the Club.

SYLVESTER. Exactly!

MRS. HEEGAN. The chill's residin' in my bones, an' feelin's left me just the strength to shiver. He's overstayed his leave a lot, an' if he misses now the tide that's waitin', he skulks behind desertion from the colours.

SUSIE. On Active Service that means death at dawn.

MRS. HEEGAN. An' my governmental money grant would stop at once.

SUSIE. That would gratify Miss Jessie Taite, because you put her weddin' off with Harry till after the duration of the war, an' cut her out of the allowance.

SYLVESTER [*with a sickened look at* SIMON]. Dtch, dtch, dtch, the way the women wag the worst things out of happenings! [*To the women.*] My God Almighty, he'll be back in time an' fill yous all with disappointment.

MRS. HEEGAN. She's coinin' money workin' at munitions, an' doesn't need to eye the little that we get from Harry; for one evening hurryin' with him to the pictures she left her bag behind, an' goin' through it what would you think I found?

SUSIE. A saucy book, now, or a naughty picture?

MRS. HEEGAN. Lion and Unicorn standin' on their Jew ay mon draw. With all the rings an' dates, an' rules an' regulations.

SIMON. What was it, Mrs. Heegan?

MRS HEEGAN. Spaced an' lined; signed an' signatured; nestlin' in a blue envelope to keep it warm.

SYLVESTER [*testily*]. Oh, sing it out, woman, an' don't be takin' the value out of what you're goin' to tell us.

MRS. HEEGAN. A Post Office Savings Bank Book.

SYLVESTER. Oh, hairy enough, eh?

SIMON. How much, Mrs. Heegan?

MRS. HEEGAN. Pounds an' shillings with the pence missin'; backed by secrecy, an' security guaranteed by Act of Parliament.

SYLVESTER [*impatiently*]. Dtch, dtch. Yes, yes, woman, but how much was it?

MRS. HEEGAN. Two hundred an' nineteen pounds, sixteen shillings, an' no pence.

SYLVESTER. Be-God, a nice little nest-egg, right enough!

SUSIE. I hope in my heart that she came by it honestly, and that she remembers that it's as true now as when it was first spoken that it's harder for a camel to go through the eye of a needle than for a rich person to enter the kingdom of heaven.

SIMON. And she hidin' it all under a veil of silence, when there wasn't the slightest fear of any of us bein' jealous of her.

[*A tumult is heard on the floor over their heads, followed by a crash of breaking delf. They are startled, and listen attentively.*]

MRS. HEEGAN [*breaking the silence*]. Oh, there he's at it again. An she sayin' that he was a pattern husband since he came home on leave, merry-making with her an' singin' dolorously the first thing every mornin'. I was thinkin' there'd be a rough house sometime over her lookin' so well after his long absence . . . you'd imagine now, the trenches would have given him some idea of the sacredness of life!

[*Another crash of breaking delfware.*]

MRS. HEEGAN. An' the last week of his leave she was too fond of breakin' into song in front of him.

SYLVESTER. Well, she's gettin' it now for goin' round heavin' her happiness in the poor man's face.

[*A crash, followed by screams from* MRS. FORAN.]

SUSIE. I hope he won't be running down here as he often does.

SIMON [*a little agitated*]. I couldn't stay here an' listen to that; I'll go up and stop him: he might be killing the poor woman.

MRS. HEEGAN. Don't do anything of the kind, Simon; he might down you with a hatchet or something.

SIMON. Phuh, I'll keep him off with the left and hook him with the right. [*Putting on his hat and coat as he goes to the door.*] Looking prim and careless'll astonish him. Monstrous to stay here, while he may be killing the woman.

MRS. HEEGAN [*to* SIMON *as he goes out*]. For God's sake mind yourself, Simon.

SYLVESTER [*standing beside closed door on right with his ear close to one of the panels, listening intently*]. Simon's a tidy little man with his fists, an' would make Teddy Foran feel giddy if he got home with his left hook. [*Crash.*] I wonder is that Simon knockin' down Foran, or Foran knockin' down Simon?

MRS. HEEGAN. If he came down an' we had the light low, an' kept quiet, he might think we were all out.

SYLVESTER. Shush. I can hear nothin' now. Simon must have awed him. Quiet little man, but when Simon gets goin'. Shush? No, nothin' . . . Something unusual has happened. O, oh, be-God!

[*The door against which* SYLVESTER *is leaning bursts suddenly in.* SYLVESTER *is flung headlong to the floor, and* MRS. FORAN, *her hair falling wildly over her shoulders, a cut over her eye, frantic with fear, rushes in and scrambles in a frenzy of haste under the bed.* MRS. HEEGAN, *quickened by fear, runs like a good one, followed by* SUSIE, *into the room, the door of which they bang after them.* SYLVESTER *hurriedly fights his way under the bed with* MRS. FORAN.]

MRS. FORAN [*speaking excitedly and jerkily as she climbs under the bed*]. Flung his dinner into the fire—and started to smash the little things in the room. Tryin' to save the dresser, I got a box in the eye. I locked the door on him as I rushed out, an' before I was half-way down, he had one of the panels flyin' out with—a hatchet!

SYLVESTER [*under the bed—out of breath*]. Whythehell didn't-you sing out beforeyousent thedoor flyin' inontop o' me!

MRS. FORAN. How could I an' flyin' before danger to me—life?

SYLVESTER. Yes, an'you'vegot meinto a nice extremity now!

MRS. FORAN. An' I yelled to Simon Norton when he had me—down, but the boyo only ran the faster out of the—house!

SYLVESTER. Oh, an' the regal-like way he went out to fight! Oh, I'm findin' out that everyone who wears a cocked hat isn't a Napoleon!

[TEDDY FORAN, MRS. FORAN'S *husband, enters by door, with a large, fancy, vividly yellow-coloured bowl, ornamented with crimson roses, in one hand and a hatchet in the other. He is big and powerful, rough and hardy. A man who would be dominant in a public-house, and whose opinions would be listened to with great respect. He is dressed in the khaki uniform of a soldier home on leave.*]

TEDDY. Under the bed, eh? Right place for a guilty conscience. I should have thrown you out of the window with the dinner you put before me. Out with you from under there, an' come up with your husband.

SUSIE [*opening suddenly door right, putting in her head, pulling it back and shutting door again*]. God is looking at you, God is looking at you!

MRS. FORAN. I'll not budge an inch from where I am.

TEDDY [*looking under the bed and seeing* SYLVESTER]. What are you doin' there encouragin' her against her husband?

SYLVESTER. You've no right to be rippin' open the poor woman's life of peace with violence.

TEDDY [*with indignation*]. She's my wife, isn't she?

MRS. FORAN. Nice thing if I lose the sight of my eye with the cut you gave me!

TEDDY. She's my wife, isn't she? An' you've no legal right to be harbourin' her here, keepin' her from her household duties. Stunned I was when I seen her lookin' so well after me long absence. Blowin' her sighin' in me face all day, an' she sufferin' the tortures of hell for fear I'd miss the boat!

SYLVESTER. Go on up to your own home; you've no right to be violatin' this place.

TEDDY. You'd like to make her your cheery amee, would you? It's napoo, there, napoo, you little pip-squeak. I seen you an' her goin' down the street arm-in-arm.

SYLVESTER. Did you expect to see me goin' down the street leg-in-leg with her?

TEDDY. Thinkin' of her Ring-papers instead of her husband. [*To* MRS. FORAN.] I'll teach you to be rippling with joy an' your husband goin' away! [*He shows the bowl.*] Your weddin' bowl, look at it; pretty, isn't it? Take your last eyeful of it now, for it's goin' west quick!

SUSIE [*popping her head in again*]. God is watching you, God is watching you!

MRS. FORAN [*appealingly*]. Teddy, Teddy, don't smash the poor weddin' bowl.

TEDDY [*smashing the bowl with a blow of the hatchet*]. It would be a pity, wouldn't it? Damn it, an' damn you. I'm off now to smash anything I missed, so that you'll have a gay time fittin' up the little home again by the time your loving husband comes back. You can come an' have a look, an' bring your mon amee if you like.

[*He goes out, and there is a pause as* MRS. FORAN *and* SYL-VESTER *peep anxiously towards the door.*]

SYLVESTER. Cautious, now cautious; he might be lurking outside that door there, ready to spring on you the minute you show'd your nose!

MRS. FORAN. Me lovely little weddin' bowl, me lovely little weddin' bowl!

[TEDDY *is heard breaking things in the room above.*]

SYLVESTER [*creeping out from under the bed*]. Oh, he is gone up. He was a little cow'd, I think, when he saw me.

MRS. FORAN. Me little weddin' bowl, wrapp'd in tissue paper, an' only taken out for a few hours every Christmas—me poor little weddin' bowl.

SUSIE [*popping her head in*]. God is watching—oh, he's gone!

SYLVESTER [*jubilant*]. Vanished! He was a little cow'd, I think, when he saw me.

[MRS. HEEGAN *and* SUSIE *come into the room.*]

MRS. FORAN. He's makin' a hash of every little thing we have in the house, Mrs. Heegan.

MRS. HEEGAN. Go inside to the room, Mrs. Foran, an' if he comes down again, we'll say you ran out to the street.

MRS. FORAN [*going into room*]. My poor little weddin' bowl that I might have had for generations!

SUSIE [*who has been looking out of the window, excitedly*]. They're comin', they're comin': a crowd with a concertina;

some of them carrying Harry on their shoulders, an' others
are carrying that Jessie Taite too, holding a silver cup in
her hands. Oh, look at the shameful way she's showing her
legs to all who like to have a look at them!

MRS. HEEGAN. Never mind Jessie's legs—what we have to do
is to hurry him out in time to catch the boat.

[*The sound of a concertina playing in the street outside has
been heard, and the noise of a marching crowd. The crowd
stop at the house. Shouts are heard—"Up the Avondales!";
"Up Harry Heegan and the Avondales!" Then steps are
heard coming up the stairs, and first* SIMON NORTON *enters,
holding the door ceremoniously wide open to allow* HARRY
to enter, with his arm around JESSIE, *who is carrying a
silver cup joyously, rather than reverentially elevated, as
a priest would elevate a chalice.* HARRY *is wearing khaki
trousers, a military cap stained with trench mud, a vivid
orange-coloured jersey with black collar and cuffs. He is
twenty-three years of age, tall, with the sinewy muscles of
a manual worker made flexible by athletic sport. He is a
typical young worker, enthusiastic, very often boisterous,
sensible by instinct rather than by reason. He has gone to
the trenches as unthinkingly as he would go to the polling
booth. He isn't naturally stupid; it is the stupidity of persons in high places that has stupefied him. He has given all
to his masters, strong heart, sound lungs, healthy stomach,
lusty limbs, and the little mind that education has permitted
to develop sufficiently to make all the rest a little more
useful. He is excited now with the sweet and innocent in-
sanity of a fine achievement, and the rapid lowering of a
few drinks.*

JESSIE *is twenty-two or so, responsive to all the animal
impulses of life. Ever dancing around, in and between the
world, the flesh, and the devil. She would be happy climbing with a boy among the heather on Howth Hill, and could
play ball with young men on the swards of the Phoenix
Park. She gives her favour to the prominent and popular.*
HARRY *is her favourite: his strength and speed have won the
Final for his club, he wears the ribbon of the D.C.M. It is a
time of spiritual and animal exaltation for her.*

BARNEY BAGNAL, *a soldier mate of* HARRY's, *stands a little
shyly near the door, with a pleasant, good-humoured grin
on his rather broad face. He is the same age as* HARRY, *just*

as strong, but not so quick, less finely formed, and not so sensitive; able to take most things quietly, but savage and wild when he becomes enraged. He is fully dressed, with topcoat buttoned on him, and he carries HARRY's *on his arm.*]

HARRY [*joyous and excited*]. Won, won, won, be-God; by the odd goal in five. Lift it up, lift it up, Jessie, sign of youth, sign of strength, sign of victory!

MRS. HEEGAN [*to* SYLVESTER]. I knew, now, Harry would come back in time to catch the boat.

HARRY [*to* JESSIE]. Leave it here, leave it down here, Jessie, under the picture, the picture of the boy that won the final.

MRS. HEEGAN. A parcel of sandwiches, a bottle of whisky, an' some magazines to take away with you an' Barney, Harry.

HARRY. Napoo sandwiches, an' napoo magazines: look at the cup, eh? The cup that Harry won, won by the odd goal in five! [*To* BARNEY.] The song that the little Jock used to sing, Barney, what was it? The little Jock we left shrivellin' on the wire after the last push.

BARNEY. "Will ye no come back again?"

HARRY. No, no, the one we all used to sing with him, "The Silver Tassie." [*Pointing to cup.*] There it is, the Silver Tassie, won by the odd goal in five, kicked by Harry Heegan.

MRS. HEEGAN. Watch your time, Harry, watch your time.

JESSIE. He's watching it, he's watching it—for God's sake don't get fussy, Mrs. Heegan.

HARRY. They couldn't take their beatin' like men. . . . Play the game, play the game, why the hell couldn't they play the game? [*To* BARNEY.] See the President of the Club, Dr. Forby Maxwell, shaking hands with me, when he was giving me the cup, "Well done, Heegan!" The way they yell'd and jump'd when they put in the equalizing goal in the first half!

BARNEY. Ay, a fluke, that's what it was; a lowsey fluke.

MRS. HEEGAN [*holding* HARRY's *coat up for him to put it on*]. Here, your coat, Harry, slip it on while you're talkin'.

HARRY [*putting it on*]. All right, keep smiling, don't fuss. [*To the rest.*] Grousing the whole time they were chasing the ball; an' when they lost it, "Referee, referee, offside, referee . . . foul there; ey, open your eyes, referee!"

JESSIE. And we scream'd and shouted them down with "Play the game, Primrose Rovers, play the game!"

BARNEY. You ran them off their feet till they nearly stood still.

MRS. FORAN [*has been peeping twice in timidly from the room and now comes in to the rest*]. Somebody run up an' bring Teddy down for fear he'd be left behind.

SYLVESTER [*to* HARRY]. Your haversack an' trench tools, Harry; haversack first, isn't it?

HARRY [*fixing his haversack*]. Haversack, haversack, don't rush me. [*To the rest.*] But when I got the ball, Barney, once I got the ball, the rain began to fall on the others. An' the last goal, the goal that put us one ahead, the winning goal, that was a-a-eh-a stunner!

BARNEY. A beauty, me boy, a hot beauty.

HARRY. Slipping by the back rushing at me like a mad bull, steadying a moment for a drive, seeing in a flash the goalie's hands sent with a shock to his chest by the force of the shot, his half-stunned motion to clear, a charge, and then carrying him, the ball and all with a rush into the centre of the net!

BARNEY [*enthusiastically*]. Be-God, I did get a thrill when I seen you puttin' him sittin' on his arse in the middle of the net!

MRS. FORAN [*from the door*]. One of yous do go up an' see if Teddy's ready to go.

MRS. HEEGAN [*to* HARRY]. Your father'll carry your kit-bag, an' Jessie'll carry your rifle as far as the boat.

HARRY [*irritably*]. Oh, damn it, woman, give your wailin' over for a minute!

MRS. HEEGAN. You've got only a few bare minutes to spare, Harry.

HARRY. We'll make the most of them, then. [*To* BARNEY.] Out with one of them wine-virgins we got in "The Mill in the Field," Barney, and we'll rape her in a last hot moment before we set out to kiss the guns!

[SIMON *has gone into room and returned with a gun and a kit-bag. He crosses to where* BARNEY *is standing.*]

BARNEY [*taking a bottle of wine from his pocket*]. Empty her of her virtues, eh?

HARRY. Spill it out, Barney, spill it out. . . . [*Seizing Silver Cup, and holding it towards* BARNEY.] Here, into the cup, be-God. A drink out of the cup, out of the Silver Tassie!

BARNEY [*who has removed the cap and taken out the cork*]. Here she is now. . . . Ready for anything, stripp'd to the skin!

JESSIE. No double-meaning talk, Barney.

SUSIE [*haughtily, to* JESSIE]. The men that are defending us have leave to bow themselves down in the House of Rimmon, for the men that go with the guns are going with God.

[BARNEY *pours wine into the cup for* HARRY *and into a glass for himself.*]

HARRY [*to* JESSIE]. Jessie, a sup for you. [*She drinks from the cup.*] An' a drink for me. [*He drinks.*] Now a kiss while our lips are wet. [*He kisses her.*] Christ, Barney, how would you like to be retreating from the fairest face and [*lifting* JESSIE'S *skirt a little*]—and the trimmest, slimmest little leg in the parish? Napoo, Barney, to everyone but me!

MRS. FORAN. One of you go up, an' try to get my Teddy down.

BARNEY [*lifting* SUSIE'S *skirt a little*]. Napoo, Harry, to everyone but——

SUSIE [*angrily, pushing* BARNEY *away from her*]. You khaki-cover'd ape, you, what are you trying to do? Manhandle the lassies of France, if you like, but put on your gloves when you touch a woman that seeketh not the things of the flesh.

HARRY [*putting an arm round* SUSIE *to mollify her*]. Now, Susie, Susie, lengthen your temper for a passing moment, so that we may bring away with us the breath of a kiss to the shell-bullied air of the trenches. . . . Besides, there's nothing to be ashamed of—it's not a bad little leggie at all.

SUSIE [*slipping her arm round* HARRY'S *neck, and looking defiantly at* BARNEY]. I don't mind what Harry does; I know he means no harm, not like other people. Harry's different.

JESSIE. You'll not forget to send me the German helmet home from France, Harry?

SUSIE [*trying to rest her head on* HARRY'S *breast*]. I know Harry, he's different. It's his way. I wouldn't let anyone else touch me, but in some way or another I can tell Harry's different.

JESSIE [*putting her arm round* HARRY *under* SUSIE'S *in an effort to dislodge it*]. Susie, Harry wants to be free to keep his arm round me during his last few moments here, so don't be pulling him about!

SUSIE [*shrinking back a little*]. I was only saying that Harry was different.

MRS. FORAN. For God's sake, will someone go up for Teddy, or he won't go back at all!

TEDDY [*appearing at door*]. Damn anxious for Teddy to go back! Well, Teddy's goin' back, an' he's left everything tidy upstairs so that you'll not have much trouble sortin' things out. [*To* HARRY.] The Club an' a crowd's waitin' outside to bring us to the boat before they go to the spread in honour of the final. [*Bitterly*.] A party for them while we muck off to the trenches!

HARRY [*after a slight pause, to* BARNEY]. Are you game, Barney?

BARNEY. What for?

HARRY. To go to the spread and hang the latch for another night?

BARNEY [*taking his rifle from* SIMON *and slinging it over his shoulder*]. No, no, napoo desertin' on Active Service. Deprivation of pay an' the rest of your time in the front trenches. No, no. We must go back!

MRS. HEEGAN. No, no, Harry. You must go back.

SIMON,
SYLVESTER, } [*together*]. You must go back.
and SUSIE

VOICES OF CROWD OUTSIDE. They must go back!

[*The ship's siren is heard blowing.*]

SIMON. The warning signal.

SYLVESTER. By the time they get there, they'll be unslinging the gangways!

SUSIE [*handing* HARRY *his steel helmet*]. Here's your helmet, Harry.

[*He puts it on.*]

MRS. HEEGAN. You'll all nearly have to run for it now!

SYLVESTER. I've got your kit-bag, Harry.

SUSIE. I've got your rifle.

SIMON. I'll march in front with the cup, after Conroy with the concertina.

TEDDY. Come on: ong avong to the trenches!

HARRY [*recklessly*]. Jesus, a last drink, then! [*He raises the Silver Cup, singing*]:
    Gae bring to me a pint of wine,
    And fill it in a silver tassie;

BARNEY [*joining in vigorously*]:
    . . . . a silver tassie.

HARRY:

> That I may drink before I go,
> A service to my bonnie lassie.

BARNEY:

> . . . . bonnie lassie.

HARRY:

> The boat rocks at the pier o' Leith,
> Full loud the wind blows from the ferry;
> The ship rides at the Berwick Law,
> An' I must leave my bonnie Mary!

BARNEY:

> . . . . . . leave my bonnie Mary!

HARRY:

> The trumpets sound, the banners fly,
> The glittering spears are ranked ready;

BARNEY:

> . . . glittering spears are ranked ready;

HARRY:

> The shouts of war are heard afar,
> The battle closes thick and bloody.

BARNEY:

> . . . . . . closes thick and bloody.

HARRY:

> It's not the roar of sea or shore,
> That makes me longer wish to tarry,
> Nor shouts of war that's heard afar—
> It's leaving thee, my bonnie lassie!

BARNEY:

> . . leaving thee, my bonnie lassie!

TEDDY. Come on, come on.

[SIMON, SYLVESTER, *and* SUSIE *go out.*]

VOICES OUTSIDE:

> Come on from your home to the boat;
> Carry on from the boat to the camp.

[TEDDY *and* BARNEY *go out.* HARRY *and* JESSIE *follow; as*
  HARRY *reaches the door, he takes his arm from round*
  JESSIE *and comes back to* MRS. HEEGAN.]

VOICES OUTSIDE. From the camp up the line to the trenches.
HARRY [*shyly and hurriedly kissing* MRS. HEEGAN]. Well, good-
  bye, old woman.
MRS. HEEGAN. Good-bye, my son.

[HARRY *goes out. The chorus of "The Silver Tassie," accompanied by a concertina, can be heard growing fainter till it ceases.* MRS. FORAN *goes out timidly.* MRS. HEEGAN *pokes the fire, arranges the things in the room, and then goes to the window and looks out. After a pause, the loud and long blast of the ship's siren is heard. The light on the masthead, seen through the window, moves slowly away, and* MRS. HEEGAN *with a sigh, "Ah dear," goes over to the fire and sits down. A slight pause, then* MRS. FORAN *returns to the room.*]

MRS. FORAN. Every little bit of china I had in the house is lyin' above in a mad an' muddled heap like the flotsum an' jetsum of the seashore!

MRS. HEEGAN [*with a deep sigh of satisfaction*]. Thanks be to Christ that we're after managin' to get the three of them away safely.

ACT TWO

[*In the war zone: a scene of jagged and lacerated ruin of what was once a monastery. At back a lost wall and window are indicated by an arched piece of broken coping pointing from the left to the right, and a similar piece of masonry pointing from the right to the left. Between these two lacerated fingers of stone can be seen the country stretching to the horizon where the front trenches are. Here and there heaps of rubbish mark where houses once stood. From some of these, lean, dead hands are protruding. Further on, spiky stumps of trees which were once a small wood. The ground is dotted with rayed and shattered shell-holes. Across the horizon in the red glare can be seen the criss-cross pattern of the barbed wire bordering the trenches. In the sky sometimes a green star, sometimes a white star, burns. Within the broken archway to the left is an arched entrance to another part of the monastery, used now as a Red Cross Station. In the wall, right, near the front is a stained-glass window, background green, figure of the Virgin, white-faced, wearing a black robe, lights inside making the figure vividly apparent. Further up from this window is a life-size crucifix. A shell has released an arm from the cross, which has caused the upper part of the figure to lean forward with the released arm outstretched towards the figure of the Virgin. Underneath the crucifix on a pedestal, in red letters, are the words:* PRINCEPS PACIS. *Almost opposite the crucifix is a gunwheel to which* BARNEY *is tied. At the back, in the centre, where the span of the arch should be, is the shape of a big howitzer gun, squat, heavy underpart, with a long, sinister barrel now pointing towards the front at an angle of forty-five degrees. At the base of the gun a piece of wood is placed on which is chalked,* HYDE PARK CORNER. *On another piece of wood near the entrance of the Red Cross Station is chalked,* NO HAWKERS OR STREET CRIES PERMITTED HERE. *In the near centre is a brazier in which a fire is burning. Crouching above, on a ramp, is a soldier whose clothes are covered with mud and splashed with blood. Every feature of the scene seems a little distorted from its*]

original appearance. Rain is falling steadily; its fall worried
now and again by fitful gusts of cold wind. A small organ
is heard playing slow and stately notes as the curtain rises.
After a pause, the CROUCHER, *without moving, intones*
dreamily]:

CROUCHER. And the hand of the Lord was upon me, and
    carried me out in the spirit of the Lord, and set me down
    in the midst of a valley.

And I looked and saw a great multitude that stood upon
    their feet, an exceeding great army.

And he said unto me, Son of man, can this exceeding great
    army become a valley of dry bones?

[*The music ceases, and a voice, in the part of the monastery*
    left standing, intones: Kyr . . . ie . . . e . . . eleison. Kyr . . .
    ie . . . e . . . eleison, *followed by the answer:* Christe . . .
    eleison.]

CROUCHER [*resuming*]. And I answered, O Lord God, thou
    knowest. And he said, prophesy and say unto the wind,
    come from the four winds a breath and breathe upon
    these living that they may die.

[*As he pauses the voice in the monastery is heard again:*
    Gloria in excelsis Deo et in terra pax hominibus bonae
    voluntatis.]

CROUCHER [*resuming*]. And I prophesied, and the breath came
    out of them, and the sinews came away from them, and
    behold a shaking, and their bones fell asunder, bone from
    his bone, and they died, and the exceeding great army
    became a valley of dry bones.

[*The voice from the monastery is heard, clearly for the first*
    half of the sentence, then dying away towards the end:
    Accendat in nobis Dominus ignem sui amoris, et flammam
    aeternae caritatis.

    [*A group of soldiers come in from fatigue, bunched to-*
    gether as if for comfort and warmth. They are wet and
    cold, and they are sullen-faced. They form a circle around
    the brazier and stretch their hands toward the blaze.]

1ST SOLDIER. Cold and wet and tir'd.
2ND SOLDIER. Wet and tir'd and cold.
3RD SOLDIER. Tir'd and cold and wet.

4TH SOLDIER [*very like* TEDDY]. Twelve blasted hours of am-
munition transport fatigue!

1ST SOLDIER. Twelve weary hours.

2ND SOLDIER. And wasting hours.

3RD SOLDIER. And hot and heavy hours.

1ST SOLDIER. Toiling and thinking to build the wall of force
that blocks the way from here to home.

2ND SOLDIER. Lifting shells.

3RD SOLDIER. Carrying shells.

4TH SOLDIER. Piling shells.

1ST SOLDIER. In the falling, pissing rine and whistling wind.

2ND SOLDIER. The whistling wind and falling, drenching rain.

3RD SOLDIER. The God-dam rain and blasted whistling wind.

1ST SOLDIER. And the shirkers sife at home coil'd up at ease.

2ND SOLDIER. Shells for us and pianos for them.

3RD SOLDIER. Fur coats for them and winding-sheets for us.

4TH SOLDIER. Warm.

2ND SOLDIER. And dry.

1ST SOLDIER. An' 'appy.

[*A slight pause.*]

BARNEY. An' they call it re-cu-per-at-ing!

1ST SOLDIER [*reclining near the fire*]. Gawd, I'm sleepy.

2ND SOLDIER [*reclining*]. Tir'd and lousy.

3RD SOLDIER [*reclining*]. Damp and shaking.

4TH SOLDIER [*murmuringly, the rest joining him*]. Tir'd and
lousy, an' wet an' sleepy, but mother call me early in the
morning.

1ST SOLDIER [*dreamily*]. Wen I thinks of 'ome, I thinks of a
field of dysies.

THE REST [*dreamily*]. Wen 'e thinks of 'ome, 'e thinks of a
field of dysies.

1ST SOLDIER [*chanting dreamily*]:

    I sees the missus paryding along Walham Green,
    Through the jewels an' silks on the costers' carts,
    Emmie a-pulling her skirt an' muttering,
    "A balloon, a balloon, I wants a balloon,"
    The missus a-tugging 'er on, an' sying,
    "A balloon, for shime, an' your father fighting:
    You'll wait till 'e's 'ome, an' the bands a-plying!"

                        [*He pauses.*]

[*Suddenly.*] But wy'r we 'ere, wy'r we 'ere—that's wot we
wants to know!

2ND SOLDIER. God only knows—or else, perhaps, a red-cap.

1ST SOLDIER [*chanting*]:

> Tabs'll murmur, 'em an' 'aw, an' sy: "You're 'ere because
>   you're
>
> Point nine double o, the sixth platoon an' forty-eight
>   battalion,
>
> The Yellow Plumes that pull'd a bow at Crecy,
>
> And gave to fame a leg up on the path to glory;
>
> Now with the howitzers of the Twenty-first Division,
>
> Tiking life easy with the Army of the Marne,
>
> An' all the time the battered Conchie squeals,
>
> 'It's one or two men looking after business'."

3RD SOLDIER. An' saves his blasted skin!

1ST SOLDIER [*chanting*]. The padre gives a fag an' softly
whispers:

> "Your king, your country an' your muvver 'as you 'ere."
>
> An' last time 'ome on leave, I awsks the missus:
>
> "The good God up in heaven, Bill, 'e knows,
>
> An' I gets the seperytion moneys reg'lar."

>   [*He sits up suddenly.*]

> But wy'r we 'ere, wy'r we 'ere,—that's wot I wants to
>   know!

THE REST [*chanting sleepily*]. Why 's 'e 'ere, why 's 'e 'ere—
that's wot 'e wants to know!

BARNEY [*singing to the air of second bar in chorus of "Auld
Lang Syne"*]. We're here because we're here, because we're
here, because we're here!

[*Each slides into an attitude of sleep—even* BARNEY'S *head
droops a little. The* CORPORAL, *followed by the* VISITOR,
appears at back. The VISITOR *is a portly man with a rubi-
cund face; he is smiling to demonstrate his ease of mind,
but the lines are a little distorted with an ever-present sense
of anxiety. He is dressed in a semi-civilian, semi-military
manner—dark worsted suit, shrapnel helmet, a haversack
slung round his shoulder, a brown belt round his middle,
black top boots and spurs, and he carries a cane. His head is
bent between his shoulders, and his shoulders are crouched
a little.*]

VISITOR. Yes, to-morrow, I go a little further. Penetrate a
little deeper into danger. Foolish, yes, but then it's an experience; by God, it's an experience. The military authorities
are damned strict—won't let a . . . man . . . plunge!

CORPORAL. In a manner of speakin', sir, only let you see the arses of the guns.

VISITOR [*not liking the remark*]. Yes, no; no, oh yes. Damned strict, won't let a . . . man . . . plunge! [*Suddenly, with alarm.*] What's that, what was that?

CORPORAL. Wha' was what?

VISITOR. A buzz, I thought I heard a buzz.

CORPORAL. A buzz?

VISITOR. Of an aeroplane.

CORPORAL. Didn't hear. Might have been a bee.

VISITOR. No, no; don't think it was a bee. [*Arranging helmet with his hands.*] Damn shrapnel helmet; skin tight; like a vice; hurts the head. Rather be without it; but, regulations, you know. Military authorities damn particular—won't let a . . . man . . . plunge!

VISITOR [*seeing* BARNEY]. Aha, what have we got here, what have we got here?

CORPORAL [*to* BARNEY]. 'Tshun! [*To the* VISITOR.] Regimental misdemeanour, sir.

VISITOR [*to* BARNEY]. Nothing much, boy, nothing much?

BARNEY [*chanting softly*]:
  A Brass-hat pullin' the bedroom curtains
  Between himself, the world an' the Estaminay's daughter.
  In a pyjama'd hurry ran down an' phon'd
  A Tommy was chokin' an Estaminay cock,
  An' I was pinch'd as I was puttin' the bird
  Into a pot with a pint of peas.

CORPORAL [*chanting hoarsely*]:
  And the hens all droop, for the loss has made
  The place a place of desolation!

VISITOR [*reprovingly, to the Corporal*]. Seriously, Corporal, seriously, please. Sacred, sacred: property of the citizen of a friendly State, sacred. On Active Service, serious to steal a fowl, a cock. [*To* BARNEY.] The uniform, the cause, boy, the corps. *Infra dignitatem, boy, infra dignitatem.*

BARNEY. Wee, wee.

VISITOR [*pointing to reclining soldiers*]. Taking it easy, eh?

CORPORAL. Done in; transport fatigue; twelve hours.

VISITOR. Um, not too much rest, Corporal. Dangerous. Keep 'em moving much as possible. Too much rest—bad. Sap, sap, sap.

CORPORAL [*pointing to the left*]. Bit of monastery left intact. Hold services there; troops off to front line. Little organ plays.

VISITOR. Splendid. Bucks 'em up. Gives 'em peace.

[*A Staff Officer enters suddenly, passing by the* VISITOR *with a springing hop, so that he stands in the centre with the* VISITOR *on his right and the* CORPORAL *on his left. He is prim, pert, and polished, superfine khaki uniform, gold braid, crimson tabs, and gleaming top-boots. He speaks his sentences with a gasping importance.*]

CORPORAL [*stiffening*]. 'Shun! Staff!

SOLDIERS [*springing to their feet—the* CROUCHER *remains as he is, with a sleepy alertness*]. Staff! 'Shun!

CORPORAL [*bellowing at the* CROUCHER]. Eh, you there: 'shun! Staff!

CROUCHER [*calmly*]. Not able. Sick. Privilege. Excused duty.

STAFF-WALLAH [*reading document*]:
          Battery Brigade Orders, F.A., 31 D 2.
Units presently recuperating, parade eight o'clock P.M.
Attend Lecture organized by Society for amusement and mental development, soldiers at front.
Subject: Habits of those living between Frigid Zone and Arctic Circle.
Lecturer: Mr. Melville Sprucer.
Supplementary Order: Units to wear gas-masks.
As you were. [*The* STAFF-WALLAH *departs as he came with a spring hop.*]

[*The* VISITOR *and the* CORPORAL *relax, and stroll down towards the R.C. Station. The soldiers relax too, seeking various positions of ease around the fire.*]

VISITOR [*indicating R.C. Station*]. Ah, in here. We'll just pop in here for a minute. And then pop out again.

[*He and the* CORPORAL *go into the R.C. Station. A pause.*]

1ST SOLDIER [*chanting and indicating that he means the* VISITOR *by looking in the direction of the R.C. Station*]:
          The perky bastard's cautious nibbling
          In a safe, safe shelter at danger queers me.
          Furiously feeling he's up to the neck in
          The whirl and the sweep of the front-line fighting.

2ND SOLDIER [*chanting*]:
          In his full-blown, chin-strapp'd, shrapnel helmet,
          He'll pat a mug on the back and murmur,
          "Here's a stand-fast Tauntonshire before me,"
          And the mug, on his feet, 'll whisper "yessir."

3RD SOLDIER [*chanting*]:

> Like a bride, full-flush'd, 'e'll sit down and listen
> To every word of the goddam sermon,
> From the cushy-soul'd, word-spreading, yellow-streaked
>   dud.

BARNEY [*chanting*]. Who wouldn't make a patch on a Tommy's
    backside.   [*A pause.*]

1ST SOLDIER. 'Ow long have we been resting 'ere?

2ND SOLDIER. A month.

3RD SOLDIER. Twenty-nine days, twenty-three hours and [*look-ing at watch*] twenty-three minutes.

4TH SOLDIER. Thirty-seven minutes more'll make it thirty days.

CROUCHER:

> Thirty days hath September, April, June, and Novem-
>   ber—
> November—that's the month when I was born—
>   November.
> Not the beginning, not the end, but the middle of
>   November.
> Near the valley of the Thames, in the middle of No-
>   vember.
> Shall I die at the start, near the end, in the middle
>   of November?

1ST SOLDIER [*nodding towards the* CROUCHER]. One more
    scrap, an' 'e'll be Ay one in the kingdom of the bawmy.

2ND SOLDIER. Perhaps they have forgotten.

3RD SOLDIER. Forgotten.

4TH SOLDIER. Forgotten us.

1ST SOLDIER. If the blighters at the front would tame their
    grousing.

THE REST. Tame their grousing.

2ND SOLDIER. And the wounded cease to stare their silent
    scorning.

THE REST. Passing by us, carried cushy on the stretchers.

3RD SOLDIER. We have beaten out the time upon the duck-
    board.

4TH SOLDIER. Stiff standing watch'd the sunrise from the
    firestep.

2ND SOLDIER. Stiff standing from the firestep watch'd the
    sunset.

3RD SOLDIER. Have bless'd the dark wiring of the top with
    curses.

2ND SOLDIER. And never a ray of leave.

3RD SOLDIER. To have a quiet drunk.

1ST SOLDIER. Or a mad mowment to rustle a judy.

[3RD SOLDIER *takes out a package of cigarettes; taking one
himself he hands the package round. Each takes one, and
the man nearest to* BARNEY, *kneeling up, puts one in his
mouth and lights it for him. They all smoke silently for a
few moments, sitting up round the fire.*]

2ND SOLDIER [*chanting very earnestly and quietly*]:
    Would God I smok'd an' walk'd an' watch'd th'
    Dance of a golden Brimstone butterfly,
    To the saucy pipe of a greenfinch resting
    In a drowsy, brambled lane in Cumberland.

1ST SOLDIER:
    Would God I smok'd and lifted cargoes
    From the laden shoulders of London's river-way;
    Then holiday'd, roaring out courage and movement
    To the muscled machines of Tottenham Hotspur.

3RD SOLDIER:
    To hang here even a little longer,
    Lounging through fear-swell'd, anxious moments;
    The hinderparts of the god of battles
    Shading our war-tir'd eyes from his flaming face.

BARNEY:
    If you creep to rest in a clos'd-up coffin,
    A tail of comrades seeing you safe home;
    Or be a kernel lost in a shell exploding—
    It's all, sure, only in a lifetime.

ALL TOGETHER:
    Each sparrow, hopping, irresponsible,
    Is indentur'd in God's mighty memory;
    And we, more than they all, shall not be lost
    In the forgetfulness of the Lord of Hosts.

[*The* VISITOR *and the* CORPORAL *come from the Red Cross
Station.*]

VISITOR [*taking out a cigarette-case*]. Nurses too gloomy. Sur-
geons too serious. Doesn't do.

CORPORAL. All lying-down cases, sir. Pretty bad.

VISITOR [*who is now standing near the crucifix*]. All the more
reason make things merry and bright. Lift them out of
themselves. [*To the soldiers.*] See you all to-morrow at
lecture?

1ST SOLDIER [*rising and standing a little sheepishly before the Visitor*]. Yessir, yessir.

THE REST. Yessir, yessir.

THE VISITOR. Good. Make it interesting. [*Searching in pocket.*] Damn it, have I none? Ah, saved.

[*He takes a match from his pocket and is about to strike it carelessly on the arm of the crucifix, when the 1ST SOLDIER, with a rapid frightened movement, knocks it out of his hand.*]

1ST SOLDIER [*roughly*]. Blarst you, man, keep your peace-white paws from that!

2ND SOLDIER. The image of the Son of God.

3RD SOLDIER. Jesus of Nazareth, the King of the Jews.

1ST SOLDIER [*reclining by the fire again*]. There's a Gawd knocking abaht somewhere.

4TH SOLDIER. Wants Him to be sending us over a chit in the shape of a bursting shell.

THE VISITOR. Sorry put it across you. [*To* CORPORAL.] Too much time to think. Nervy. Time to brood, brood; bad. Sap. Sap. Sap. [*Walking towards where he came in.*] Must return quarters; rough and ready. Must stick it. There's a war on. Cheerio. Straight down road instead of round hill: shorter?

CORPORAL. Less than half as long.

THE VISITOR. Safe?

CORPORAL. Yes. Only drop shells off and on, cross-roads. Ration party wip'd out week ago.

THE VISITOR. Go round hill. No hurry. General Officer's orders, no unnecessary risks. Must obey. Military Authorities damned particular—won't let a . . . man . . . plunge!

[*He and the* CORPORAL *go off. The soldiers in various attitudes are asleep around the fire. After a few moments' pause, two* STRETCHER-BEARERS *come in slowly from left, carrying a casualty. They pass through the sleeping soldiers, going towards the Red Cross Station. As they go they chant a verse, and as the verse is ending, they are followed by another pair carrying a second casualty.*]

1ST BEARERS [*chanting*]:
    Oh, bear it gently, carry it softly—
    A bullet or a shell said stop, stop, stop.
    It's had its day, and it's left the play,

Since it gamboll'd over the top, top, top.
It's had its day and it's left the play,
Since it gamboll'd over the top.

2ND BEARERS [*chanting*]:

Oh, carry it softly, bear it gently—
The beggar has seen it through, through, through.
If it 'adn't been 'im, if it 'adn't been 'im,
It might 'ave been me or you, you, you.
If it 'adn't been 'im, if it 'adn't been 'im,
It might 'ave been me or you.

VOICE [*inside R.C. Station*]. Easy, easy there; don't crowd.

1ST STRETCHER-BEARER [*to man behind*]. Woa, woa there,
Bill, 'ouse full.

STRETCHER-BEARER [*behind, to those following*]. Woa, woa;
traffic blocked.

[*They leave the stretchers on the ground.*]

THE WOUNDED ON THE STRETCHERS [*chanting*]:

Carry on, carry on to the place of pain,
Where the surgeon spreads his aid, aid, aid.
And we show man's wonderful work, well done,
To the image God hath made, made, made,
And we show man's wonderful work, well done,
To the image God hath made!

When the future hours have all been spent,
And the hand of death is near, near, near,
Then a few, few moments and we shall find
There'll be nothing left to fear, fear, fear,
Then a few, few moments and we shall find
There'll be nothing left to fear.

The power, the joy, the pull of life,
The laugh, the blow, and the dear kiss,
The pride and hope, the gain and loss,
Have been temper'd down to this, this, this,
The pride and hope, the gain and loss,
Have been temper'd down to this.

1ST STRETCHER-BEARER [*to* BARNEY]. Oh, Barney, have they
liced you up because you've kiss'd the Colonel's judy?

BARNEY. They lit on me stealin' Estaminay poulthry.

1ST STRETCHER-BEARER. A hen?

2ND STRETCHER-BEARER. A duck, again, Barney?

3RD STRETCHER-BEARER. A swan this time.

BARNEY [*chanting softly*]:
> A Brass-hat pullin' the bedroom curtains
> Between himself, the world an' the Estaminay's daughter,
> In a pyjama'd hurry ran down and phon'd
> A Tommy was chokin' an Estaminay cock;
> An' I was pinch'd as I was puttin' the bird
> Into a pot with a pint of peas.

1ST STRETCHER-BEARER. The red-tabb'd squit!

2ND STRETCHER-BEARER. The lousy map-scanner!

3RD STRETCHER-BEARER. We must keep up, we must keep up the morale of the awmy.

2ND STRETCHER-BEARER [*loudly*]. Does 'e eat well?

THE REST [*in chorus*]. Yes, 'e eats well!

2ND STRETCHER-BEARER. Does 'e sleep well?

THE REST [*in chorus*]. Yes, 'e sleeps well!

2ND STRETCHER-BEARER. Does 'e whore well?

THE REST [*in chorus*]. Yes 'e whores well!

2ND STRETCHER-BEARER. Does 'e fight well?

THE REST [*in chorus*]. Napoo; 'e 'as to do the thinking for the Tommies!

VOICE [*from the R.C. Station*]. Stretcher Party—carry on!

[*The Bearers stoop with precision, attach their supports to the stretchers, lift them up and march slowly into the R.C. Station, chanting.*]

STRETCHER-BEARERS [*chanting*]:
> Carry on—we've one bugled reason why—
> We've 'eard and answer'd the call, call, call.
> There's no more to be said, for when we are dead,
> We may understand it all, all, all.
> There's no more to be said, for when we are dead,
> We may understand it all.

[*They go out, leaving the scene occupied by the* CROUCHER *and the soldiers sleeping around the fire. The* CORPORAL *re-enters. He is carrying two parcels. He pauses, looking at the sleeping soldiers for a few moments, then shouts.*]

CORPORAL [*shouting*]. Hallo, there, you sleepy blighters! Number 2, a parcel; and for you, Number 3. Get a move on—parcels!

[*The* SOLDIERS *wake up and spring to their feet.*]

CORPORAL. For you, Number 2. [*He throws a parcel to* 2ND SOLDIER.] Number 3. [*He throws the other parcel to* 3RD SOLDIER.]

3RD SOLDIER [*taking paper from around his parcel*]. Looks like a bundle of cigarettes.

1ST SOLDIER. Or a pack of cawds.

4TH SOLDIER. Or a prayer-book.

3RD SOLDIER [*astounded*]. Holy Christ, it is!

THE REST. What?

3RD SOLDIER. A prayer-book!

4TH SOLDIER. In a green plush cover with a golden cross.

CROUCHER. Open it at the Psalms and sing that we may be saved from the life and death of the beasts that perish.

BARNEY. *Per omnia saecula saeculorum.*

2ND SOLDIER [*who has opened his parcel*]. A ball, be God!

4TH SOLDIER. A red and yellow coloured rubber ball.

1ST SOLDIER. And a note.

2ND SOLDIER [*reading*]. To play your way to the enemies' trenches when you all go over the top. Mollie.

1ST SOLDIER. See if it 'ops.

[*The* 2ND SOLDIER *hops the ball, and then kicks it from him. The* CORPORAL *intercepts it, and begins to dribble it across the stage. The* 3RD SOLDIER *tries to take it from him. The* CORPORAL *shouts "Offside, there!" They play for a few minutes with the ball, when suddenly the* STAFF-WALLAH *springs in and stands rigidly in centre.*]

CORPORAL [*stiff to attention as he sees the* STAFF-WALLAH]. 'Shun. Staff!

[*All the soldiers stiffen. The* CROUCHER *remains motionless.*]

CORPORAL [*shouting to the* CROUCHER]. You: 'shun. Staff!

CROUCHER. Not able. Sick. Excused duty.

STAFF-WALLAH [*reading document*]:

Brigade Orders, C/X 143. B/Y 341. Regarding gas-masks. Gas-masks to be worn round neck so as to lie in front $2\frac{1}{2}$ degrees from socket of left shoulderblade, and $2\frac{3}{4}$ degrees from socket of right shoulderblade, leaving bottom margin to reach $\frac{1}{4}$ of an inch from second button of lower end of tunic. Order to take effect from 6 A.M. following morning of date received. Dismiss! [*He hops out again, followed by* CORPORAL.]

1ST SOLDIER [*derisively*]. Comprenneemoy.

3RD SOLDIER. Tray bong.

2ND SOLDIER [*who is standing in archway, back, looking scorn-
    fully after the* STAFF-WALLAH, *chanting*]:

> Jazzing back to his hotel he now goes gaily,
> Shelter'd and safe where the clock ticks tamely.
> His backside warming a cushion, down-fill'd,
> Green clad, well splash'd with gold birds red-beak'd.

1ST SOLDIER:

> His last dim view of the front-line sinking
> Into the white-flesh'd breasts of a judy;
> Cuddling with proud, bright, amorous glances
> The thing salved safe from the mud of the trenches.

2ND SOLDIER:

> His tunic reared in the lap of comfort
> Peeps at the blood-stain'd jackets passing,
> Through colour-gay bars of ribbon jaunty,
> Fresh from a posh shop snug in Bond Street.

CROUCHER:

> Shame and scorn play with and beat them,
> Till we anchor in their company;
> Then the decorations of security
> Become the symbols of self-sacrifice.

[*A pause.*]

2ND SOLDIER:

> A warning this that we'll soon be exiles
> From the freedom chance of life can give,
> To the front where you wait to be hurried breathless,
> Murmuring how, how do you do, to God.

3RD SOLDIER:

> Where hot with the sweat of mad endeavour,
> Crouching to scrape a toy-deep shelter,
> Quick-tim'd by hell's fast, frenzied drumfire
> Exploding in flaming death around us.

2ND SOLDIER:

> God, unchanging, heart-sicken'd, shuddering,
> Gathereth the darkness of the night sky
> To mask His paling countenance from
> The blood dance of His self-slaying children.

3RD SOLDIER:

> Stumbling, swiftly cursing, plodding,

Lumbering, loitering, stumbling, grousing,
Through mud and rain, and filth and danger,
Flesh and blood seek slow the front line.

2ND SOLDIER:

Squeals of hidden laughter run through
The screaming medley of the wounded
Christ, who bore the cross, still weary,
Now trails a rope tied to a field gun.

[As the last notes of the chanting are heard the CORPORAL comes rapidly in; he is excited but steady; pale-faced and grim.]

CORPORAL. They attack. Along a wide front the enemy attacks. If they break through it may reach us even here.
SOLDIERS [in chorus as they all put on gas-masks]. They attack. The enemy attacks.
CORPORAL. Let us honour that in which we do put our trust.
SOLDIERS [in chorus]:

That it may not fail us in our time of need.

[The CORPORAL goes over to the gun and faces towards it, standing on the bottom step. The soldiers group around, each falling upon one knee, their forms crouched in a huddled act of obeisance. They are all facing the gun with their backs to the audience. The CROUCHER rises and joins them.]

CORPORAL [singing]:

Hail, cool-hardened tower of steel emboss'd
With the fever'd, figment thoughts of man;
Guardian of our love and hate and fear,
Speak for us to the inner ear of God!

SOLDIERS:

We believe in God and we believe in thee.

CORPORAL:

Dreams of line, of colour, and of form;
Dreams of music dead for ever now;
Dreams in bronze and dreams in stone have gone
To make thee delicate and strong to kill.

SOLDIERS:

We believe in God and we believe in thee.

CORPORAL:
>Jail'd in thy steel are hours of merriment
>Cadg'd from the pageant-dream of children's play;
>Too soon of the motley stripp'd that they may sweat
>With them that toil for the glory of thy kingdom.

SOLDIERS:
>We believe in God and we believe in thee.

CORPORAL:
>Remember our women, sad-hearted, proud-fac'd,
>Who've given the substance of their womb for shadows;
>Their shrivel'd, empty breasts war tinselléd
>For patient gifts of graves to thee.

SOLDIERS:
>We believe in God and we believe in thee.

CORPORAL:
>Dapple those who are shelter'd with disease,
>And women labouring with child,
>And children that play about the streets,
>With blood of youth expiring in its prime.

SOLDIERS:
>We believe in God and we believe in thee.

CORPORAL:
>Tear a gap through the soul of our mass'd enemies;
>Grant them all the peace of death;
>Blow them swiftly into Abram's bosom,
>And mingle them with the joys of paradise!

SOLDIERS:
>For we believe in God and we believe in thee.

[*The sky has become vexed with a crimson glare, mixed with yellow streaks, and striped with pillars of rising brown and black smoke. The* STAFF-WALLAH *rushes in, turbulent and wild, with his uniform disordered.*]

STAFF-WALLAH:
>The enemy has broken through, broken through, broken through!
>Every man born of woman to the guns, to the guns.

SOLDIERS:
>To the guns, to the guns, to the guns!

STAFF-WALLAH:

> Those at prayer, all in bed, and the swillers drinking
> deeply in the pubs.

SOLDIERS:

> To the guns, to the guns.

STAFF-WALLAH:

> All the batmen, every cook, every bitch's son that hides
> A whiff of courage in his veins,
> Shelter'd vigour in his body,
> That can run, or can walk, even crawl—
> Dig him out, dig him out, shove him on—

SOLDIERS:

> To the guns!

[*The* SOLDIERS *hurry to their places led by the* STAFF-WALLAH
*to the gun. The gun swings around and points to the horizon; a shell is swung into the breech and a flash indicates
the firing of the gun, searchlights move over the red glare
of the sky; the scene darkens, stabbed with distant flashes
and by the more vivid flash of the gun which the* SOLDIERS
*load and fire with rhythmical movements while the scene is
closing. Only flashes are seen; no noise is heard.*]

ACT THREE

[*The upper end of an hospital ward. At right angles from back wall are two beds, one covered with a red quilt and the other with a white one. From the centre of the head of each bed is an upright having at the top a piece like a swan's neck, curving out over the bed, from which hangs a chain with a wooden cross-piece to enable weak patients to pull themselves into a sitting posture. To the left of these beds is a large glass double-door which opens on to the ground: one of the doors is open and a lovely September sun, which is setting, gives a glow to the garden.*

Through the door two poplar trees can be seen silhouetted against the sky. To the right of this door is another bed covered with a black quilt. Little white discs are fixed to the head of each bed: on the first is the number 26, on the second 27, and on the third 28. Medical charts hang over each on the wall. To the right is the fireplace, facing down the ward. Farther on, to the right of the fire, is a door of a bathroom. In the corner, between the glass door and the fire, is a pedestal on which stands a statue of the Blessed Virgin; under the statue is written, "Mater Misericordiae, ora pro nobis." An easy-chair, on which are rugs, is near the fire. In the centre is a white, glass-topped table on which are medicines, drugs, and surgical instruments. On one corner is a vase of flowers. A locker is beside the head, and a small chair by the foot of each bed. Two electric lights, green-shaded, hang from the ceiling, and a bracket light with a red shade projects from the wall over the fireplace. It is dusk, and the two lights suspended from the ceiling are lighted. The walls are a brilliant white.

SYLVESTER *is in the bed numbered "26"; he is leaning upon his elbow looking towards the glass door.*

SIMON, *sitting down on the chair beside bed numbered "27"; is looking into the grounds.*]

SYLVESTER [*after a pause*]. Be God, isn't it a good one!

SIMON. Almost, almost, mind you, Sylvester, incomprehensible.

SYLVESTER. To come here and find Susie Monican fashion'd

[204]

like a Queen of Sheba. God moves in a mysterious way, Simon.

SIMON. There's Surgeon Maxwell prancing after her now.

SYLVESTER [*stretching to see*]. Heads together, eh? Be God, he's kissing her behind the trees! Oh, Susannah, Susannah, how are the mighty fallen, and the weapons of war perished!

[HARRY HEEGAN *enters crouched in a self-propelled invalid chair; he wheels himself up to the fire.* SYLVESTER *slides down into the bed, and* SIMON *becomes interested in a book that he takes off the top of his locker.* HARRY *remains for a few moments beside the fire, and then wheels himself round and goes out as he came in;* SYLVESTER *raises himself in the bed, and* SIMON *leaves down the book to watch* HARRY.]

SYLVESTER. Down and up, up and down.

SIMON. Up and down, down and up.

SYLVESTER. Never quiet for a minute.

SIMON. Never able to hang on to an easy second.

SYLVESTER. Trying to hold on to the little finger of life.

SIMON. Half-way up to heaven.

SYLVESTER. And him always thinking of Jessie.

SIMON. And Jessie never thinking of him.

[SUSIE MONICAN, *in the uniform of a V.A.D. nurse, enters the ward by the glass door. She is changed, for it is clear that she has made every detail of the costume as attractive as possible. She has the same assertive manner, but dignity and a sense of importance have been added. Her legs, encased in silk stockings, are seen (and shown) to advantage by her short and smartly cut skirt. Altogether she is now a very handsome woman. Coming in she glances at the bed numbered 28, then pauses beside* SYLVESTER *and* SIMON.]

SUSIE. How is Twenty-eight?

SIMON AND SYLVESTER [*together*]. Travelling again.

SUSIE. Did he speak at all to you?

SYLVESTER. Dumb, Susie, dumb.

SIMON. Brooding, Susie; brooding, brooding.

SYLVESTER. Cogitatin', Susie; cogitatin', cogitatin'.

SUSIE [*sharply, to* SYLVESTER]. It's rediculous, Twenty-six, for you to be in bed. The Sister's altogether too indulgent to you. Why didn't you pair of lazy devils entice him down to sit and cogitate under the warm wing of the sun in the garden?

SYLVESTER. Considerin' the low state of his general health.

SIMON. Aided by a touch of frost in the air.

SYLVESTER. Thinkin' it over we thought it might lead——

SIMON. To him getting an attack of double pneumonia.

SYLVESTER AND SIMON [*together*]. An' then he'd go off like—
[*they blow through their lips*] poof—the snuff of a candle!

SUSIE. For the future, during the period you are patients here,
I am to be addressed as "Nurse Monican," and not as
"Susie." Remember that, the pair of you, please.

[HARRY *wheels himself in again, crossing by her, and, going
over to the fire, looks out into grounds.*]

SUSIE [*irritatedly, to Sylvester*]. Number Twenty-six, look at
the state of your quilt. You must make an effort to keep it
tidy. Dtch, dtch, dtch, what would the Matron say if she
saw it!

SIMON [*with a nervous giggle*]. He's an uneasy divil, Nurse
Monican.

SUSIE [*hotly, to* SIMON]. Yours is as bad as his, Twenty-seven.
You mustn't lounge on your bed; it must be kept perfectly
tidy [*she smoothes the quilts*]. Please don't make it necessary to mention this again. [*To* HARRY.] Would you like to
go down for a little while into the garden, Twenty-eight?

[HARRY *crouches silent and moody.*]

SUSIE [*continuing*]. After the sober rain of yesterday it is good
to feel the new grace of the yellowing trees, and to get the
fresh smell of the grass.

[HARRY *wheels himself round and goes out by the left.*]

SUSIE [*to* SYLVESTER *as she goes out*]. Remember, Twenty-six,
if you're going to remain in a comatose condition, you'll
have to keep your bed presentable.   [*A pause.*]

SYLVESTER [*mimicking* SUSIE]. Twenty-six, if you're going to
remeen in a comatowse condition, you'll have to keep your
bed in a tidy an' awdahly mannah.

SIMON. Dtch, dtch, dtch, Twenty-seven, it's disgriceful. And
as long as you're heah, in the capacity of a patient, please
remember I'm not to be addressed as "Susie," but as "Nurse
Monican."

SYLVESTER. Twenty-seven, did you tike the pills the doctah
awdahed?

VOICE OF SUSIE, *left*. Twenty-six!

SYLVESTER. Yes, Nurse?

VOICE OF SUSIE. Sister says you're to have a bawth at once; and you, Twenty-seven, see about getting it ready for him.

[*A fairly long pause.*]

SYLVESTER [*angrily*]. A bawth: well, be God, that's a good one! I'm not in a fit condition for a bath!

[*Another pause.*]

SYLVESTER [*earnestly, to* SIMON]. You haven't had a dip now for nearly a week, while I had one only the day before yesterday in the late evening: it must have been you she meant, Simon.

SIMON. Oh, there was no dubiety about her bellowing out Twenty-six, Syl.

SYLVESTER [*excitedly*]. How the hell d'ye know, man, she didn't mix the numbers up?

SIMON. Mix the numbers up! How could the woman mix the numbers up?

SYLVESTER. How could the woman mix the numbers up! What could be easier than to say Twenty-six instead of Twenty-seven? How could the woman mix the numbers up! Of course the woman could mix the numbers up!

SIMON. What d'ye expect me to do—hurl myself into a bath that was meant for you?

SYLVESTER. I don't want you to hurl yourself into anything; but you don't expect me to plunge into a bath that maybe wasn't meant for me?

SIMON. Nurse Monican said Twenty-six, and when you can alter that, ring me up and let me know. [*A pause; then* SIMON *gets up and goes toward bathroom door.*]

SYLVESTER [*snappily*]. Where are you leppin' to now?

SIMON. I want to get the bath ready.

SYLVESTER. You want to get the bawth ready! Turn the hot cock on, and turn the cold cock on for Number Twenty-six, mixin' them the way a chemist would mix his medicines—sit still, man, till we hear the final verdict.

[SIMON *sits down again.* SUSIE *comes in left, and, passing to the door leading to grounds, pauses beside* SIMON *and* SYLVESTER.]

SUSIE [*sharply*]. What are the two of you doing? Didn't I tell you, Twenty-six, that you were to take a bawth; and you, Twenty-seven, that you were to get it ready for him?

SYLVESTER [*sitting brightly up in bed*]. Oh, just goin' to spring
  up, Nurse Monican, when you popped in.

SUSIE. Well, up with you, then, and take it. [*To* SIMON.] You
  go and get it ready for him.

[SIMON *goes into the bathroom.*]

SYLVESTER [*venturing a last hope as* SUSIE *goes towards the
  entrance to grounds*]. I had a dip, Nurse, only the day
  before yesterday in the late evening.

SUSIE [*as she goes out*]. Have another one now, please.

[*The water can be heard flowing in the bathroom, and a light
  cloud of steam comes out by the door which* SIMON *has left
  open.*]

SYLVESTER [*mimicking* SUSIE]. Have another one, now, please!
  One to be taken before and after meals. The delicate
  audacity of the lip of that one since she draped her shoulders with a crimson cape!

[SIMON *appears and stands leaning against the side of the
  bathroom door.*]

SIMON [*gloating*]. She's steaming away now, Sylvester, full
  cock.

SYLVESTER [*scornfully, to* SIMON]. Music to you, the gurgling
  of the thing, music to you. Gaugin' the temperature for me.
  Dtch, dtch, dtch [*sitting up*], an hospital's the last place
  that God made. Be damn it, I wouldn't let a stuffed bird
  stay in one!

SIMON. Come on, man, before the hot strength bubbles out
  of it.

SYLVESTER [*getting out of bed*]. Have you the towels hot an'
  everything ready for me to spring into?

SIMON [*with a bow*]. Everything's ready for your enjoyment,
  Sir.

SYLVESTER [*as he goes towards the bathroom*]. Can't they be
  content with an honest to God cleanliness, an' not be tryin'
  to gild a man with soap and water.

SIMON [*with a grin, as* SYLVESTER *passes*]. Can I do anything
  more for you, Sir?

SYLVESTER [*almost inarticulate with indignation, as he goes
  in*]. Now I'm tellin' you, Simon Norton, our cordiality's
  gettin' a little strained!

[HARRY *wheels himself in, goes again to the fireplace, and*

looks into grounds. SIMON *watches him for a moment, takes
a package of cigarettes from his pocket and lights one.*]

SIMON [*awkwardly, to* HARRY]. Have a fag, Harry, oul' son?

HARRY. Don't want one; tons of my own in the locker.

SIMON. Like me to get you one?

HARRY. I can get them myself if I want one. D'ye think my
arms are lifeless as well as my legs?

SIMON. Far from that. Everybody's remarking what a great
improvement has taken place in you during the last few
days.

HARRY. Everybody but myself.

SIMON. What with the rubbing every morning and the rubbing
every night, and now the operation to-morrow as a grand
finally, you'll maybe be in the centre of the football field
before many months are out.

HARRY [*irritably*]. Oh, shut up, man! It's a miracle I want—
not an operation. The last operation was to give life to my
limbs, but no life came, and again I felt the horrible sickness of life only from the waist up. [*Raising his voice.*]
Don't stand there gaping at me, man. Did you never before
clap your eyes on a body dead from the belly down? Blast
you, man, why don't you shout at me, "While there's life
there's hope!"

[SIMON *edges away to his corner.* SUSIE *comes in by the glass
door and goes over to the table.*]

HARRY [*to* SUSIE]. A package of fags. Out of the locker. Will
you, Susie?

[SUSIE *goes to* HARRY'S *locker, gets the cigarettes and gives
them to him. As he lights the cigarette, his right arm gives
a sudden jerk.*]

SUSIE. Steady. What's this?

HARRY [*with a nervous laugh*]. Barred from my legs it's flowing back into my arms. I can feel it slyly creeping into my
fingers.

VOICE OF PATIENT, *out left* [*plaintively*]. Nurse!

SUSIE [*turning her head in direction of the voice*]. Shush, you
Twenty-three; go asleep, go asleep.

HARRY. A soft, velvety sense of distance between my fingers
and the things I touch.

SUSIE. Stop thinking of it. Brooding checks the chance of your
recovery. A good deal may be imagination.

HARRY [*peevishly*]. Oh, I know the different touches of iron [*he touches the bed-rail*]; of wood [*he touches the chair*]; of flesh [*he touches his cheek*]; and to my fingers they're giving the same answers—a feeling of numb distance between me and the touches of them all.

VOICE OF PATIENT, *out left*. Nurse!

SUSIE. Dtch, dtch. Go asleep, Twenty-three.

VOICE, *out left*. The stab in the head is worse than ever, Nurse.

SUSIE. You've got your dose of morphia, and you'll get no more. You'll just have to stick it.

[*Resident Surgeon* FORBY MAXWELL *enters from the grounds. He is about thirty years of age, and good-looking. His white overalls are unbuttoned, showing war ribbons on his waistcoat, flanked by the ribbon of the D.S.O. He has a careless, jaunty air, and evidently takes a decided interest in* SUSIE. *He comes in singing softly.*]

SURGEON MAXWELL:
  Stretched on the couch, Jessie fondled her dress,
  That hid all her beauties just over the knee;
  And I wondered and said, as I sigh'd, "What a shame,
  That there's no room at all on the couch there for me."

SUSIE [*to* SURGEON MAXWELL]. Twenty-three's at it again.

SURGEON MAXWELL. Uh, hopeless case. Half his head in Flanders. May go on like that for another month.

SUSIE. He keeps the patients awake at night.

SIMON. With his "God have mercys on me," running after every third or fourth tick of the clock.

HARRY. 'Tisn't fair to me, 'tisn't fair to me; I must get my bellyful of sleep if I'm ever going to get well.

SURGEON MAXWELL. Oh, the poor devil won't trouble any of you much longer. [*Singing*]:
  Said Jess, with a light in the side of her eyes,
  "A shrewd, mathematical fellow like you,
  With an effort of thought should be able to make
  The couch wide enough for the measure of two."

SUSIE. Dtch, dtch, Surgeon Maxwell.

SURGEON MAXWELL [*singing*]:
  I fixed on a plan, and I carried it through,
  And the eyes of Jess gleam'd as she whisper'd to me:
  "The couch, made for one, that was made to hold two,
  Has, maybe, been made big enough to hold three!"

[SURGEON MAXWELL *catches* SUSIE'S *hand in his.* SYLVESTER

*bursts in from the bathroom, and rushes to his bed, colliding
with the* SURGEON *as he passes him.*]

SURGEON MAXWELL. Hallo, hallo there, what's this?

SYLVESTER [*flinging himself into bed, covering himself rapidly
with the clothes, blowing himself warm*]. Pooh, pooh, I feel
as if I was sittin' on the doorstep of pneumonia! Pooh, oh!

SURGEON MAXWELL [*to* SYLVESTER]. We'll have a look at you
in a moment, Twenty-six, and see what's wrong with you.

[SYLVESTER *subsides down into the bed, and* SIMON *edges
towards the entrance to grounds, and stands looking into
the grounds, or watching* SURGEON MAXWELL *examining*
SYLVESTER.]

SURGEON MAXWELL [*to* HARRY, *who is looking intently out
into the grounds*]. Well, how are we to-day, Heegan?

HARRY. I imagine I don't feel quite so dead in myself as I've
felt these last few days back.

SURGEON MAXWELL. Oh, well, that's something.

HARRY. Sometimes I think I feel a faint, fluttering kind of a
buzz in the top of my thighs.

SURGEON MAXWELL [*touching* HARRY'S *thigh*]. Where, here?

HARRY. No; higher up, doctor; just where the line is that
leaves the one part living and the other part dead.

SURGEON MAXWELL. A buzz?

HARRY. A timid, faint, fluttering kind of a buzz.

SURGEON MAXWELL. That's good. There might be a lot in that
faint, fluttering kind of a buzz.

HARRY [*after a pause*]. I'm looking forward to the operation
to-morrow.

SURGEON MAXWELL. That's the way to take it. While there's
life there's hope [*with a grin and a wink at* SUSIE]. And
now we'll have a look at Twenty-six.

[HARRY, *when he hears "while there's life there's hope," wheels
himself madly out left; half-way out he turns his head and
stretches to look out into the grounds, then he goes on.*]

SUSIE. Will the operation to-morrow be successful?

SURGEON MAXWELL. Oh, of course; very successful.

SUSIE. Do him any good, d'ye think?

SURGEON MAXWELL. Oh, blast the good it'll do him.

[SUSIE *goes over to* SYLVESTER *in the bed.*]

SUSIE [*to* SYLVESTER]. Sit up, Twenty-six, Surgeon Maxwell
wants to examine you.

SYLVESTER [*sitting up with a brave effort but a woeful smile*]. Righto. In the pink!

[SURGEON MAXWELL *comes over, twirling his stethoscope.* SIMON *peeps round the corner of the glass door.*]

SUSIE [*to* SURGEON MAXWELL]. What was the cause of the row between the Matron and Nurse Jennings? [*To* SYLVESTER.] Open your shirt, Twenty-six.

SURGEON MAXWELL [*who has fixed the stethoscope in his ears, removing it to speak to* SUSIE]. Caught doing the tango in the Resident's arms in the Resident's room. Naughty girl, naughty girl. [*To* SYLVESTER.] Say "ninety-nine."

SYLVESTER. Ninety-nine.

SUSIE. Oh, I knew something like that would happen. Daughter of a Dean, too.

SURGEON MAXWELL [*to* SYLVESTER]. Say "ninety-nine."

SYLVESTER. Ninety-nine. U-u-uh, it's gettin' very cold here, sitting up!

SURGEON MAXWELL [*to* SYLVESTER]. Again. Don't be frightened; breathe quietly.

SYLVESTER. Ninety-nine. Cool as a cucumber, Doctor. Ninety-nine.

SURGEON MAXWELL [*to* SUSIE]. Damn pretty little piece. Not so pretty as you, though.

SYLVESTER [*to* SURGEON MAXWELL]. Yesterday Doctor Joyce, givin' me a run over, said to a couple of medical men that were with him lookin' for tips, that the thing was apparently yieldin' to treatment, and that an operation wouldn't be necessary.

SURGEON MAXWELL. Go on; ninety-nine, ninety-nine.

SYLVESTER. Ninety-nine, ninety-nine.

SURGEON MAXWELL [*to* SUSIE]. Kicks higher than her head, and you should see her doing the splits.

SYLVESTER [*to* SURGEON MAXWELL]. Any way of gettin' rid of it'll do for me, for I'm not one of them that'll spend a night before an operation in a crowd of prayers.

SUSIE. Not very useful things to be doing and poor patients awaiting attention.

SURGEON MAXWELL [*putting stethoscope into pocket*]. He'll do all right; quite fit. Great old skin. [*To* SYLVESTER.] You can cover yourself up, now. [*To* SUSIE.] And don't tell me, Nurse Susie, that you've never felt a thrill or left a bedside for a kiss in a corner. [*He tickles her under the arm.*] Kiss in a corner, Nurse!

SUSIE [*pleased, but coy*]. Please don't, Doctor Maxwell, please.

SURGEON MAXWELL [*tickling her again as they go out*]. Kiss in a corner; ta-ra-ra-ra, kiss in a corner!   [*A pause.*]

SYLVESTER [*to* SIMON]. Simon, were you listenin' to that conversation?

SIMON. Indeed I was.

SYLVESTER. We have our hands full, Simon, to keep alive. Think of sinkin' your body to the level of a hand that, ta-ra-ra-ra, would plunge a knife into your middle, haphazard, hurryin' up to run away after a thrill from a kiss in a corner. Did you see me dizzied an' wastin' me time pumpin' ninety-nines out of me, unrecognized, quiverin' with cold an' equivocation!

SIMON. Everybody says he's a very clever fellow with the knife.

SYLVESTER. He'd gouge out your eye, saw off your arm, lift a load of vitals out of your middle, rub his hands, keep down a terrible desire to cheer lookin' at the ruin, an' say, "Twenty-six, when you're a little better, you'll feel a new man!"

[MRS. HEEGAN, MRS. FORAN, *and* TEDDY *enter from the grounds.* MRS. FORAN *is leading* TEDDY, *who has a heavy bandage over his eyes, and is dressed in the blue clothes of military hospitals.*]

MRS. FORAN [*to* TEDDY]. Just a little step here, Ted; upsh! That's it; now we're on the earth again, beside Simon and Sylvester. You'd better sit here. [*She puts him sitting on a chair.*]

SYLVESTER [*to* MRS. HEEGAN, *as she kisses him*]. Well, how's the old woman, eh?

MRS. HEEGAN. A little anxious about poor Harry.

SIMON. He'll be all right. To-morrow'll tell a tale.

SUSIE [*coming in, annoyed*]. Who let you up here at this hour? Twenty-eight's to have an operation to-morrow, and shouldn't be disturbed.

MRS. HEEGAN. Sister Peter Alcantara said we might come up, Nurse.

MRS. FORAN [*loftily*]. Sister Peter Alcantara's authority ought to be good enough, I think.

MRS. HEEGAN. Sister Peter Alcantara said a visit might buck him up a bit.

MRS. FORAN. Sister Peter Alcantara knows the responsibility

she'd incur by keeping a wife from her husband and a mother from her son.

SUSIE. Sister Peter Alcantara hasn't got to nurse him. And remember, nothing is to be said that would make his habit of introspection worse than it is.

MRS. FORAN [*with dignity*]. Thanks for the warnin', Nurse, but them kind of mistakes is unusual with us.

[SUSIE *goes out left, as* HARRY *wheels himself rapidly in. Seeing the group, he stops suddenly, and a look of disappointment comes on to his face.*]

MRS. HEEGAN [*kissing* HARRY]. How are you, son?

MRS. FORAN. I brought Teddy, your brother in arms, up to see you, Harry.

HARRY [*impatiently*]. Where's Jessie? I thought you were to bring her with you?

MRS. HEEGAN. She's comin' after us in a moment.

HARRY. Why isn't she here now?

MRS. FORAN. She stopped to have a word in the grounds with someone she knew.

HARRY. It was Barney Bagnal, was it? Was it Barney Bagnal?

TEDDY. Maybe she wanted to talk to him about gettin' the V.C.

HARRY. What V.C.? Who's gettin' the V.C.?

TEDDY. Barney. Did he not tell you? [MRS. FORAN *prods his knee.*] What's up?

HARRY [*intensely, to* TEDDY]. What's he gettin' it for? What's he gettin' the V.C. for?

TEDDY. For carryin' you wounded out of the line of fire. [MRS. FORAN *prods his knee.*] What's up?

HARRY [*in anguish*]. Christ Almighty, for carryin' me wounded out of the line of fire!

MRS. HEEGAN [*rapidly*]. Harry, I wouldn't be thinkin' of anything till we see what the operation'll do tomorrow.

SIMON [*rapidly*]. God, if it gave him back the use even of one of his legs.

MRS. FORAN [*rapidly*]. Look at all the places he could toddle to, an' all the things he could do then with the prop of a crutch.

MRS. HEEGAN. Even at the worst, he'll never be dependin' on anyone, for he's bound to get the maximum allowance.

SIMON. Two quid a week, isn't it?

SYLVESTER. Yes, a hundred per cent total incapacitation.

HARRY. She won't come up if one of you don't go down and bring her up.

MRS. HEEGAN. She's bound to come up, for she's got your ukelele.

HARRY. Call her up, Simon, call her up—I must see Jessie.

[SIMON *goes over to the door leading to the grounds, and looks out.*]

MRS. FORAN [*bending over till her face is close to* HARRY's]. The drawn look on his face isn't half as bad as when I seen him last.

MRS. HEEGAN [*bending and looking into* HARRY's *face*]. Look, the hollows under his eyes is fillin' up, too.

TEDDY. I'm afraid he'll have to put Jessie out of his head, for when a man's hit in the spine . . . [MRS. FORAN *prods his knee.*] What's up, woman?

HARRY [*impatiently, to* SIMON]. Is she coming? Can you see her anywhere?

SIMON. I see someone like her in the distance, under the trees.

HARRY. Call her; can't you give her a shout, man?

SIMON [*calling*]. Jessie. Is that you, Jessie? Jessie-e!

MRS. HEEGAN [*to* HARRY]. What time are you goin' under the operation?

HARRY [*to* SIMON]. Call her again, call her again, can't you!

SIMON [*calling*]. Jessie, Jessie-e!

TEDDY. Not much of a chance for an injury to the spine, for . . .

MRS. FORAN [*putting her face close to* TEDDY's]. Oh, shut up, you!

HARRY. Why did you leave her in the grounds? Why didn't you wait till she came up with you?

MRS. FORAN [*going over to* SIMON *and calling*]. Jessie, Jessie-e!

JESSIE'S VOICE, *in distance*. Yehess!

MRS. FORAN [*calling*]. Come up here at once; we're all waitin' for you!

JESSIE'S VOICE. I'm not going up!

MRS. FORAN [*calling*]. Bring up that ukelele here at once, miss!

JESSIE'S VOICE. Barney'll bring it up!

[HARRY, *who has been listening intently, wheels himself rapidly to where* SIMON *and* MRS. FORAN *are, pushing through them hurriedly.*]

HARRY [*calling loudly*]. Jessie! Jessie! Jessie-e!

MRS. FORAN. Look at that, now; she's runnin' away, the young rip!

HARRY [*appealingly*]. Jessie, Jessie-e!

[SUSIE *enters quickly from left. She goes over to* HARRY *and pulls him back from the door.*]

SUSIE [*indignantly*]. Disgraceful! Rousing the whole ward with this commotion! Dear, dear, dear, look at the state of Twenty-eight. Come along, come along, please; you must all go at once.

HARRY. Jessie's coming up for a minute, Nurse.

SUSIE. No more to come up. We've had enough for one night, and you for a serious operation to-morrow. Come on, all out, please.

[SUSIE *conducts* MRS. HEEGAN, MRS. FORAN, *and* TEDDY *out left.*]

MRS. FORAN [*going out*]. We're goin', we're goin', thank you. A nice way to treat the flotsum and jetsum of the battle-fields!

SUSIE [*to* HARRY]. To bed now, Twenty-eight, please. [*To* SIMON.] Help me get him to bed, Twenty-seven.

[SUSIE *pushes* HARRY *to his bed, right;* SIMON *brings portion of a bed-screen which he places around* HARRY, *hiding him from view.*]

SUSIE [*turning to speak to* SYLVESTER, *who is sitting up in bed, as she arranges screen*]. You're going to have your little operation in the morning, so you'd better go to sleep too.

[SYLVESTER *goes pale and a look of dismay and fear crawls over his face.*]

SUSIE. Don't funk it now. They're not going to turn you inside out. It'll be over in ten minutes.

SYLVESTER [*with a groan*]. When they once get you down your only hope is in the infinite mercy of God!

SIMON. If I was you, Sylvester, I wouldn't take this operation too seriously. You know th' oul' song—Let Me like a Soldier Fall! If I was you, I'd put it completely out of me mind.

SYLVESTER [*subsiding on to the pillow—with an agonised look on his face*]. Let me like a soldier fall! Did anyone ever hear th' equal o' that! Put it out of me mind completely! [*He sits up, and glares at* SIMON.] Eh, you, look! If you can't think sensibly, then thry to think without talkin'! [*He sinks back on the pillow again.*] Let me like a soldier fall. Oh, it's not a fair trial for a sensible man to be stuck down in a world like this!

[SYLVESTER *slides down till he lies prone and motionless on the bed.* HARRY *is in bed now.* SIMON *removes the screen, and* SUSIE *arranges* HARRY'S *quilt for the night.*]

SUSIE [*to* SIMON]. Now run and help get the things together for supper. [SIMON *goes out left.*] [*Encouragingly to* HARRY.] After the operation, a stay in the air of the Convalescent may work wonders.

HARRY. If I could mingle my breath with the breeze that blows from every sea, and over every land, they wouldn't widen me into anything more than the shrivell'd thing I am.

SUSIE [*switching off the two hanging lights, so that the red light over the fireplace alone remains*]. Don't be foolish, Twenty-eight. Wheeling yourself about among the beeches and the pines, when the daffodils are hanging out their blossoms, you'll deepen your chance in the courage and renewal of the country.

[*The bell of a Convent in grounds begins to ring for Compline.*]

HARRY [*with intense bitterness*]. I'll say to the pine, "Give me the grace and beauty of the beech"; I'll say to the beech, "Give me the strength and stature of the pine." In a net I'll catch butterflies in bunches; twist and mangle them between my fingers and fix them wriggling on to mercy's banner. I'll make my chair a Juggernaut, and wheel it over the neck and spine of every daffodil that looks at me, and strew them dead to manifest the mercy of God and the justice of man!

SUSIE [*shocked*]. Shush, Harry, Harry!

HARRY. To hell with you, your country, trees, and things, you jibbering jay!

SUSIE [*as she is going out*]. Twenty-eight!

HARRY [*vehemently*]. To hell with you, your country, trees, and things, you jibbering jay!

[SUSIE *looks at him, pauses for a few moments, as if to speak, and then goes out.*

[*A pause; then* BARNEY *comes in by door from grounds. An overcoat covers his military hospital uniform of blue. His left arm is in a sling. Under his right arm he carries a ukelele, and in his hand he has a bunch of flowers. Embarrassed, he goes slowly to* HARRY'S *bed, drops the flowers at the foot, then he drops the ukelele there.*]

BARNEY [*awkwardly*]. Your ukelele. An' a bunch of flowers from Jessie.

[HARRY *remains motionless on the bed.*]

BARNEY. A bunch of flowers from Jessie, and . . . your . . . ukelele.

[*The* SISTER OF THE WARD *enters, left, going to the chapel for Compline. She wears a cream habit with a white coif; a large set of Rosary beads hangs from her girdle. She pauses on her way, and a brass Crucifix flashes on her bosom.*]

SISTER [*to* HARRY]. Keeping brave and hopeful, Twenty-eight?
HARRY [*softly*]. Yes, Sister.
SISTER. Splendid. And we've got a ukelele too. Can you play it, my child?
HARRY. Yes, Sister.
SISTER. Splendid. You must play me something when you're well over the operation. [*To* BARNEY.] Standing guard over your comrade, Twenty-two, eh?
BARNEY [*softly and shyly*]. Yes, Sister.
SISTER. Grand. Forasmuch as ye do it unto the least of these my brethren, ye do it unto me. Well, God be with you both, my children. [*To* HARRY.] And Twenty-eight, pray to God, for wonderful He is in His doing toward the children of men. [*Calm and dignified she goes out into the grounds.*]
BARNEY [*pausing as he goes out left*]. They're on the bed; the ukelele, and the bunch of flowers from . . . Jessie.

[*The* SISTERS *are heard singing in the Convent the hymn of Salve Regina.*]
SISTERS:

> Salve Regina, mater misericordiae;
> Vitae dulcedo et spes nostra, salve!
> Ad te clamamus, exules filii Hevae;
> Ad te suspiramus, gementes et flentes in hac lacrymarum valle.
> Eia ergo Advocata nostra,
> Illos tuos misericordes oculos ad nos converte,
> Et Jesum, benedictum fructum ventris tui—

HARRY. God of the miracles, give a poor devil a chance, give a poor devil a chance!
SISTERS:

> Nobis post hoc exsilium ostende,
> O clemens, o pia, o dulcis Virgo Maria!

ACT FOUR

[*A room of the dance hall of the Avondale Football Club. At back, left, cutting corners of the back and side walls, is the arched entrance, divided by a slim pillar, to the dance hall. This entrance is hung with crimson and black striped curtains; whenever these are parted the dancers can be seen swinging or gliding past the entrance if a dance be taking place at the time. Over the entrance is a scroll on which is printed: "Up the Avondales!" The wall back has a wide, tall window which opens to the garden, in which the shrubs and some sycamore trees can be seen. It is hung with apple-green casement curtains, which are pulled to the side to allow the window to be open as it is at present. Between the entrance to hall and the window is a Roll of Honour containing the names of five members of the Club killed in the war. Underneath the Roll of Honour a wreath of laurel tied with red and black ribbon. To the front left is the fireplace. Between the fireplace and the hall entrance is a door on which is an oval white enamel disc with "Caretaker" painted on it. To the right a long table, covered with a green cloth, on which are numerous bottles of wine and a dozen glasses. On the table, too, is a telephone. A brown carpet covers the floor. Two easy and one ordinary chairs are in the room. Hanging from the ceiling are three lanterns; the centre one is four times the length of its width, the ones at the side are less than half as long as the centre lantern and hang horizontally; the lanterns are black, with a broad red stripe running down the centre of the largest and across those hanging at each side, so that, when they are lighted, they suggest an illuminated black cross with an inner one of gleaming red. The hall is vividly decorated with many coloured lanterns, looped with coloured streamers.*

When the scene is revealed the curtains are drawn, and the band can be heard playing a fox-trot. Outside in the garden, near the window, SIMON *and* SYLVESTER *can be seen smoking, and* TEDDY *is walking slowly up and down the path. The band is heard playing for a few moments, then the curtains are pulled aside, and* JESSIE, *with* BARNEY *holding her hand, comes in and walks rapidly to the table where*

*the wine is standing. They are quickly followed by Harry,
who wheels himself a little forward, then stops, watching
them. The curtains part again, and* MRS. HEEGAN *is seen
watching* HARRY. SIMON *and* SYLVESTER, *outside, watch
those in the room through the window.* BARNEY *wears a
neat navy-blue suit, with a rather high, stiff collar and black
tie. Pinned on the breast of his waistcoat are his war medals,
flanked by the Victoria Cross.* HARRY *is also wearing his
medals.* JESSIE *has on a very pretty, rather tight-fitting
dance frock, with the sleeves falling widely to the elbow,
and cut fairly low on her breast. All the dancers, and*
HARRY *too, wear coloured, fantastically shaped paper hats.*]

JESSIE [*hot, excited, and uneasy, as with a rapid glance back
she sees the curtains parted by* HARRY]. Here he comes
prowling after us again! His watching of us is pulling all
the enjoyment out of the night. It makes me shiver to feel
him wheeling after us.

BARNEY. We'll watch for a chance to shake him off, an' if he
starts again we'll make him take his tangled body somewhere else. [*As* HARRY *moves forward from the curtained
entrance.*] Shush, he's comin' near us. [*In a louder tone to*
JESSIE.] Red wine, Jessie, for you, or white wine?

HARRY. Red wine first, Jessie, to the passion and the power
and the pain of life, an' then a drink of white wine to the
melody that is in them all!

JESSIE. I'm so hot.

HARRY. I'm so cold; white wine for the woman warm to make
her cold; red wine for the man that's cold to make him
warm!

JESSIE. White wine for me.

HARRY. For me the red wine till I drink to men puffed up with
pride of strength, for even creeping things can praise the
Lord!

BARNEY [*gently to* HARRY, *as he gives a glass of wine to*
JESSIE]. No more for you now, Harry.

HARRY [*mockingly*]. Oh, please, your lusty lordship, just another, an' if I seek a second, smack me well. [*Wheeling his
chair viciously against* BARNEY.] Get out, you trimm'd-up
clod. There's medals on my breast as well as yours! [*He
fills a glass.*]

JESSIE. Let us go back to the dancing, Barney. [BARNEY *hesitates.*] Please, Barney, let us go back to the dancing!

HARRY. To the dancing, for the day cometh when no man can play. And legs were made to dance, to run, to jump, to carry you from one place to another; but mine can neither walk, nor run, nor jump, nor feel the merry motion of a dance. But stretch me on the floor fair on my belly, and I will turn over on my back, then wriggle back again on to my belly; and that's more than a dead, dead man can do!

BARNEY. Jessie wants to dance, an' so we'll go, and leave you here a little.

HARRY. Cram pain with pain, and pleasure cram with pleasure. I'm going too. You'd cage me in from seeing you dance, and dance, and dance, with Jessie close to you, and you so close to Jessie. Though you wouldn't think it, yes, I have— I've hammer'd out many a merry measure upon a polish'd floor with a sweet, sweet heifer. [*As* BARNEY *and* JESSIE *are moving away he catches hold of* JESSIE'S *dress.*] Her name? Oh, any name will do—we'll call her Jessie!

JESSIE. Oh, let me go. [*To* BARNEY.] Barney, make him let me go, please.

[BARNEY, *without a word, removes* HARRY'S *hand from* JESSIE'S *dress.* JESSIE *and* BARNEY *then go out to the dance hall through the curtained entrance. After a while* MRS. HEEGAN *slips away from the entrance into the hall. After a moment's pause* HARRY *follows them into the hall.* SIMON *and* SYLVESTER *come in from the garden, leaving* TEDDY *still outside smoking and walking to and fro in the cautious manner of the blind.* SIMON *and* SYLVESTER *sit down near the fire and puff in silence for a few moments.*]

SYLVESTER [*earnestly*]. I knew it. I knew it, Simon—strainin' an' strainin' his nerves; driftin' an' driftin' towards an hallucination!

SIMON. Jessie might try to let him down a little more gently, but it would have been better, I think, if Harry hadn't come here to-night.

SYLVESTER. I concur in that, Simon. What's a decoration to an hospital is an anxiety here.

SIMON. To carry life and colour to where there's nothing but the sick and helpless is right; but to carry the sick and helpless to where there's nothing but life and colour is wrong.

[*The telephone bell rings.*]

SYLVESTER. There's the telephone bell ringing.

SIMON. Oh, someone'll come in and answer it in a second.

SYLVESTER. To join a little strength to a lot of weakness is
what I call sensible; but to join a little weakness to a lot of
strength is what I call a . . .

SIMON. A cod.

SYLVESTER. Exactly.

[*The telephone continues to ring.*]

SYLVESTER. There's that telephone ringin' still.

SIMON. Oh, someone'll come in and answer it in a second.

[TEDDY *has groped his way to French window.*]

TEDDY. The telephone's tinklin', boys.

SYLVESTER. Thanks, Teddy. We hear it, thanks. [*To* SIMON.]
When he got the invitation from the Committay to come,
wearin' his decorations, me an' the old woman tried to
persuade him that, seein' his condition, it was better to stop
at home, an' let me represent him, but [*with a gesture*]
no use!

[TEDDY *resumes his walk to and fro.*]

SIMON. It was natural he'd want to come, since he was the
means of winning the Cup twice before for them, leading
up to their keeping the trophy for ever by the win of a year
ago.

SYLVESTER. To bring a boy so helpless as him, whose memory
of agility an' strength time hasn't flattened down, to a place
wavin' with joy an' dancin', is simply, simply——

SIMON. Devastating, I'd say.

SYLVESTER. Of course it is! Is that god-damn telephone goin'
to keep ringin' all night?

[MRS. FORAN *enters from hall quickly.*]

MRS. FORAN. Miss Monican says that one of you is to answer
the telephone, an' call her if it's anything important.

SYLVESTER [*nervously*]. I never handled a telephone in my
life.

SIMON. I chanced it once and got so hot and quivery that I
couldn't hear a word, and didn't know what I was saying
myself.

MRS. FORAN. Have a shot at it and see.

[*The three of them drift over to the telephone.*]

SYLVESTER. Chance it again, Simon, an' try to keep steady.

[*As* SIMON *stretches his hand to the receiver.*]

SYLVESTER. Don't rush, don't rush, man, an' make a mess of it. Take it in your stride.

SIMON [*pointing to receiver*]. When you lift this down, you're connected, I think.

SYLVESTER. No use of thinkin' on this job. Don't you turn the handle first?

SIMON [*irritably*]. No, you don't turn no handle, man!

MRS. FORAN. Let Simon do it now; Simon knows.

[SIMON *tremblingly lifts down the receiver, almost letting it fall.*]

SYLVESTER. Woa, woa, Simon; careful, careful!

SIMON [*speaking in receiver*]. Eh, hallo! Eh, listen there. Eh, hallo! listen.

SYLVESTER. You listen, man, an' give the fellow at the other end a chance to speak.

SIMON. If you want me to manipulate the thing, let me manipulate it in tranquillity.

MRS. FORAN [*to* SYLVESTER]. Oh, don't be puttin' him out, Sylvester.

SIMON [*waving them back*]. Don't be crushing in on me; give me room to manipulate the thing.

[*Dead silence for some moments.*]

MRS. FORAN. Are you hearin' anything from the other end?

SIMON. A kind of a buzzing and a roaring noise.

[SYLVESTER *suddenly gives the cord a jerk and pulls the receiver out of* SIMON'S *hand.*]

[*Angrily.*] What the hell are you trying to do, man? You're after pulling it right out of my mit.

SYLVESTER [*heatedly*]. There was a knot or a twist an' a tangle in it that was keepin' the sound from travellin'.

SIMON. If you want me to work the thing properly, you'll have to keep yourself from interfering. [*Resuming surlily.*] Eh, hallo, listen, yes? Ha! ha! ha! ha! Yes, yes, yes. No, no, no. Cheerio! Yes. Eh, hallo, listen, eh. Hallo.

SYLVESTER. What is it? What're they sayin'?

SIMON [*hopelessly, taking the receiver from his ear*]. I don't
seem to be able to hear a damn sound.

SYLVESTER. An' Holy God, what are you yessin' and noin' and
cheerioin' out of you for then?

SIMON. You couldn't stand here like a fool and say nothing,
could you?

SYLVESTER. Show it to me, Simon, show it to me—you're not
holdin' it at the proper angle.

MRS. FORAN. Give it to Syl, Simon; it's a delicate contrivance
that needs a knack in handlin'.

SYLVESTER [*as he is taking the receiver from* SIMON *and carefully placing it to his ear*]. You have always to preserve an
eqwee-balance between the speakin' mouth and the hearin'
ear. [*Speaking into receiver.*] Hallo! Anybody there at the
other end of this? Eh, wha's that? Yes, yes, I've got you
[*taking the receiver from his ear and speaking to* SIMON *and*
MRS. FORAN]: Something like wine, or dine, or shine, or
something—an' a thing that's hummin'.

SIMON. I can see no magnificent meaning jumping out of that!

MRS. FORAN. They couldn't be talkin' about bees, could they?

SYLVESTER [*scornfully*]. Bees! No, they couldn't be talkin'
about bees! That kind of talk, Mrs. Foran, only tends to
confuse matters. Bees! Dtch, dtch, dtch—the stupidity of
some persons is . . . terrifyin'!

SIMON. Ask them quietly what they want.

SYLVESTER [*indignantly*]. What the hell's the use of askin'
them that, when I can hear something only like a thing
that's hummin'?

MRS. FORAN. It wouldn't be, now, comin', or even bummin'?

SYLVESTER. It might even possibly be drummin'. Personally,
Mrs. Foran, I think, since you can't help, you might try to
keep from hinderin'.

SIMON. Put it back, Syl, where it was, an' if it rings again,
we'll only have to slip quietly out of this.

MRS. FORAN. Yes, put it back, an' say it never rang.

SYLVESTER. Where was it? Where do I put it back?

SIMON. On that thing stickin' out there. Nice and gently now.

[SYLVESTER *cautiously puts receiver back. They look at the
telephone for a few moments, then go back to the fire, one
by one.* SYLVESTER *stands with his back to it;* SIMON *sits in
a chair, over the back of which* MRS. FORAN *leans.*]

MRS. FORAN. Curious those at the other end of the telephone
couldn't make themselves understood.

SIMON. Likely they're not accustomed to it, and it's a bit difficult if you're not fully conscious of its manipulation.

SYLVESTER. Well, let them study an' study it then, or abide by the consequences, for we can't be wastin' time teachin' them.

[*The curtains at entrance of dance hall are pulled aside, and* TEDDY, *who has disappeared from the garden a little time before, comes in. As he leaves the curtains apart, the dancers can be seen gliding past the entrance in the movements of a tango.* TEDDY *comes down, looks steadily but vacantly towards the group around the fire, then goes over carefully to the table, where he moves his hand about till it touches a bottle, which he takes up in one hand, feeling it questioningly with the other.*]

SIMON. How goes it, Teddy?

TEDDY [*with a vacant look towards them*]. Sylvester—Simon —well. What seest thou, Teddy? Thou seest not as man seeth. In the garden the trees stand up; the green things showeth themselves and fling out flowers of divers hues. In the sky the sun by day and the moon and the stars by night—nothing. In the hall the sound of dancing, the eyes of women, grey and blue and brown and black, do sparkle and dim and sparkle again. Their white breasts rise and fall, and rise again. Slender legs, from red and black, and white and green, come out, go in again—nothing. Strain as you may, it stretches from the throne of God to the end of the hearth of hell.

SIMON. What?

TEDDY. The darkness.

SIMON [*knowing not what to say*]. Yes, oh yes.

TEDDY [*holding up a bottle of wine*]. What colour, Syl? It's all the same, but I like the red the best.

MRS. FORAN [*going over to* TEDDY]. Just one glass, dear, and you'll sit down quietly an' take it in sips.

[MRS. FORAN *fills a glass of wine for* TEDDY, *leads him to a chair, puts him sitting down, and gives the glass of wine carefully to him. The band in the hall has been playing, and through the parted curtains the dancers are seen gliding past.* JESSIE *moves by now in the arms of* BARNEY, *and in a few moments is followed along the side of the hall by* HARRY *wheeling himself in his chair and watching them.* MRS. FORAN *and the two men look on and become more attentive when among the dancers* SUSIE, *in the arms of* SURGEON

MAXWELL, JESSIE *partnered with* BARNEY, *and* HARRY *move past.*

SYLVESTER [*as* SUSIE *goes by*]. Susie Monican's lookin' game enough to-night for anything.

SIMON. Hardly remindful of her one-time fear of God.

SYLVESTER [*as* JESSIE *goes by followed by* HARRY]. There he goes, still followin' them.

SIMON. And Jessie's looking as if she was tired of her maiden-hood, too.

MRS. FORAN. The thin threads holdin' her dress up sidlin' down over her shoulders, an' her catchin' them up again at the tail end of the second before it was too late.

SIMON [*grinning*]. And Barney's hand inching up, inching up to pull them a little lower when they're sliding down.

MRS. FORAN. Astonishin' the way girls are advertisin' their immodesty. Whenever one of them sits down, in my heart I pity the poor men havin' to view the disedifyin' sight of the full length of one leg couched over another.

TEDDY [*forgetful*]. A damn nice sight, all the same, I think.

MRS. FORAN [*indignantly*]. One would imagine such a thought would jar a man's mind that had kissed goodbye to the sight of his eyes.

TEDDY. Oh, don't be tickin' off every word I say!

MRS. FORAN [*after an astonished pause, whipping the glass out of* TEDDY's *hand*]. Damn the drop more, now, you'll get for the rest of the evenin'.

[*The band suddenly stops playing, and the couples seen just then through the doorway stop dancing and look attentively up the hall. After a slight pause,* HARRY *in his chair, pushed by* SUSIE, *comes in through the entrance; his face is pale and drawn, his breath comes in quick faint gasps, and his head is leaning sideways on the back of the chair.* MRS. HEEGAN *is on one side of* HARRY, *and* SURGEON MAXWELL, *who is in dinner-jacket style of evening dress, wearing his medals, including the D.S.O., walks on the other.* HARRY *is wheeled over near the open window.* BARNEY *and* JESSIE *standing in the entrance, look on and listen.*]

MAXWELL. Here near the window. [*To* MRS. HEEGAN.] He'll be all right, Mrs. Heegan, in a second; a little faint—too much excitement. When he recovers a little, I'd get him home.

HARRY [*faintly but doggedly*]. Napoo home, napoo. Not yet. I'm all right. I'll spend a little time longer in the belly of an hour bulgin' out with merriment. Carry on.

MAXWELL. Better for you to go home, Heegan.

HARRY. When they drink to the Club from the Cup—the Silver Tassie—that I won three times, three times for them—that first was filled to wet the lips of Jessie and of me—I'll go, but not yet. I'm all right; my name is yet only a shadow on the Roll of Honour.

MRS. HEEGAN. Come home, Harry; you're gettin' your allowance only on the understandin' that you take care of yourself.

HARRY. Get the Cup. I'll mind it here till you're ready to send it round to drink to the Avondales—on the table here beside me. Bring the Cup; I'll mind it here on the table beside me.

MAXWELL. Get the Cup for him, someone.

[SIMON *goes to the hall and returns with the Cup, which he gives to* HARRY.]

HARRY [*holding the Cup out*]. A first drink again for me, for me alone this time, for the shell that hit me bursts for ever between Jessie and me. [*To* SIMON.] Go on, man, fill out the wine!

MAXWELL [*to* SIMON]. A little—just a glass. Won't do him any harm. [*To* HARRY.] Then you'll have to remain perfectly quiet, Heegan.

HARRY. The wine—fill out the wine!

SIMON [*to* HARRY]. Red wine or white?

HARRY. Red wine, red like the faint remembrance of the fires in France; red wine like the poppies that spill their petals on the breasts of the dead men. No, white wine, white like the stillness of the millions that have removed their clamours from the crowd of life. No, red wine; red like the blood that was shed for you and for many for the commission of sin! [*He drinks the wine.*] Steady, Harry, and lift up thine eyes unto the hills. [*Roughly to those around him.*] What are you all gaping at?

MAXWELL. Now, now, Heegan—you must try to keep quiet.

SUSIE. And when you've rested and feel better, you will sing for us a Negro Spiritual, and point the melody with the ukelele.

MRS. HEEGAN. Just as he used to do.

SYLVESTER. Behind the trenches.

SIMON. In the Rest Camps.

MRS. FORAN. Out in France.

HARRY. Push your sympathy away from me, for I'll have none of it. [*He wheels his chair quickly towards the dance hall.*] Go on with the dancing and keep the ball a-rolling. [*Calling loudly at the entrance.*] Trumpets and drum begin! [*The band begins to play.*] Dance and dance and dance. [*He listens for a moment.*] Sink into merriment again, and sling your cares to God! [*He whirls round in the chair to the beat of the tune. Dancers are seen gliding past entrance.*] Dear God, I can't. [*He sinks sideways on his chair.*] I must, must rest. [*He quietly recites*]:

> For a spell here I will stay,
> Then pack up my body and go—
> For mine is a life on the ebb,
> Yours a full life on the flow!

[HARRY *goes over to far side of window and looks out into garden.* MRS. HEEGAN *is on his right and* TEDDY *on his left;* SIMON *and* SYLVESTER *a little behind, looking on.* MRS. FORAN *to the right of* MRS. HEEGAN. SURGEON MAXWELL *and* SUSIE, *who are a little to the front, watch for a moment, then the* SURGEON *puts his arm round* SUSIE *and the pair glide off into the dance hall.*

[*When* SURGEON MAXWELL *and* SUSIE *glide in to the motions of the dance through the entrance into the dance hall, the curtains are pulled together. A few moments' pause.* TEDDY *silently puts his hand on* HARRY'S *shoulder, and they both stare into the garden.*]

SIMON. The air'll do him good.

SYLVESTER. An' give him breath to sing his song an' play the ukelele.

MRS. HEEGAN. Just as he used to do.

SYLVESTER. Behind the trenches.

SIMON. In the Rest Camps.

MRS. FORAN. Out in France.

HARRY. I can see, but I cannot dance.

TEDDY. I can dance, but I cannot see.

HARRY. Would that I had the strength to do the things I see.

TEDDY. Would that I could see the things I've strength to do.

HARRY. The Lord hath given and the Lord hath taken away.

TEDDY. Blessed be the name of the Lord.

MRS. FORAN. I do love the ukelele, especially when it goes tinkle, tinkle, tinkle in the night-time.

SYLVESTER. Bringin' before you glistenin' bodies of blacks, coilin' themselves an' shufflin' an' prancin' in a great jungle dance; shakin' assegais an' spears to the rattle, rattle, rattle an' thud, thud, thud of the tom-toms.

MRS. FORAN. There's only one possible musical trimmin' to the air of a Negro Spiritual, an' that's the tinkle, tinkle, tinkle of a ukelele.

HARRY. The rising sap in trees I'll never feel.

TEDDY. The hues of branch or leaf I'll never see.

HARRY. There's something wrong with life when men can walk.

TEDDY. There's something wrong with life when men can see.

HARRY. I never felt the hand that made me helpless.

TEDDY. I never saw the hand that made me blind.

HARRY. Life came and took away the half of life.

TEDDY. Life took from me that half he left with you.

HARRY. The Lord hath given and the Lord hath taken away.

TEDDY. Blessed be the name of the Lord.

[SUSIE *comes quickly in by entrance, goes over to the table and, looking at several bottles of wine, selects one. She is going hurriedly back, when, seeing* HARRY, *she goes over to him.*]

SUSIE [*kindly*]. How are you now, Harry?

HARRY. All right, thank you.

SUSIE. That's good.

[SUSIE *is about to hurry away, when* MRS. FORAN *stops her with a remark.*]

MRS. FORAN [*with a meaning gesture*]. He's takin' it cushy till you're ready to hear him singin' his Negro Spiritual, Miss.

SUSIE. Oh, God, I'd nearly forgotten that. They'll be giving out the balloons at the next dance, and when that fox-trot's over he'll have to come in and sing us the Spiritual.

MRS. HEEGAN. Just as he used to do.

SIMON. Behind the trenches.

SYLVESTER. In the Rest Camps.

MRS. FORAN. Out in France.

SUSIE. As soon as the Baloon Dance is over, Harry, out through the garden and in by the front entrance with you, so that you'll be ready to start as they all sit down. And after the song, we'll drink to the Club from the Silver

Tassie. [*She hurries back to the hall with the bottle of wine.*]

MRS. FORAN. I'm longin' to hear Harry on the ukelele.

HARRY. I hope I'll be able to do justice to it.

MRS. HEEGAN. Of course you will, Harry.

HARRY [*nervously*]. Before a crowd. Forget a word and it's all up with you.

SIMON. Try it over now, softly; the sound couldn't carry as far as the hall.

SYLVESTER. It'll give you confidence in yourself.

HARRY [*to* SIMON]. Show us the ukelele, Simon.

[SIMON *gets the ukelele and gives it to* HARRY.]

TEDDY. If I knew the ukelele it might wean me a little way from the darkness.

[HARRY *pulls a few notes, turning the ukelele, then he softly sings.*]

HARRY:
    Swing low, sweet chariot, comin' for to carry me home,
    Swing low, sweet chariot, comin' for to carry me home.
    I looked over Jordan, what did I see, comin' for to carry
        me home?
    A band of angels comin' after me—comin' for to carry
        me home.

[*A voice in the hall is heard shouting through a megaphone.*]

VOICE. Balloons will be given out now! Given out now—the balloons!

MRS. FORAN [*excitedly*]. They're goin' to send up the balloons! They're going to let the balloons fly now!

HARRY [*singing*]:
    Swing low, sweet chariot, comin' for to carry me home.
    Swing low, sweet chariot, comin' for to carry me home.

MRS. FORAN [*as* HARRY *is singing*]. Miss Monican wants us all to see the flyin' balloons. [*She catches* TEDDY'S *arm and runs with him into the hall.*]

SIMON. We must all see the flyin' balloons.

MRS. HEEGAN [*running into hall*]. Red balloons and black balloons.

SIMON [*following* MRS. HEEGAN.] Green balloons and blue balloons.

SYLVESTER [*following* SIMON]. Yellow balloons and puce balloons.

[*All troop into the hall, leaving the curtains apart, and* HARRY *alone with his ukelele. Through the entrance various coloured balloons that have been tossed into the air can be seen, mid sounds of merriment and excitement.*]

HARRY [*softly and slowly*]. Comin' for to carry me home. [*He throws the ukelele into an armchair, sits still for a moment, then goes to the table, takes up the Silver Cup, and wheels himself into the garden.*]

[*After a pause* BARNEY *looks in, then enters pulling* JESSIE *by the hand, letting the curtains fall together again. Then he goes quickly to window, shuts and bolts it, drawing-to one half of the curtains, goes back to* JESSIE, *catches her hand again, and tries to draw her towards room on the left. During the actions that follow the dance goes merrily on in the hall.*]

JESSIE [*holding up a broken shoulder-strap and pulling back towards the hall*]. Barney, no. God, I'd be afraid he might come in on us alone.

[*Hands part the curtains and throw in coloured streamers that encircle* JESSIE *and* BARNEY.]

BARNEY. Damn them! . . . He's gone, I tell you, to sing the song an' play the ukelele.

JESSIE [*excited and afraid*]. See, they're watching us. No, Barney. You mustn't. I'll not go! [BARNEY *seizes* JESSIE *in his arms and forces her towards the door on the left.*] You wouldn't be good. I'll not go into that room.

BARNEY. I will be good, I tell you! I just want to be alone with you for a minute.

[BARNEY *loosens* JESSIE'S *other shoulder-strap, so that her dress leaves her shoulders and bosom bare.*]

JESSIE [*near the door left, as* BARNEY *opens it*]. You've loosened my dress—I knew you weren't going to be good. [*As she kisses him passionately.*] Barney, Barney—you shouldn't be making me do what I don't want to do!

BARNEY [*holding her and trying to pull her into room*]. Come on, Jessie, you needn't be afraid of Barney—we'll just rest a few minutes from the dancing.

[*At that part of the window uncurtained* HARRY *is seen peering in. He then wheels his chair back and comes on to the centre of the window-frame with a rush, bursting the catch and speeding into the room, coming to a halt, angry and savage, before* BARNEY *and* JESSIE.]

HARRY. So you'd make merry over my helplessness in front of my face, in front of my face, you pair of cheats! You couldn't wait till I'd gone, so that my eyes wouldn't see the joy I wanted hurrying away from me over to another? Hurt her breast pulling your hand quick out of her bodice, did you? [*To* JESSIE.] Saved you in the nick of time, my lady, did I? [*To* BARNEY.] Going to enjoy yourself on the same little couch where she, before you formed an image in her eye, acted the part of an amateur wife, and I acted the part of an amateur husband—the black couch with the green and crimson butterflies, in the yellow bushes, where she and me often tired of the things you're dangling after now!

JESSIE. He's a liar, he's a liar, Barney! He often tried it on with coaxing first and temper afterwards, but it always ended in a halt that left him where he started.

HARRY. If I had my hands on your white neck I'd leave marks there that crowds of kisses from your Barney wouldn't moisten away.

BARNEY. You half-baked Lazarus, I've put up with you all the evening, so don't force me now to rough-handle the bit of life the Jerries left you as a souvenir!

HARRY. When I wanted to slip away from life, you brought me back with your whispered "Think of the tears of Jess, think of the tears of Jess," but Jess has wiped away her tears in the ribbon of your Cross, and this poor crippled jest gives a flame of joy to the change; but when you get her, may you find in her the pressed-down emptiness of a whore!

BARNEY [*running over and seizing* HARRY]. I'll tilt the leaking life out of you, you jealous, peering pimp!

JESSIE [*trying to hold* BARNEY *back*]. Barney, Barney, don't! don't!

HARRY [*appealingly*]. Barney, Barney! My heart—you're stopping it!

JESSIE [*running to entrance and shouting in*]. Help! help! They're killing each other!

[*In the hall the dance stops.* SURGEON MAXWELL *runs in,*

followed by SUSIE, SIMON, SYLVESTER, MRS. FORAN, MRS.
HEEGAN, *and lastly* TEDDY *finding his way over to the window. Dancers gather around entrance and look on.*

[SURGEON MAXWELL, *running over, separates* BARNEY
from HARRY.]

MAXWELL. What's this? Come, come—we can't have this sort
of thing going on.

MRS. HEEGAN. He was throttlin' him, throttlin' a poor helpless
creature, an' if anything happens, he and that painted slug
Jessie Taite'll be held accountable!

MAXWELL. This can't be allowed to go on. You'll have to
bring him home. Any more excitement would be dangerous.

MRS. HEEGAN. This is what he gets from Jessie Taite for sittin'
on the stairs through the yawnin' hours of the night, racin'
her off to the play an' the pictures, an' plungin' every
penny he could keep from me into presents for the consoli-
dation of the courtship!

MAXWELL. Bring the boy home, woman, bring the boy home.

SYLVESTER [*fiercely to* JESSIE]. And money of mine in one of
the gewgaws scintillatin' in her hair!

JESSIE. What gewgaw? What gewgaw?

[*Coloured streamers are thrown in by those standing at entrance, which fall on and encircle some of the group around*
HARRY.]

SYLVESTER. The tiarara I gave you two Christmases ago with
the yellow berries and the three flutterin' crimson swallows!

HARRY [*faintly and bitterly, with a hard little laugh*]. Napoo
Barney Bagnal and napoo Jessie Taite. A merry heart throbs
coldly in my bosom; a merry heart in a cold bosom—or is
it a cold heart in a merry bosom? [*He gathers a number
of the coloured streamers and winds them round himself
and chair.*] Teddy! [HARRY *catches* TEDDY *by the sleeve and
winds some more streamers round him.*] Sing a song, man,
and show the stuff you're made of!

MAXWELL [*catching hold of* MRS. HEEGAN's *arm*]. Bring him
home, woman. [MAXWELL *catches* SYLVESTER's *arm.*] Get
him home, man.

HARRY. Dear God, this crippled form is still your child. [*To
MRS. HEEGAN.*] Dear mother, this helpless thing is still your
son. Harry Heegan, me, who, on the football field, could
crash a twelve-stone flyer off his feet. For this dear Club

three times I won the Cup, and grieve in reason I was just too weak this year to play again. And now, before I go, I give you all the Cup, the Silver Tassie, to have and to hold for ever, evermore. [*From his chair he takes the Cup with the two sides hammered close together, and holds it out to them.*] Mangled and bruised as I am bruised and mangled. Hammered free from all its comely shape. Look, there is Jessie writ, and here is Harry, the one name safely separated from the other. [*He flings it on the floor.*] Treat it kindly. With care it may be opened out, for Barney there to drink to Jess, and Jessie there to drink to Barney.

TEDDY. Come, Harry, home to where the air is soft. No longer can you stand upon a hill-top; these empty eyes of mine can never see from one. Our best is all behind us—what's in front we'll face like men, dear comrade of the blood-fight and the battle-front!

HARRY. What's in front we'll face like men! [HARRY *goes out by the window*, SYLVESTER *pushing the chair*, TEDDY'S *hand on* HARRY'S *shoulder*, MRS. HEEGAN *slowly following. Those left in the room watch them going out through the garden, turning to the right till they are all out of sight. As he goes out of window.*] The Lord hath given and man hath taken away!

TEDDY [*heard from the garden*]. Blessed be the name of the Lord!

[*The band in the hall begins to play again. Those in hall begin to dance.*]

MAXWELL. Come on, all, we've wasted too much time already.

SUSIE [*to* JESSIE, *who is sitting quietly in a chair*]. Come on, Jessie—get your partner; [*roguishly*] you can have a quiet time with Barney later on.

JESSIE. Poor Harry!

SUSIE. Oh nonsense! If you'd passed as many through your hands as I, you'd hardly notice one. [*To* JESSIE.] Jessie, Teddy Foran and Harry Heegan have gone to live their own way in another world. Neither I nor you can lift them out of it. No longer can they do the things we do. We can't give sight to the blind or make the lame walk. We would if we could. It is the misfortune of war. As long as wars are waged, we shall be vexed by woe; strong legs shall be made useless and bright eyes made dark. But we, who have come through the fire unharmed, must go on living. [*Pulling*

JESSIE *from the chair.*] Come along, and take your part in life! [*To* BARNEY.] Come along, Barney, and take your partner into the dance!

[BARNEY *comes over, puts his arm round* JESSIE, *and they dance into the hall.* SUSIE *and* SURGEON MAXWELL *dance together. As they dance the Waltz "Over the Waves," some remain behind drinking. Two of these sing the song to the same tune as the dance.*]

MAXWELL:

> Swing into the dance,
> Take joy when it comes, ere it go;
> For the full flavour of life
> Is either a kiss or a blow.
> He to whom joy is a foe,
> Let him wrap himself up in his woe;
> For he is a life on the ebb,
> We a full life on the flow!

[*All in the hall dance away with streamers and balloons flying.* SIMON *and* MRS. FORAN *sit down and watch the fun through the entrance.* MRS. FORAN *lights a cigarette and smokes. A pause as they look on.*]

MRS. FORAN. It's a terrible pity Harry was too weak to stay an' sing his song, for there's nothing I love more than the ukelele's tinkle, tinkle in the night-time.

CURTAIN

SONGS AND CHANTS IN
THE SILVER TASSIE

1st CHANT.

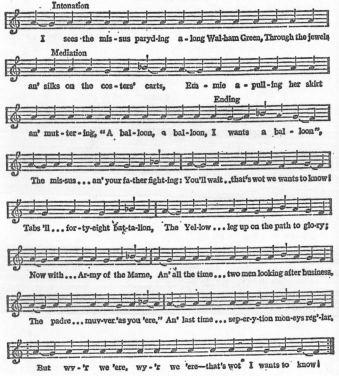

2nd CHANT.

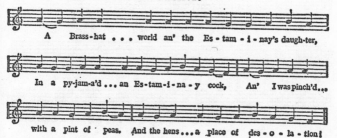

A Brass-hat ... world an' the Es-tam-i-nay's daugh-ter,

In a py-jam-a'd ... an Es-tam-i-na-y cock, An' I was pinch'd...

with a pint of peas. And the hens...a place of des-o-la-tion!

3rd CHANT.

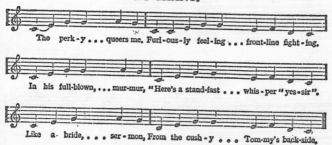

The perk-y ... queers me. Fu-ri-ous-ly feel-ing ... front-line fight-ing.

In his full-blown,... mur-mur, "Here's a stand-fast ... whis-per "yes-sir".

Like a bride, ... ser-mon, From the cush-y ... Tom-my's back-side.

4th CHANT.

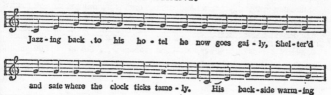

Jazz-ing back .to his ho-tel he now goes gai-ly, Shel-ter'd

and safe where the clock ticks tame-ly. His back-side warm-ing

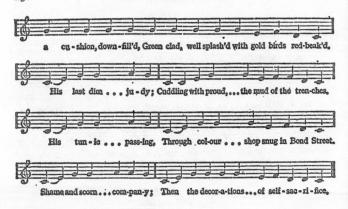

a cu-shion, down-fill'd, Green clad, well splash'd with gold birds red-beak'd.

His last dim ... ju-dy; Cuddling with proud, ... the mud of the tren-ches.

His tun-ic ... pass-ing, Through col-our ... shop snug in Bond Street.

Shame and scorn ... com-pan-y; Then the decor-a-tions ... of self-sac-ri-fice.

5th CHANT.

A warn-ing ... give, To the front ... do, to God.

God, un-chang-ing, ... night sky To mask ... His self-slay-ing chil-dren.

Stumbling, swiftly ... grous-ing, Through mud ... seek slow the front line.

Squeals of hid-den ... wounded—Christ who bore ... tied to a field gun.

WOULD GOD I SMOK'D.

Would God I smok'd and walk'd and watch'd . . The dance of a
Would God I smok'd and lift-ed car-goes From the lad-en
To hang here ev-en a lit-tle lon-ger, Loung-ing
If you creep to rest-in a clos'd-up cof-fin, A tail of
Each spar-row, hop-ping, ir-re-sponsible, Is in-den-tur'd

gol-den Brim-stone but-ter-fly, . . To the
shoul-ders of Lon-don's riv-er-way; . . Then
through fear-swell'd, anx-ious moments; The
com-rades see-ing you safe home; . Or be a
in God's migh-ty mem-o-ry; . . And we,

sau-cy pipe of a green-finch rest-ing In a
holi-day'd, roar-ing out courage and move-ment To the
hin-der-parts of the god of bat-tles Shading our
ker-nel lost .in a shell ex-plod-ing— It's all,
more than they all, shall not be lost In the for-

drowsy, brambled lane in Cumber-land. In Cumber-land.
mus-cled ma-chines of Tottenham Hotspur. Of Tottenham Hotspur.
war-tir'd .eyes from his flam-ing face. From his flaming face.
sure, on-ly in a life-time. A life-time.
get-ful-ness of the Lord of Hosts. Of the Lord of Hosts.

STRETCHER-BEARERS' SONG.

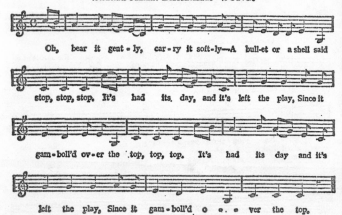

Oh, bear it gent-ly, car-ry it soft-ly—A bull-et or a shell said stop, stop, stop. It's had its day, and it's left the play, Since it gam-boll'd ov-er the top, top, top. It's had its day and it's left the play, Since it gam-boll'd o - - ver the top.

SONG TO THE GUN.

Hail, cool-hardened tower of steel em-boss'd With the fever'd, fig-ment thoughts of man; Guard-ian of our love and hate and fear, Speak for us to the in - ner ear of God! We be-lieve in God and we be-lieve in thee.

THE ENEMY HAS BROKEN THROUGH

The en-em-y has brok-en through, brok-en through, brok-en through! Ev-ery man born of wo-man to the guns, to the guns. To the guns, to the guns, to the guns! Those at prayer, all in bed and the swillers drinking deeply in the pubs. To the guns, to the guns. All the bat-men, ev-ery cook, ev-ery bitch's son that hides A whiff of cour-age in his veins, Shelter'd vig-our in his bod-y, That can run, or can walk, ev-en crawl— Dig him out, dig him out, shove him on— To the guns!

SURGEON'S SONG.

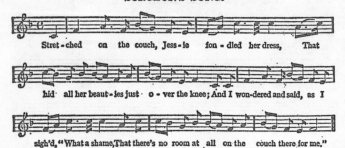

Stret - ched on the couch, Jess - ie fon - dled her dress, That

hid all her beaut - ies just o - ver the knee; And I won-dered and said, as I

sigh'd, "What a shame, That there's no room at all on the couch there for me."

COCK-A-DOODLE DANDY

by SEAN O'CASEY

1949

COCK-A-DOODLE DANDY[1]

CHARACTERS

THE COCK

MICHAEL MARTHRAUN, *a small farmer, now the owner of a lucrative bog*

SAILOR MAHAN, *once a sailor, now the owner of a fleet of lorries carrying turf from bog to town*

LORNA, *second young wife of Marthraun*

LORELEEN, *Marthraun's daughter by his first young wife*

MARION, *helper in Lorna's house*

SHANAAR, *a "very wise old crawthumper," really a dangerous old cod*

FIRST ROUGH FELLOW

SECOND ROUGH FELLOW, *peasants working on the bog*

FATHER DOMINEER, *the parish priest of Nyadnanave*

THE SERGEANT, *of the Civic Guard*

JACK, *Mahan's foreman lorry driver*

JULIA, *Lorna's sister, a paralytic on a visit to Lourdes*

HER FATHER

ONE-EYED LARRY, *a peasant lad and potential sacristan*

A MAYOR

A MACE-BEARER

THE MESSENGER, *in love with Marion*

THE BELLMAN, *a kind of town crier*

A PORTER, *of a general store in the near-by town*

SCENE 1—*The front garden outside Michael Marthraun's house, in Nyadnanave. Morning.*

SCENE 2—*The same. Midday.*

SCENE 3—*The same. Dusk.*

[1] Reprinted with permission of The Macmillan Company from *Collected Plays, Volume IV* by Sean O'Casey. First printed in Great Britain.

Scene 1

[*Part of the garden outside the house of* MICHAEL MARTHRAUN.
*It is rough and uncared for, with tough grass everywhere,
sprinkled with buttercups and daisies. It is surrounded by
a stone wall, three to four feet high, which is pierced by a
wooden gate to the right of any visitor entering the garden.
To the left, a little way from the gate, a clump of sunflowers, in full bloom, stand stiff and stately, their blossoms
big as shields, the petals raying out widely and sharply, like
rays from an angry sun. Glancing farther to the left, a
visitor would see the gable end of the house, with a porch
jutting from it, and a window above the porch. The porch
is supported by twisted pillars of wood, looking like snakes,
which are connected with latticework shaped like noughts
and crosses. These are painted a dazzling white. The framework of the window above is a little on the skew, and the
sashwork holding the glass is twisted into irregular lines.
A little way from the porch, towards the wall, is a dignified-
looking bronze urn holding a standoffish, cynical-looking
evergreen. Farther up, near the wall, the Irish Tricolour
flutters from a flagpole. The house itself is black in colour,
the sash and frame of the window in it is a brilliant red.*

*It is a brilliantly fine day in summer, and as there is
nothing in the garden to provide a shade, the place is a
deep pool of heat, which, seemingly, has lasted for some
time, for the grass has turned to a deep yellow hue, save
where the house and porch throw a rich black shadow.
Stretching away in the distance, beyond the wall, is a bog
of a rich purple colour, dabbed here and there with black
patches. The sky above it is a silvery grey, glittering like
an Oriental canopy.*

*Some little distance away, an accordion is heard playing
a dance tune, and, a few moments after, the* COCK *comes
dancing in around the gable of the house, circles the dignified urn, and disappears round the farther end of the gable
end as the music ceases.*

*He is of a deep black plumage, fitted to his agile and
slender body like a glove on a lady's hand; yellow feet and
ankles, bright green flaps like wings, and a stiff cloak falling*

[245]

like a tail behind him. A big crimson crest flowers over his head, and crimson flaps hang from his jaws. His face has the look of a cynical jester.

MICHAEL MARTHRAUN, *followed by* SAILOR MAHAN, *comes into the garden by the porch. Each carries a kitchen chair, which he sets down some way from the house.* MICHAEL *is a man who is well over sixty years of age, clean-shaven, lean, and grim-looking. His lips twitch nervously whenever he forgets to keep his mouth tightly closed. He is dressed in a blackish tweed suit, and his legs are encased in black leggings. A heavy gold chain stretches across his waistcoat, and he wears a wide-leafed collar, under which a prim black bow is tied.*

SAILOR MAHAN *is a little over fifty, stouter than his companion, and of a more serene countenance. He has a short, pointed beard, just beginning to show signs of greyness. His face is of a ruddier hue, and shows that the wind and the stress of many storms have made it rugged, but in no way unpleasant. There is, maybe, a touch of the sea breeze in his way of talking and his way of walking. He is wearing light grey flannel trousers, a double-breasted royal blue coat, and has a white scarf round his neck, over a light blue shirt. They come to the two chairs, and stand there facing each other.*]

MICHAEL. Come out here, come on out here, where a body can talk free. There's whispers an' whispers in that house, upsettin' a man's mind.

MAHAN [*puzzled*]. Whispers? What kinda whispers?

MICHAEL. Sthrange kinds; whispers good for neither soul nor body.

MAHAN. But there's no-one in the house but your wife, Lorna, Marion the maid, and your own girl Loreleen?

MICHAEL. Ay, so you think; but I know different.

MAHAN [*breezily*]. Nonsense, Mick; you're haulin' on a rope that isn't there!

MICHAEL [*raising his voice*]. You don't live in th' house, do you?

[MAHAN *is silent.*]

You don't live in th' house, do you?

MAHAN [*raising his voice too*]. I know I don't live in it, an' if it's like what you say, I don't want to live in it!

MICHAEL. Well, then, keep quiet when a man speaks of what he knows.

MAHAN. I know as much about a whisper as you do.

MICHAEL. You know about th' whispers of wind an' wave, harmless an' innocent things; but I'm talkin' about whispers ebbin' an flowin' about th' house, with an edge of evil on them, since that painted one, that godless an' laughin' little bitch left London to come here for a long an' leering holiday.

MAHAN. Loreleen? Why, man, she's your own daughter by your first young wife!

MICHAEL. So it was said at th' time, an' so it's believed still; but I had me doubts then, and I've more doubts now. I dhread meetin' her, dhread it, dhread it. [*With a frightened laugh.*] Michael Marthraun's daughter! [*Gripping* MAHAN's *arm.*] Is she anyone's daughter, man?

MAHAN [*impatiently*]. She must be somebody's daughter, man!

MICHAEL [*impatiently*]. Why must she be, man? Remember what th' Missioner said last night: Sthrange things are foisted by the powers of evil into th' life o' man. Since that one come back from England, where evil things abound, there's sinisther signs appearin' everywhere, evil evocations floatin' through every room.

MAHAN [*puzzled*]. What kinda evocation an' significality is there?

MICHAEL [*looking suspiciously at the porch, then at the window above it, and drawing* MAHAN *farther away from the house*]. Looka, Sailor Mahan, [*he speaks furtively*] there's always a stern commotion among th' body objects of th' house, when that one, Loreleen, goes sailin' by; an invisible wind blows th' pictures out, an' turns their frenzied faces to th' wall; once I seen the statue of St. Crankarius standin' on his head to circumvent th' lurin' quality of her presence; an' another time, I seen th' image of our own St. Pathrick makin' a skelp at her with his crozier; fallin' flat on his face, stunned, when he missed!

MAHAN [*doubtful, but a little impressed*]. Good God, them's serious things, Michael Marthraun! [*A pause.*] Are you sure, now, Mick, you're not deludin' yourself?

MICHAEL. Have sense, man! An' me own wife, Lorna Marthraun, is mixin' herself with th' disordher, fondlin' herself with all sorts o' dismayin' decorations. Th' other day, I caught her gapin' into a lookin'-glass, an' when I looked meself, I seen gay-coloured horns branchin' from her head!

MAHAN. No! Oh, Mick, you're fancyin' things. Lorna's a fine, upstandin' woman, an' should be respected.

MICHAEL. Are you gone on her, too? I tell you, I seen the way th' eyes of young men stare at her face, an' follow th' movements of her lurin' legs—there's evil in that woman!

MAHAN. But there's nothin' evil in a pretty face, or in a pair of lurin' legs.

MICHAEL. Oh, man, your religion should tell you th' biggest fight th' holy saints ever had was with temptations from good-lookin' women.

MAHAN [getting nervous, and eager to change the subject]. Looka, let's sit down, an' thry to settle about what you're willin' to pay for th' cartage of th' turf.

MICHAEL [ignoring MAHAN'S attempt to change the tide of talk]. Up there in that room [he points to the window above the porch] she often dances be herself, but dancin' in her mind with hefty lads, plum'd with youth, an' spurred with looser thoughts of love. [As he speaks, the sounds of a gentle waltz are heard, played by harp, lute, or violin, or by all three, the sounds coming, apparently, from the room whose window is above the porch. Bitterly.] There, d'ye hear that, man! Mockin' me. She'll hurt her soul, if she isn't careful.

MAHAN. She's young enough yet to nourish th' need o' dancin'. An' anyway, why did you insist on marryin' her, an' she so young; an' she so gay? She was all again' it herself.

MICHAEL. She consented to it, at last, didn't she?

MAHAN. Ay, when you, her father, an' th' priest had badgered th' girl's mind into disordered attention over th' catch she was gettin'.

MICHAEL. Oh, well you know, Sailor Mahan, that she had her blue eye on th' fat little farm undher me feet; th' taut roof over me head; an' the kind cushion I had in th' bank, against a hard day.

MAHAN. I seen you meself throtting afther her from starboard to port, from poop to quarther-deck, hoistin' before her th' fancy of ribbon an' lace, silver-buckled shoes, an' a silk dhress for Sunday.

MICHAEL. An' what had she but a patched petticoat, a worn look, an' broken brogues to wear to Mass on Sundays? An' didn't I give her oul' fella fifty solid pounds so that her ailin' sisther could thravel to Lourdes to get undher th' aegis of th' Blessed Virgin? An' what did I get for them but a scraggy oul' bog of two hundhred acres?

MAHAN. An' you're makin' a good thing out of it since turf came into its own. It's made you a Councillor, a Justice of the Peace, an' th' fair-haired boy of th' clergy.

MICHAEL. As you mentioned turf, we'd better settle this question of you demandin', for carting it, an exthra amount I couldn't possibly pay.

MAHAN [*stiffness coming into his voice*]. You'll have to, Michael Marthraun, for it can't be done now for a cent less.

MICHAEL. We'll have a drink while we're discussin'. I have a bottle of th' best, ten years maturin', inside. Sit down there till I get it. [*He goes into the porch and, after a few moments, comes quickly out again, his mouth twitching, his voice toned to fear and hate.*] That one, Loreleen's comin' down th' stairs, an' I don't want to come too near her. We'll wait till she goes. Let's talk of our affairs, quietly, while she passes by. Th' thing to do, as Shanaar would tell you, when you hear a sound or see a shape of anything evil, is to take no notice of it. [*Whispering impatiently.*] Sit down, man!

MAHAN [*sitting down—dubiously*]. Are you sure, Mick, you have a close-hauled comprehension of th' way you're thinkin'?

MICHAEL. Ay, am I sure; as sure as I am that a cock crows!

[*A cock suddenly crows lustily as* LORELEEN *appears in the doorway of the porch. She is a very attractive young woman with an air of her own. A jaunty air it is, indicating that it is the sign of a handsome, gay, and intelligent woman. She is dressed in a darkish green dress, with dark red flashes on bodice and side of skirt. A saucy hat of a brighter green than the dress sports a scarlet ornament, its shape suggestive of a cock's crimson crest. Her legs—very charming ones—are clad in brown silk stockings; brown that flashes a golden sheen.* MICHAEL, *who has sat down, jumps startled to his feet at the sudden sound of the cock's crow and, stretching over the table, grips* MAHAN *by the shoulder.*]

MICHAEL. What's that, what's that?

MAHAN [*startled by* MICHAEL'S *frightened movement*]. What's what, man?

MICHAEL [*trying to recover himself*]. Nothin', I heard nothin'.

What was it you were sayin'? [*In a whisper.*] Get goin' on th' turf, man.

MAHAN [*mystified, but doing his best*]. You'll have to grant th' two shillin's additional on each load, Mick. I'd work me lorries at a loss if I took less. [*Placing an affectionate hand on* MICHAEL's *shoulder.*] An' you know well, you're such an oul' an' valued friend, I'd do it for affection's sake, if I only could.

MICHAEL [*forgetting about* LORELEEN]. Don't I know that well, Sailor Mahan; an' I'd do th' same, an' more, be you; but if I surrendhered two shillin's, I might as well give you th' bog as well. I have to live, Sailor Mahan.

MAHAN. Damn it, man, haven't I to live too? How th' hell am I to give th' men a shillin' more without th' exthra two shillin's from you? Pray to th' saints to let them fall like rain from heaven, eh?

MICHAEL [*putting his face closer to* MAHAN's, *hotly*]. Looka here, Sailor Mahan, you're not goin' magicfy me into th' dhream of believin' you're not addin', every hurryin' week, a fine bundle o' notes to th' jubilant store you've there already, forcin' overtime on th' poor men o' th' bank, flickin' th' notes into imperial ordher.

MAHAN [*as fiercely—standing up to say it, his face close to the face of* MICHAEL]. An' you yourself, Michael Marthraun, aren't worn away with th' punishment of poverty! Puttin' on a poor mouth, an' if you set out to count graciously all you have in hidlins, you'd be workin' many a long, glad day, without supper or sleep, be daylight an' candlelight, till your mind centhred on th' sum dominated be th' last note fluttherin' from your fingers!

LORELEEN [*who has strolled slowly over to the gate, listening to the talk the while, turning at the gate to watch as well as listen*]. Lay not up for yourselves treasures upon earth, where moth and rust doth corrupt, and where thieves break through and steal!

MICHAEL [*in a frightened whisper*]. Don't turn your head; take no notice. Don't pretend to hear her lyin' hallucinations!

[*A young, rough-looking fellow, well set and strong, comes running along the pathway to the gate. He is wearing dark brown corduroy trousers, belted at waist, grey shirt, and scarf of bright green, with yellow dots. He pushes* LORELEEN *aside.*]

FIRST ROUGH FELLOW [*pushing* LORELEEN *out of his way*].
Outa me way, woman! [*He sees how charming she is as he
swings her aside.*] Be God, but you're th' good-lookin' lass!
What are you doin' in this hole?

LORELEEN. Seeking happiness, an' failing to find it.

FIRST ROUGH FELLOW. It isn't here you should be, lost among
th' rough stones, th' twisty grass, an' the moody misery
of th' brown bog; but it's lyin' laughin' you should be where
th' palms are tall, an' wherever a foot is planted, a scarlet
flower is crushed; where there's levity living its life, an' not
loneliness dyin' as it is here.

LORELEEN [*dropping him a deep curtsy*]. Thank you, sir
knight, for th' silken compliments to your handmaiden.

[*She turns to go out, and the* ROUGH FELLOW *hurries in
through the gate, down to the two men.*]

FIRST ROUGH FELLOW [*going through the gate down to where
the two men are, and turning to speak up to* LORELEEN,
still standing at the gate]. If you wait till I'm done with
these fellas [*he indicates* MICHAEL *and* MAHAN] I could go
to th' bend o' the road with you, for it's meself would
surrendher a long spell of heaven's ease to go a long day's
journey with a lass like you!

[*Another* ROUGH FELLOW *hurries in along the pathway outside to the gate, pulling* LORELEEN *aside when he finds her
in his way. He wears light brown corduroy trousers, check
shirt, and has a scarf of light yellow, with green stripes,
round his neck.*]

SECOND ROUGH FELLOW [*pulling* LORELEEN *out of his way*].
Eh, there, woman—outa me way! [*He sees, as she swings
around, how charming she is.*] Arra, what winsome wind
blew such a flower into this dread, dhried-up desert?
Deirdre come to life again, not to sorrow, but to dance!
If Eve was as you are, no wondher Adam fell, for a lass
like you could shutther th' world away with a kiss! [*He
goes through the gate, and down to the other men, pausing
to look up at* LORELEEN *again.*]

SECOND ROUGH FELLOW [*to* LORELEEN]. Wait, lass, till I'm
done with these fellas, an' I'll go with you till youth's a
shadow a long way left behind!

LORELEEN [*down to the two* ROUGH FELLOWS]. I'm not for
you, friends, for I'm not good for decent men. The two old
cronies will tell you a kiss from me must be taken undher

a canopy of dangerous darkness. [*She kisses a hand to them.*] Good-bye! [*She goes out.*]

MICHAEL ⎱ [*together*].   What d'ye th' two of yous want here?
MAHAN ⎰   Why aren't yous at work?

FIRST ROUGH FELLOW [*laying a hand sternly on the shoulder of* MAHAN]. Looka, you; you give us the' exthra shillin', or we leave your lorries standin', helpless an' naked on th' roads!

SECOND ROUGH FELLOW [*laying a hand sternly on* MICHAEL'S *shoulder*]. Looka, you; looka that! [*He throws a cheque contemptuously on to the table.*] D'ye think a good week's wages is in a cheque for tuppence?

MICHAEL. You didn't work a week, because of th' rain, an' canteen contribution an' insurance brought your wage for the week to tuppence.

SECOND ROUGH FELLOW. Tell me how I'm goin' to live a week on tuppence?

FIRST ROUGH FELLOW. Seein' th' both of them's Knights o' Columbanus, they should be able to say.

MICHAEL. That's a social question to be solved by th' Rerum novarum.

SECOND ROUGH FELLOW. Fifty years old; not worth much when it was born, an' not worth a damn now. You give a guaranteed week, or th' men come off your bog! [*He goes off towards the gate.*]

FIRST ROUGH FELLOW [*going to the gate—to* MAHAN]. Take our demand serious, or your lorries stand still on th' highways!

SECOND ROUGH FELLOW [*impatiently*]. Looka, there she is! [*He points a finger in front.*]
Let's hurry, an' we'll ketch up on th' fine, fair lady.

[*They hurry along the path, but suddenly stop to stare ahead.*]

FIRST ROUGH FELLOW [*with awe in his voice*]. What's happenin' to her? A cloud closin' in on her, flashes like lightning whirlin' round her head, an' her whole figure ripplin'!

SECOND ROUGH FELLOW [*frightened*]. Jasus, she's changin' into th' look of a fancy-bred fowl! It's turnin' to face us; it's openin' its bake as big as a bayonet!

[*The crow of a cock is heard in the distance.*]

FIRST ROUGH FELLOW [*frightened*]. Here, man, th' other way for us! It's an omen, a warnin', a reminder of what th' Missioner said last night that young men should think of good-

lookin' things in skirts only in th' presence of, an' undher
the guidance of, old and pious people.

[*The two of them hurry away in the opposite direction.*]

MICHAEL [*to* MAHAN]. Did you hear that? I'm askin' you,
Sailor Mahan, did you hear what them two graspin' rascals
said?

MAHAN. I heard, but I can see no significality in it, unless th'
two of them had dhrink taken.

MICHAEL [*warningly*]. Looka, Sailor Mahan, if you aren't careful, your wilful disbelief in things'll lead you astray!
Loreleen isn't me daughter; she isn't even a woman: she's
either undher a spell, or she's a possessed person.

MAHAN [*with contempt*]. Aw, for God's sake, Mick, have
sense, an' get that bottle o' whiskey out to put a spell
on us.

MICHAEL [*almost shouting*]. Have you forgotten already th'
case of th' Widow Malone who could turn, twinklin', into
a dog or a hare, when she wanted to hide herself? An' how,
one day, th' dogs followed what they thought was a hare
that made for th' widow's cottage, an' dived through an
open window, one o' the dogs snappin' a leg off before it
could get through? An' when th' door was burst open, there
was th' oul' witch-widow screamin' on her oul' bed, one
leg gone, with blood spoutin' from th' stump, so that all
th' people heard her last screechin' as she went sliddherin'
down to hell!

MAHAN. I heard tell of it months after, when I come back
from Valparaiso.

MICHAEL. Well, if you heard of it, you know it must have
happened. An' here you are, thinkin' only of whiskey, and
showin' how ready you are to ruin me be askin' more than
I'm able to give. You, a good Christian, a Knight of
Columbanus, a student in th' Circle studyin' th' Rerum
novarum, you should show a sign of charity an' justice,
recognisin' the needs of th' people rather than your own.
[*Suddenly.*] Here, I'll add thruppence, an' make th' offer
ninepence. Hold out th' hand, an' clinch th' bargain.

MAHAN. I'll be scuppered if I will! You'll not use me like th'
oul' father of th' good woman within, who sold you th' bog
when he thought it was derelict, though you're makin'
thousands out of it now.

MICHAEL. You forget I gave th' oul' cod enough to bring his
other daughter to Lourdes for a cure!

MAHAN. You know th' way th' men are actin' now—goin' slow, an' doin' two journeys where they used to do three.

MICHAEL. An' aren't my men threatenin' to come off th' bog altogether? It's this materialism's doin' it—edgin' into revolt against Christian conduct. If they'd only judge o' things in th' proper Christian way, as we do, there'd be no disputes. Now let's be good sons of Columbanus—you thinkin' of my difficulties, an' me thinkin' of yours.

MAHAN. Make your offer one an' sixpence, an' I'll hoist th' pennant of agreement?

MICHAEL. I couldn't. Looka, Sailor Mahan, it would ruin me.

MAHAN [viciously]. You'd rather throw th' money after a tall-hat so that you could controvert yourself into a dapper disturbance th' time the President comes to view th' workin' of th' turf. Talk about Loreleen castin' a spell! Th' whole disthrict'll be paralysed in a spell when your top-hat comes out to meet the President's top-hat, th' two poor things tryin' to keep people from noticin' what's undher them! Two shillin's, now, or nothin'.

[He sits down in disgust. Behind the wall, SHANAAR is seen coming along the road; he opens the gate, and comes slowly down to where the two men are. He is a very, very old man, wrinkled like a walnut, bent at the shoulders, with longish white hair, and a white beard—a bit dirty— reaching to his belly. He is dressed peasant-wise, thin, threadbare frieze coat, patched blackish corduroy trousers, thick boots, good and strong, a vivid blue muffler round his neck, and a sackcloth waistcoat, on which hangs a brass cross, suspended round his neck by twine. A round, wide-brimmed, black hat is on his head.]

SHANAAR [lifting his hat as he comes in by the gate]. God save all here! God save all that may be in th' house, barrin' th' cat an' th' dog!

MICHAEL [with great respect]. An' you, too, Shanaar, old, old man, full of wisdom an' th' knowledge of deeper things.

SHANAAR. Old, is it? Ever so old, thousands of years, thousands of years if all were told.

MICHAEL. Me an' Sailor Mahan here were talkin' some time ago about th' sthrange dodges of unseen powers, an' of what the Missioner said about them last night, but th' easiness of his mind hasn't been hindhered.

SHANAAR [*bending lower, and shoving his bearded face between the two men*]. If it doesn't hindher th' easiness of his mind now, it will one day! Maybe this very day in this very place.

MICHAEL [*to* MAHAN]. What d'ye say to that, now?

MAHAN [*trying to be firm, but a little uneasy*]. Nothin', nothin'.

SHANAAR [*shoving his face closer to* MAHAN's]. Ah, me friend, for years an' years I've thravelled over hollow lands an' hilly lands, an' I know. Big powers of evil, with their little powers, an' them with their littler ones, an' them with their littlest ones, are everywhere. You might meet a bee that wasn't a bee; a bird that wasn't a bird; or a beautiful woman who wasn't a woman at all.

MICHAEL [*excitedly*]. I'm tellin' him that, I'm tellin' him that all along.

MAHAN [*a little doubtfully—to* SHANAAR]. An' how's a poor body to know them?

SHANAAR [*looking round cautiously, then speaking in a tense whisper*]. A sure sign, if only you can get an all-round glimpse of them. [*He looks round him again.*] *Daemones posteriora non habent*—they have no behinds!

MICHAEL [*frightened a lot*]. My God, what an awe-inspiring, expiring experience!

MAHAN [*frightened too, but trying to appear brave*]. That may be, but I wouldn't put innocent birds or bees in that category.

SHANAAR [*full of pitying scorn for ignorance*]. You wouldn't! Innocent birds! Listen all: There was a cuckoo once that led a holy brother to damnation. Th' cuckoo's call enticed th' brother to a silent glade where th' poor man saw a lovely woman, near naked, bathin' her legs in a pool, an' in an instant th' holy man was taken with desire. Lost! She told him he was handsome, but he must have money if he wanted to get her. Th' brother entered a noble's house, an' demanded a hundhred crowns for his convent; but the noble was a wise old bird, an' said he'd have to see the prior first. Thereupon, th' brother up with an axe, hidden under his gown, an' cleft th' noble from skull to chin; robbed th' noble, dhressed himself in rare velvets, an' searched out all th' rosy rottenness of sin with th' damsel till th' money was gone. Then they caught him. Then they hanged him, an', mind you [*the three heads come closer together*] while this poor brother sobbed on the scaffold,

everyone heard th' mocking laughter of a girl and th' calling
of a cuckoo!

[*As* SHANAAR *is speaking the three last things, the mocking
laughter of a girl is heard, the call of a cuckoo, and a young
man's sobbing, one after the other, at first, then they blend
together for a few moments, and cease.* SHANAAR *stands as
stiff as his bent back will allow, and the other two rise
slowly from their chairs, stiff, too, and frightened.*]

SHANAAR [*in a tense whisper*]. Say nothing; take no notice. Sit
down. Thry to continue as if yous hadn't heard!

MAHAN [*after a pause*]. Ay, a cuckoo, maybe; but that's a
foreign bird: no set harbour or home. No genuine decent
Irish bird would do a thing like that on a man.

MICHAEL. Looka here, Sailor Mahan, when th' powers of evil
get goin', I wouldn't put anything past an ordinary hen!

SHANAAR. An' you'd be right, Mr. Marthraun, though, as a
rule, hens is always undher th' eye an' comprehension of a
Christian. Innocent-looking things are often th' most dangerous. Looka th' lad whose mother had set her heart on
him bein' a priest, an' one day, at home, he suddenly saw
a corn crake flyin' into a house be an open window.
Climbin' in afther it, he spied a glittherin' brooch on a
table, an' couldn't resist th' temptation o' thievin' it. That
lad spent th' next ten years in a reformatory; his mother
died of a broken heart, and his father took to dhrink.

[*During the recital of* SHANAAR'S *story, the "crek crek, crek
crek" of a corn crake is heard.*]

MICHAEL [*in a tense whisper—to* MAHAN]. D'ye hear that,
Sailor Mahan?

SHANAAR [*warningly*]. Hush! Take no vocal notice. When yous
hear anything or see anything suspicious, give it no notice,
unless you know how to deal with it.

MICHAEL [*solemnly*]. A warnin' we'll remember. But supposin'
a hen goes wrong, what are we to do?

SHANAAR [*thoughtfully*]. It isn't aysey to say, an' you have
to go cautious. The one thing to do, if yous have the knowledge, is to parley with th' hens in a Latin dissertation. If
among the fowl there's an illusion of a hen from Gehenna,
it won't endure th' Latin. She can't fact th' Latin. The
Latin downs here. She tangles herself in a helluva disordher.
She busts asundher, an' disappears in a quick column of

black an' blue smoke, a thrue ear ketchin' a screech of
agony from its centre!

MICHAEL [*tremendously impressed*]. Looka that now. See what
it is to know!

[*A commotion is heard within the house: a loud cackling,
mingled with a short, sharpened crow of a cock; the breaking of delf; the half-angry, half-frightened cries of women.
A cup, followed by a saucer, flies out through the open
window, over the porch, past the heads of the three men,
who duck violently, and then crouch, amazed, and a little
frightened.*]

What th' hell's happenin' now?

[MARION *rushes to the door of the porch, frightened and
alarmed. She is a young girl of twenty or so, and very good-
looking. Her skirts come just to her knees, for they are nice
legs, and she likes to show them—and why shouldn't she?
And when she does so, she can add the spice of a saucy
look to her bright blue eyes. Instead of the usual maid's cap,
she wears a scarf-bandeau round her head, ornamented
with silver strips, joined in the center above her forehead
with an enamelled stone, each strip extending along the
bandeau as far as either ear. She wears a dark green
uniform, flashed with a brighter green on the sleeves and
neck, and the buttons of the bodice are of the same colour.
Her stockings and shoes are black. A small, neat, white
apron, piped with green, protects her uniform.*]

MARION [*excitedly—to the men*]. It's flyin' about th' house, an'
behavin' outrageous! I guessed that that Loreleen's cluck,
cluck, cluckin' would upset th' bird's respectable way of
livin'!

MICHAEL [*frightened*]. What's wrong with you, girl; what's up?

MARION. Will one of yous come in, an' ketch it, for God's
sake, before it ruins th' house?

MAHAN [*shouting*]. Ketch what, ketch what, woman?

MARION. A wild goose! It's sent th' althar light flyin'; it's
clawed the holy pictures; an' now it's peckin' at th' tall-hat!

MICHAEL. A wild goose? Are you sure it was a wild one?

MARION [*in great distress*]. I dunno, I dunno—maybe it's a
wild duck. It's some flyin' thing tearin' th' house asundher.

MICHAEL [*trembling—to* SHANAAR]. D'ye think it might be
what you know?

SHANAAR [*his knees shaking a little*]. It might be, Mr. Marthraun! It might be, God help us!

MAHAN [*nervous himself*]. Keep your heads, keep your heads!
It's nothin'.

MICHAEL [*beside himself with anxiety and dread—shaking*
MARION *roughly by the shoulders*]. Conthrol yourself, girl,
an' speak sensibly. Is it a goose or a duck or a hen, or what
is it?

MARION [*wildly*]. It's a goose—no, it's a hen, it must be a hen!
We thried to dhrive it out with flyin' cups and flyin' saucers,
but it didn't notice them. Oh, someone should go in, or it'll
peck th' place to pieces!

SHANAAR [*prayerfully*]. So long as it's not transmuted, so long
as it's not been transmuted!

MICHAEL [*shaking* MARION *again*]. Where's Lorna, where's
Lorna?

MARION [*responding to the shaking listlessly*]. Last I seen of
her, she was barricadin' herself undher th' banisters!

MICHAEL [*pleadingly—to* MAHAN]. You've been free with
whales an' dolphins an' octopususas, Sailor Mahan—you
run in, like a good man, an' enthrone yourself on top of
th' thing!

MAHAN [*indignant*]. Is it me? I'm not goin' to squandher
meself conthrollin' live land fowl!

MICHAEL [*to* SHANAAR—*half-commandingly*]. In case it's what
we're afraid of, you pop in, Shanaar, an' liquidate whatever
it is with your Latin.

SHANAAR [*backing towards the wall*]. No good in th' house:
it's effective only in th' open air.

MICHAEL [*in a fury—to* MARION—*pushing her violently towards the gate*]. You go, you gapin', frightened fool, an'
bring Father Domineer quick!

[*All this time, intermittent cackling has been heard, cackling
with a note of satisfaction, or even victory in it, interspersed
with the whirring sound of wings.*

As MARION *rushes out through the gate, she runs into the
arms of the* MESSENGER, *who carries a telegram in his hand.
He clasps* MARION *tight in his arms, and kisses her. He
wears a silvery-grey coat, buttoned over his breast, and
trousers. On the right side of the coat is a flash of a pair of
scarlet wings. A bright green beret is set jauntily on his head
and he is wearing green-coloured sandals.*

MICHAEL *and* MAHAN *have moved farther from the house,
and* SHANAAR *has edged to the gateway, where he stares at
the house, ready to run if anything happens. His hands are
piously folded in front of him, and his lips move as if he
prayed.*]

MESSENGER [*to* MARION]. Ah, lovely one of grace an' gladness,
whose kiss is like a honied flame, where are you rushin' to
in such a hurry?

MICHAEL [*angrily—up to the* MESSENGER]. Let her go, you—
she's runnin' for th' priest!

MESSENGER. Th' priest—why?

[*The cackling breaks into intensity, the whirring of wings
becomes louder, and a plate flies out through the window,
followed by a squeal from* LORNA.]

MESSENGER [*astonished, but not startled*]. What's goin' on in
th' house?

MICHAEL. There's a wild goose, or somethin', asthray in th'
house, an' it's set th' althar bowl flyin'!

MARION. An' it's peckin' th' holy pictures hangin' on th' walls.

MAHAN. Some think it's a wild duck.

SHANAAR. It may be a hen, only a hen.

MESSENGER [*releasing* MARION, *and handing the telegram to*
MICHAEL]. Here's a telegram for you.

MICHAEL [*takes it mechanically, and stuffs it in a pocket*]. Is it
losin' your senses yous are to be afraid of a hen? [*He goes
towards the porch.*] I'll soon settle it!

SHANAAR [*who is now outside, behind the wall*]. If you value
your mortal life, lad, don't go in, for th' hen in there isn't
a hen at all!

MESSENGER. If th' hen, that isn't a hen, in there, isn't a hen,
then it must be a cock. I'll settle it! [*He rushes into the
house.*]

MICHAEL [*in agony*]. If it's a cock, we're done!

SHANAAR [*fervently*]. Oh, rowelum rande, horrida aidus, sed
spero spiro specialii spam!

[*The head of the* COCK, *with its huge, handsome crimson
comb, is suddenly thrust through the window above the
porch, and lets out a violent and triumphant crow.* SHANAAR
disappears behind the wall, and MAHAN *and* MICHAEL *fall
flat in the garden, as if in a dead faint.*]

MICHAEL [*as he is falling*]. Holy saints preserve us—it's th'
Cock!

SHANAAR [*from behind the wall*]. Oh, dana eirebus, heniba et
galli scatterum in multus parvum avic asthorum!

[*The* COCK'S *head is as suddenly withdrawn, and a louder
commotion is heard to be going on in the house; the*
MESSENGER *shouting, a woman's squeal. Then silence for a
few moments as puffs of blue-black smoke jet out through
the window. When the smoke has gone, the* MESSENGER
*comes from the house into the garden. His cap is awry on
his head, his face is a little flushed, and his mouth is smiling.
He carries in his right hand what might have been a broom-
stick, but is now a silver staff, topped with a rosette of
green and red ribbons. He is followed out by the* COCK,
*whom he is leading by a green ribbon, the other end cir-
cling the* COCK'S *neck. The* COCK *follows the* MESSENGER
meekly, stopping when he stops, and moving when the
MESSENGER *moves.*]

SHANAAR [*peeping over the wall*]. Boys an' girls, take no notice
of it, or you're done! Talk only of th' first thing entherin'
your minds.

MESSENGER [*looking with astonishment at the two men sitting
up now on the ground, as far as possible from the house,
and moving away when the* COCK *comes nearer*]. What's
the matther with yous? Why are yous dodgin' about on your
bums? Get up, get up, an' be sensible.

[MICHAEL *and* MAHAN *scramble to their feet, hurry out
through the gate, and stand, warily, beside* SHANAAR.
LORNA'S *head appears at the window above the porch, and
it is at once evident that she is much younger than her
husband, very good-looking still, but the bright and graceful
contours of her face are somewhat troubled by a vague
aspect of worry and inward timidity. Her face shows signs
of excitement, and she speaks rather loudly down to the*
MESSENGER.]

LORNA [*to the* MESSENGER]. Robin Adair, take that bird away
at once. Hand him over to th' Civic Guard, or someone fit
to take charge of him.

MESSENGER [*up to* LORNA]. Looka, lovely lady, there's no
danger, an' there never was. He was lonely, an' was only
goin' about in quest o' company. Instead of shyin' cups an'

saucers at him, if only you'd given him your lily-white
hand, he'd have led you through a wistful an' wondherful
dance. But you frightened th' poor thing!

LORNA. Frightened him, is it? It was me was frightened when
I seen him tossin' down delf, clawin' holy pictures, and
peckin' to pieces th' brand new tall-hat that Mr. Marthraun
bought to wear, goin' with the Mayor to greet His Brightness, th' President of Eire, comin' to inaugerate th' new
canteen for th' turf workers.

MICHAEL [*enraged*]. Is it me new hat he's destroyed?

SHANAAR [*pulling* MICHAEL's *arm in warning*]. Damnit, man,
take no notice!

MICHAEL [*turning indignantly on* SHANAAR]. How'd you like
your sumptuous, silken hat to be mangled into a mon-
strosity!

SHANAAR [*with concentrated venom*]. Hush, man, hush!

MARION [*who has been looking at the* COCK *with admiration*].
Sure, he's harmless when you know him.

MESSENGER [*stroking its back*]. 'Course he is! Just a gay bird,
that's all. A bit unruly at times, but conthrollable be th'
right persons. [*To the* COCK.] Go on, comrade, lift up th'
head an' clap th' wings, black cock, an' crow!

[*The* COCK *lifts up his head, claps his wings, and lets out a
mighty crow, which is immediately followed by a rumbling
roll of thunder.*]

MICHAEL [*almost in a state of collapse*]. Aw, we're done for!

SHANAAR [*violently*]. No notice, no notice!

LORNA [*from the window*]. God bless us, what's that? [*Down
to the* MESSENGER.] Robin, will you take that damned animal away before things happen that God won't know about!

MESSENGER [*reassuringly—up to* LORNA]. Lovely lady, you can
let your little hands lie with idle quietness in your lap, for
there's no harm in him beyond gaiety an' fine feelin'.
[*To the* COCK.] You know th' goose step done be the Irish
Militia in th' city of Cork more'n a hundhred years ago?
Well, we'll go home doin' it, to show there's nothing undher
th' sun Ireland didn't know, before th' world sensed it.
Ready? One, two—quick march!

[*The* MESSENGER *and the* COCK *march off doing the goose
step.* MARION *follows them, imitating the step, as far as the
end of the garden; then she stands looking after them,*

waving them farewell. MICHAEL *and* MAHAN *come slowly
and stealthily into the garden as the* COCK *goes out. They
go to the chairs, on which they sit, exhausted, wiping their
foreheads with their handkerchiefs.* SHANAAR *comes towards
them more slowly, keeping an eye in the direction taken by
the* COCK *and the* MESSENGER. *When the place is clear, he
anchors himself behind the table.*]

LORNA [*down to* MARION]. Marion, dear, come on in, an' help
me to straighten things up a little. [*She goes away from
the window.*]

MARION [*going slowly towards the house, after having given
a last farewell—gleefully*]. Wasn't it a saucy bird! An' th'
stately way he done th' goose step!
[*She playfully shakes* MICHAEL'*s shoulder.*] Did you see it,
sir? [MICHAEL *takes no notice.*] God forgive me, but it
gave us all an hilarious time—didn't it, sir?

MICHAEL [*coldly*]. Your misthress called you.

MARION. I heard her, sir. What a clatther it all made! An' yous
all quakin', an' even Sailor Mahan there, shakin' in his
shoes, sure it was somethin' sinisther!

MAHAN [*angrily*]. You go in to your misthress, girl!

MARION [*giggling*]. Th' bould sailor lad! An' he gettin' rocked
in th' cradle of th' deep! Me faltherin' tongue can't impart
th' fun I felt at seein' yous all thinkin' th' anchor was
bein' weighed for th' next world.

MICHAEL [*loudly*]. Go to your misthress when you're told.

MARION [*giggling more than ever*]. An' oul' dodderin' Shanaar,
there, concoctin' his Latin, an' puttin' th' wall between
himself an' th' blast! Well, while yous sit all alone there in
th' gloamin', yous won't be in heart for singin'.
[*She chants.*]
"Only to see his face again, only to hear him crow!"
[*She runs merrily in.*]

SHANAAR [*warily—in a warning whisper*]. Watch that one!

MICHAEL. Th' ignorant, mockin', saucy face of her afther us
bein' in danger of thransportation to where we couldn't
know ourselves with agony an' consternation!

SHANAAR [*fervently*]. Sweet airs of heaven be round us all!
Watch that one, Mr. Marthraun. Women is more flexible
towards th' ungodly than us men, an' well th' old saints
knew it. I'd recommend you to compel her, for a start, to
lift her bodice higher up, an' pull her skirt lower down; for

th' circumnambulatory nature of a woman's form often has a detonatin' effect on a man's idle thoughts.

MICHAEL [*pensively*]. How thrue, how thrue that is!

SHANAAR. What we have to do now is to keep thought from dwellin' on th' things seen an' heard this day; for dwellin' on it may bring th' evil back again. So don't let any thought of it, *ab initio extensio*, remain in your minds, though, as a precaution, when I'm passin' th' barracks, I'll acquaint the Civic Guard. Now I must be off, for I've a long way to thravel.

[*He goes as far as the gate, and returns.*]

Mr. Marthraun, don't forget to have th' room where th' commotion was manifested, *turbulenta concursio cockolorum*, purified an' surified be an understandin' clergyman. Good-bye.

[*Again he goes as far as the gate, and returns.*]

Be on your guard against any unfamiliar motion or peculiar conspicuosity or quasimodical addendum, perceivable in any familiar thing or creature common to your general recognisances. A cat barkin' at a dog, or a dog miaouin' be a fire would atthract your attention, give you a shock, but don't, for th' love of God, notice it! It's this scourge of materialism sweepin' th' world that's incantatin' these evils to our senses and our doorsteps.

MAHAN [*pensively*]. That's th' way th' compass is pointin', Shanaar—everyone only thinkin', thinkin' of himself.

SHANAAR. An' women's wily exhilarations are abettin' it, so that a man's measure of virtue is now made with money, used to buy ornaments, bestowed on girls to give a gaudy outside to the ugliness of hell.

MICHAEL [*fervently*]. Oh, how thrue, how thrue that is!

SHANAAR. An' th' coruscatin' conduct in th' dance halls is completin' th' ruin.

MAHAN [*solemnly*]. Wise words from a wiser man! Afther a night in one of them, there isn't an ounce of energy left in a worker!

SHANAAR [*whispering*]. A last warnin'—don't forget that six thousand six hundhred an' sixty-six evil spirits can find ready lodgin's undher th' skin of a single man!

MICHAEL [*horrified*]. What an appallin' thought!

SHANAAR. So be on your guard. Well, good-bye.

MICHAEL [*offering him a note*]. Here's a pound to help you on your way.

SHANAAR [*setting the note aside*]. No, thanks. If I took it, I couldn't fuse th' inner with th' outher vision; I'd lose th' power of spiritual scansion. If you've a shillin' for a meal in th' town till I get to the counthry, where I'm always welcome, I'll take it, an' thank you.

[MICHAEL *gives him a shilling.*]

SHANAAR. Thank you kindly. [*He goes out through the gate, and along the pathway outside. Just as he is about to disappear, he faces towards the two men, and stretches out a hand in a gesture of blessing. Fervently.*]

Ab tormentum sed absolvo, non revolvo, cockalorum credulum hibernica!

MICHAEL [*with emotion*]. You too, Shanaar, oul' son; you too!

[SHANAAR *goes off.*]

MAHAN [*after a pause—viciously*]. That Latin-lustrous oul' cod of a prayer-blower is a positive danger goin' about th' counthry!

MICHAEL [*startled and offended*]. Eh! I wouldn't go callin' him a cod, Sailor Mahan. A little asthray in a way, now an' again, but no cod. You should be th' last to call th' man a cod, for if it wasn't for his holy Latin aspirations, you mightn't be here now.

MAHAN [*with exasperation*]. Aw, th' oul' fool, pipin' a gale into every breeze that blows! I don't believe there was ever anything engenderogically evil in that cock as a cock, or denounceable either! Lardin' a man's mind with his killakee Latin! An' looka th' way he slights th' women. I seen him lookin' at Lorna an' Marion as if they'd horns on their heads!

MICHAEL [*doubtfully*]. Maybe he's too down on th' women, though you have to allow women is temptin'.

MAHAN. They wouldn't tempt man if they didn't damn well know he wanted to be tempted!

MICHAEL. Yes, yes; but we must suffer th' temptation accordin' to the cognisances of th' canon law. But let's have a dhrink, for I'm near dead with th' drouth, an' we can sensify our discussion about th' increased price you're demandin' for carryin' th' turf; though, honest to God, Sailor Mahan, I can't add a ha'penny more to what I'm givin'.

MAHAN. A dhrink would be welcome, an' we can talk over th' matter, though, honest to God, Michael Marthraun, blast th' penny less I'll take than what I'm askin'.

MICHAEL [*going to the porch, and shouting into the house*]. Marion, bring th' bottle of ten years' maturin', an' two glasses!
[*He returns.*] It's th' principle I'm thinkin' of.

MAHAN. That's what's throublin' me, too.
[MARION *comes in with the bottle of whiskey and the two glasses. She places them on the table, getting between the two men to do so. Reading the label.*]
Flanagan's First! Nyav na Nyale—th' heaven of th' clouds! An' brought be a lass who's a Flanagan's first too!

MARION [*in jovial mood*]. G'long with you—you an' your blarney!

MICHAEL [*enthusiastically*]. Had you lived long ago, Emer would have been jealous of you! [*He playfully pinches her bottom.*]

MARION [*squealing*]. Ouch!
[*She breaks away, and makes for the porch.*]
A pair o' naughty men!
[*She goes into the house.*]

MICHAEL [*calling after her*]. I forgot th' soda, Marion; bring th' siphon, lass.

MAHAN [*complacently*]. I could hold that one in me arms for a long time, Mick.

MICHAEL. Th' man would want to be dead who couldn't.

MAHAN [*enthusiastically*]. I'd welcome her, even if I seen her through th' vision of oul' Shanaar—with horns growin' out of her head!

[MARION *returns with the siphon, which she places on the table. The two men, looking in front of them, have silly, sly grins on their faces.*
The ornament which MARION *wears round her head has separated into two parts, each of which has risen over her head, forming two branching horns, apparently sprouting from her forehead. The two men, shyly gazing in front, or at the table, do not see the change.* MARION'S *face has changed too, and now seems to wear a mocking, cynical look fitting the aspect of her face to the horns.*]

MARION [*jokingly*]. Two wild men—it's afraid I am to come near yous.

MAHAN [*slyly*]. What about a kiss on your rosy mouth, darlin',
to give a honied tang to th' whiskey?

MICHAEL. An' one for me, too?

MARION [*with pretended demureness*]. A thrue gentleman'll
rise up an' never expect a thrue lady to bend down for a
kiss.
[*With vigour.*] Up an' take it, before yous grow cold!

[*They rise from their chairs, foolish grins on their faces,
settle themselves for a kiss, and then perceive the change
that has taken place. They flop back on to the chairs, fright
and dismay sweeping over their faces.*]

MAHAN } [*together*]. Good God!
MICHAEL }

[*They slump in the chairs, overcome, their hands folded in
front of their chests, palm to palm, as if in prayer. MARION
looks at them in some astonishment.*]

MARION. What ails yous? Was th' excitement too much for
yous, or what?

MICHAEL [*plaintively*]. Saints in heaven help us now!

MARION. What's come over yous? Th' way yous slumped so
sudden down, you'd think I'd horns on me, or somethin'!

MICHAEL [*hoarsely*]. G'way, g'way! Shanaar, Shanaar, where
are you now!

MARION [*going over to* MAHAN, *and putting an arm round his
neck*]. What about you, gay one?

MAHAN [*gurgling with fright*]. You're sthranglin' me! G'way,
g'way, girl!

MARION. Looka, a kiss would do yous good. Yous think too
much of th' world!

MAHAN [*chokingly*]. St. Christopher, mainstay of mariners, be
with me now!

[LORNA *thrusts her head out from the window over the porch.*]

LORNA [*down to* MARION]. Let them two oul' life-frighteners
fend for themselves, an' come in. From th' back window,
I can see th' crowd gathered to give Julia a send-off to
Lourdes, so come in to tidy if you want to join them with
me.

MARION [*half to herself—as she runs into the house*]. God forgive me—I near forgot! Here we are followin' laughter,

instead of seekin' succour from prayer! [*She runs in, and* LORNA *takes her head back into the room again.*]

MICHAEL [*frightened and very angry*]. Now, maybe, you'll quit jeerin' at oul' Shanaar! Now, maybe, you'll let your mind concentrate on higher things! Now, maybe, you won't be runnin' loose afther girls!

MAHAN [*indignantly*]. Damnit, man, you were as eager for a cuddle as I was!

MICHAEL [*lifting his eyes skywards*]. Oh, d'ye hear that! I was only toleratin' your queer declivity, like a fool. An' afther all th' warnin's given be wise oul' Shanaar! Looka, Sailor Mahan, you'll have to be more on your guard!

MAHAN [*trying to defend himself*]. How could any man suspect such a thing? We'll have to think this thing out.

MICHAEL [*with exasperation*]. Think it out! Oh, man, Sailor Mahan, have you nothin' more sensible to say than that we'll have to think it out?

MAHAN. Let's have a drink, for God's sake, to steady us down!

MICHAEL [*hurriedly putting bottle and glasses under the table*]. What're you thinkin' of, Sailor Mahan? We can't dispense ourselves through a scene of jollification an' poor Julia passin' on her way to Lourdes!

[*Along the path, on a stretcher, carried by the two* ROUGH FELLOWS, *comes* JULIA, *followed by her father. The stretcher is borne to the gate, and there laid down, so that the head of it is flush with the gateposts and the rest of it within the garden. The framework of the gate makes a frame for* JULIA, *who is half sitting up, her head supported by a high pillow. Her face is a sad yellowish mask, pierced by wide eyes, surrounded by dark circles. Her father is a sturdy fellow of fifty, a scraggly greyish beard struggling from his chin. He is roughly dressed, as a poorer peasant might be, and his clothes are patched in places. He wears a brown muffler, and a faded black trilby-hat is on his head. All the time, he looks straight in front with a passive and stony stare.*

Before the stretcher walks the MAYOR, *rather stout, clean-shaven, wearing a red robe over rough clothing; he has a very wide three-cornered hat, laced with gold, on his head. Behind him walks the* MACE-BEARER, *a big silver and black mace on his shoulder. He is tall, and wears a bright blue robe, trimmed with silver; on his head is a huge cocked*

*hat, laced, too, with silver. These two do not enter the
garden, but walk on, and stand waiting near the house,
beside the flagpole, but without the wall.*

LORNA, *followed by* MARION, *comes out of the house. Instead of the bright headgear worn before, they have black
kerchiefs, worn peasant-wise on their heads—that is, they
have been folded triangularly, draped over their heads, with
the ends tied beneath their chins.*

LORNA *runs over to the stretcher, kneels down beside it,
and kisses* JULIA.]

LORNA [*affectionately*]. My sister, my little Julia, oh, how
sorry I am that you have to go on this long, sad journey!

JULIA [*her voice is low, but there is a hectic note of hope in
it*]. A long journey, Lorna darlin', but not a sad one; oh, no,
not a sad one. Hope, Lorna, will have me be the hand all
the long way. I go to kneel at the feet of the ever Blessed
Virgin.

LORNA. Oh, she will comfort you, me darlin'.

JULIA. Yes, she will comfort me, Lorna;

[*After a pause*]

an' cure me too. Lorna, say she will cure me too.

LORNA [*stifling a sob*]. An' cure you too.

JULIA [*to* MICHAEL]. Give me your good wishes, Mr. Marthraun.

MICHAEL [*with genuine emotion*]. Julia, me best wishes go
with you, an' me best prayers'll follow all th' long way!

JULIA [*to* MAHAN]. An' you, Sailor Mahan—have you no good
wish for the poor voyager?

MAHAN [*fervently*]. Young lass, may you go through healin'
wathers, an' come back a clipper, with ne'er a spar, a sail,
or a rope asthray!

[FATHER DOMINEER *comes quickly in on the path outside. He
is a tall, rather heavily built man of forty. He has a breezy
manner now, heading the forlorn hope. He is trying to smile
now, but crack his mouth as he will, the tight, surly lines
of his face refuse to furnish one. He is dressed in the usual
clerical, outdoor garb, and his hard head is covered with
a soft, rather widely brimmed black hat.*]

FATHER DOMINEER [*as happily as he can*]. Now, now, no halts
on th' road, little daughter! The train won't wait, an' we
must have a few minutes to spare to make you comfortable.

Bring her along, Brancardiers! Forward, in th' name o' God
and of Mary, ever Virgin, ever blessed, always bending to
help poor, banished children of Eve!

[*The two* ROUGH MEN *take up the stretcher and carry it along
the pathway outside, the* MAYOR, *followed by his* MACE-
BEARER, *leading it on.* FATHER DOMINEER *follows immediately behind; then come* LORNA *and* MARION, *followed by*
MICHAEL *and* MAHAN.
*As the stretcher moves along the pathway outside, a band
in the distance is heard playing "Star of the Sea," to which
is added the voice of a crowd, singing the words:*

*Hail, Queen of Heav'n, the ocean Star!
Guide of the wand'rer here below!
Thrown on life's surge, we claim thy care—
Save us from peril and from woe.
Mother of Christ, Star of the Sea,
Pray for the wanderer, pray for me.*]

FATHER DOMINEER [*enthusiastically*]. Julia will bring us back
a miracle, a glorious miracle! To Lourdes!

End of Scene 1

Scene 2

[*The scene is the same as before, though the sunshine isn't
quite so bright and determined. The Irish Tricolour flies
breezily from its flagpole; the table and chairs stand where
they were, and the bottle and glasses are still under it.
No-one is in the garden, all, apparently, having gone to
see* JULIA *away on her long, long journey. Away in the
distance the band is playing "Star of the Sea," and the tune
can be softly heard from the garden.
After a few moments,* LORNA *and* MARION *come along the
path outside, enter by the gate, and cross over into the
house.*]

MARION [*anxiously*]. What d'ye think of th' chance of a cure?
LORNA. I'm afraid th' chance is a poor one; but we won't talk
about it.
MARION [*piously*]. Well, it was a grand send-off, an' God is
good.

LORNA [*coldly*]. An' th' devil's not a bad fella either.

[*They both go into the house, and, a few moments later,* MICHAEL *and* MAHAN *stroll along the path, come into the garden, and go to where the table and chairs are.*]

MAHAN. Well, th' anchor's weighed.

MICHAEL. It was an edifyin' spectacle, Sailor Mahan, thrustin' us outa this world for th' time bein'. Julia's asked for a sign, Sailor Mahan, an', believe me, she'll get it.

MAHAN. She will, she will, though I wouldn't like to bet on it.

MICHAEL. She'll get what she's afther—a complete cure. Me own generous gift of fifty pounds for th' oul' bog'll be rewarded; an' th' spate o' prayin' goin' on, from the Mayor to the Bellman, is bound to get the' higher saints goin', persuadin' them to furnish a suitable answer to all we're askin'.

MAHAN [*impatiently*]. Arra, man alive, d'ye think th' skipper aloft an' his glitterin' crew is goin' to bother their heads about a call from a tiny town an' disthrict thryin' hard to thrive on turf?

MICHAEL [*indignantly*]. Looka, if you were only versed in th' endurin' promulgacity of th' gospels, you'd know th' man above's concerned as much about Nyadnanave as he is about a place where a swarm of cardinals saunther secure, decoratin' th' air with all their purple an' gold!

MAHAN [*as indignantly*]. Are you goin' to tell me that th' skipper aloft an' his hierarchilogical crew are concerned about th' Mayor, the Messenger, Marion, me, an' you as much as they are about them who've been promoted to th' quarterdeck o' th' world's fame? Are you goin' to pit our palthry penances an' haltin' hummin' o' hymns against th' piercin' pipin' of th' rosary be Bing Bang Crosby an' other great film stars, who side-stepped from published greatness for a holy minute or two to send a blessed blast over th' wireless, callin' all Catholics to perpetuatin' prayer!

MICHAEL [*sitting down on a chair*]. Sailor Mahan, I ask you to thry to get your thoughts shipshaped in your mind.

[*While they have been talking, the* MESSENGER *has come running along the path outside, and is now leaning on the gate, listening to the two men, unnoticed by them.*]

MAHAN [*plumping down on the other chair—indignantly*]. D'ye remember who you're talkin' to, man? Shipshape in

me mind! Isn't a man bound to have his mind fitted together
in a shipshape way, who, forced out of his thrue course be
a nautical cathastrope, to wit, videliket, an act o' God,
ploughed a way through th' Sargasso Sea, reachin' open
wathers, long afther hope had troubled him no longer?

MICHAEL [*wearily*]. Aw, Sailor Mahan, what's them things
got to do with th' things tantamount to heaven?

MESSENGER [*over to them*]. Mick's right—them things can't
be tantamount to anything bar themselves.

MAHAN [*turning fiercely on the* MESSENGER]. What do you
want? What're you doin' here? Your coalition of ignorant
knowledge can't comprehend th' things we talk about!

MESSENGER [*with some excitement*]. Listen, boys—I've a question to ask yous.

MICHAEL [*with a gesture signifying this isn't the time to ask
it*]. Ask it some time more convenient. An' don't refer to
us as "boys"—we're gentlemen to you!

MAHAN [*to* MICHAEL]. Looka, Mick, if you only listened to
Bing Crosby, th' mighty film star, croonin' his Irish lullaby,
[*he chants*] "Tooral ooral ooral, tooral ooral ay," you'd
have th' visuality to see th' amazin' response he'd have from
millions of admirers, if he crooned a hymn!

MESSENGER. I was never sthruck be Bing Crosby's croonin'.

MICHAEL [*wrathfully—to* MESSENGER]. You were never
sthruck! An' who th' hell are you to be consulted? Please
don't stand there interferin' with the earnest colloquy of
betther men. [*To* MAHAN.] Looka, Sailor Mahan, any
priest'll tell you that in th' eyes of heaven all men are
equal an' must be held in respect an' reverence.

MAHAN [*mockingly*]. Ay, they'll say that to me an' you, but
will they say it to Bing Crosby, or any other famous film
star?

MESSENGER. Will they hell! Honour be th' clergy's regulated
by how much a man can give!

MICHAEL [*furiously—to the* MESSENGER]. Get to hell outa
here! With that kinda talk, we won't be able soon to sit
steady on our chairs. Oh! [*The chair he is sitting on collapses, and he comes down to the ground on his arse.*]

MAHAN [*astonished*]. Holy saints, what's happened?

MICHAEL [*in a fierce whisper—to* MAHAN]. Take no notice of
it, fool. Go on talkin'!

MAHAN [*a little confused*]. I'll say you're right, Mick; th' way
things are goin' we won't be able much longer to sit serene

on our chairs. Oh! [*The chair collapses under* MAHAN, *and he, too, comes down to the ground.*]

MICHAEL [*in a fierce whisper*]. Don't notice it; go on's if nothin' happened!

MESSENGER [*amused*]. Well, yous have settled down now, anyhow! Will I get yous chairs sturdy enough to uphold th' wisdom of your talkin'?

MICHAEL [*angrily—to* MESSENGER]. There's nothin' wrong with th' chairs we have! You get outa here! Nothin's wrong with th' chairs at all. Get outa here—I don't trust you either!

MESSENGER. I've somethin' important to ask yous.

MICHAEL. Well, ask it at some more convenient time.

[*To* MAHAN.] It's a blessin' that so many lively-livin' oul' holy spots are still in th' land to help us an' keep us wary.

MESSENGER [*scornfully*]. An' where are th' lively holy spots still to be found? Sure, man, they're all gone west long ago, an' the whole face o' th' land is pock-marked with their ruins!

MICHAEL [*shouting at the* MESSENGER]. Where are th' lost an' ruined holy places? We've always cared for, an' honoured, our holy spots! Mention one of them, either lost or ruined!

MESSENGER [*shouting back*]. There are thousands of them, man; places founded be Finian, Finbarr, an' th' rest; places that are now only an oul' ruined wall, blighted be nettle an' dock, their only glory th' crimson berries of th' bright arbutus! Where's th' Seven Churches of Glendalough? Where's Durrow of Offally, founded be Columkille himself? Known now only be the names of the Book of Durrow!

MICHAEL [*ferociously*]. Book o' Durrow! It's books that have us half th' woeful way we are, fillin' broody minds with loose scholasticality, infringin' th' holy beliefs an' thried impositions that our fathers' fathers' fathers gave our fathers' fathers, who gave our fathers what our fathers gave to us!

MESSENGER. Faith, your fathers' faith is fear, an' now fear is your only fun.

MAHAN [*impatiently*]. Let him go, Mick, an' let's have that dhrink you mentioned a year ago.

[MARION'S *head appears at the window, looking down at the* MESSENGER. *The decorations on her head have now declined to their first place.*]

MARION [*down to the* MESSENGER]. Hallo, Robin Adair!

[*He looks up.*]

  Where are th' two oul' woeful wondhers?

[*He points to where they are.*]

  Oh, they've brought the unsteady chairs out, and now
  they've broken them up!
  [*To* MICHAEL—*angrily.*] You knew well th' chairs in the
  hall were there only to present an appearance.

MESSENGER [*up to her*]. Oh, Marion, Marion, sweet Marion,
  come down till I give you a kiss havin' in it all the life an'
  longin' of th' greater lovers of th' past!

MARION [*leaving the window*]. Now, now, naughty boy!

MICHAEL [*sourly*]. You'd do well to remember, lad, the month
  in jail you got for kissin' Marion, an' the forty-shillin' fine
  on Marion, for kissing you in a public place at th' cross-
  roads.

[MARION *comes from the house, goes toward the* MESSENGER,
  who seizes her in his arms and kisses her.]

MESSENGER. I'd do a year an' a day in a cold cell of pressed-in
  loneliness, an' come out singin' a song, for a kiss from a
  lass like Marion!

MARION. Don't think too much of me, Robin Adair, for I've
  some of th' devil in me, an' th' two fostherers of fear, there,
  think I wear horns on holy days.

MICHAEL [*impressively*]. See—she's warnin' you, herself,
  young man!

MARION [*to the* MESSENGER]. An' what has you here arguin'
  with them two oul' fools?

MESSENGER. I came to ask a question of them, but they were
  buried in their prayers. Did you see him? Did he come
  this way?

MICHAEL [*suddenly alarmed*]. Come where?

MAHAN [*alarmed*]. See who?

MESSENGER. Th' Cock.

MAHAN   } [*together*]. Th' Cock! [*They carefully creep
MICHAEL   }   away from the broken chairs, and
stand up when they are some distance from them.*]

MESSENGER. Ay. I thought he'd make for here first.

MICHAEL [*echoing the* MESSENGER]. Make for here first!

[*In the distance, the loud, exultant crow of the* COCK *is heard.*]

MESSENGER [*excitedly*]. There he is! Away in the direction east of th' bog! I'll go get him, an' fetch him home.

MARION [*kissing the* MESSENGER]. Bring him here first, Robin, an' I'll have a wreath of roses ready to hang round his neck.

MESSENGER [*rushing away*]. I will, I will, fair one!

[*He goes off. She takes the broken chairs into the house.*]

MARION [*carrying in the chairs*]. Next time, you boyos, take out two steady ones.

MICHAEL [*horrified*]. Did you hear what she said, Sailor Mahan? Hang a wreath of roses round his neck! Well, I'll have th' gun ready! Ay, now!

[*He goes over to the porch, but* MAHAN *lays a restraining hand on his arm.*]

MAHAN. What good would th' gun be? Have you forgot what Shanaar told us? Your bullet would go clean through him, an' leave him untouched. Now that we're in peace here, let's have th' dhrink we were to have an' which we both need.

MICHAEL [*halting*]. You're right, Sailor Mahan. If he comes here, what we have to do is to take no notice. Look through him, past him, over him, but never at him. [*He prepares the bottle of whiskey and the glasses.*] There's sinisther enchantments all around us. God between us an' all harm! We'll have to be for ever on our guard.

MAHAN [*impatiently*]. Yis, yis; fill out th' dhrink, for God's sake!

MICHAEL. May it give us courage. [*He tilts the bottle over the glass, but none of it spills out.*] Good God, th' bottle's bewitched too!

MAHAN. Bottle bewitched? How could a bottle be bewitched? Steady your nerves, man. Thry given' it a shake.

MICHAEL [*who has left the bottle on the table—retreating away from it*]. Thry given it a shake yourself, since you're so darin'.

[MAHAN *goes over to the table with a forced swagger, and reaches out a cautious hand for the bottle. As he touches it, its colour changes to a glowing red.*]

MAHAN [*fervent and frightened*]. St. Christopher, pathron of all mariners, defend us—th' bottle's changed its colour!

MICHAEL. There's evil things cantherin' an' crawlin' about this place! You saw th' seal on th' bottle showin' it was untouched since it left th' store. Flanagan's finest, Jamieson's best, ten years maturin'—an' look at it now.

MAHAN. How are we goin' to prevent ourselves from bein' the victims of sorcery an' ruin? You'd think good whiskey would be exempt from injury even be th' lowest of th' low.

MICHAEL. It's th' women who're always intherceptin' our good intentions. Evil things is theatenin' us everywhere. Th' one safe method of turnin' our back to a power like this is to go forward an' meet it halfway. [*He comes close to* MAHAN, *and whispers hoarsely.*] Selah!

MAHAN [*mystified and frightened at what he thinks may be something sinister*]. Selah?

MICHAEL [*emphatically*]. Selah!

MAHAN [*agonisingly*]. Good God!

MICHAEL. Now, maybe, you'll believe what th' Missioner said last night.

MAHAN [*a little dubiously*]. He might have been exaggeratin' a bit, Mick.

MICHAEL. Look at th' bottle, man! Demons can hide in th' froth of th' beer a man's dhrinkin'. An' all th' time, my turf-workers an' your lorry drivers are screwin' all they can out of us so that they'll have more to spend on pictures an' in th' dance halls, leavin' us to face th' foe alone.

MAHAN [*abjectly*]. What's a poor, good-livin', virtuous man to do then?

MICHAEL. He must always be thinkin' of th' four last things— hell, heaven, death, an' th' judgment.

MAHAN [*pitifully*]. But that would sthrain a man's nerves, an' make life hardly worth livin'.

MICHAEL. It's plain, Sailor Mahan, you're still hankerin' afther th' things o' th' world, an' the soft, stimulatin' touch of th' flesh. You're puttin' th' two of us in peril, Sailor Mahan.

MAHAN [*protesting*]. You're exaggeratin' now.

MICHAEL. I am not. I seen your eyes followin' that Loreleen when she's about, hurtin' th' tendher muscles of your eye squintin' down at her legs. You'll have to curb your conthradictions, for you're puttin' us both in dire peril, Sailor Mahan. Looka what I've lost already! Me fine silk hat torn to shreds, so that Lorna's had to telephone th' firm for

another, that I may suitably show meself when I meet
his brightness, the President; an' looka th' whiskey there
—forced into a misundherstandin' of itself be some minor
demon devisin' a spell on it! Guess how much good money
I surrendhered to get that bottle, Sailor Mahan?

MAHAN. I've no idea of what whiskey is a gallon now.

MICHAEL [*impatiently*]. What whiskey is a gallon now? Is
there some kinda spell on you, too, Sailor Mahan? You
can't think of whiskey in gallons now; you have to think of
it in terms of sips; an' sips spaced out from each other like
th' holy days of obligation.

MAHAN. An' how are we goin' to get rid of it? We're in some
danger while it's standin' there.

MICHAEL. How th' hell do I know how we'll get rid of it?
We'll have to get Shanaar to deal with it, an', mind you,
don't go too near it.

[*The* PORTER *appears on the sidewalk outside the wall. He
is a middle-aged man with an obstinate face, the chin hidden by a grizzled beard. He is wearing a pair of old brown
trousers, an older grey coat, and an old blue shirt. On his
head is a big cap, with a long, wide peak jutting out in
front of it. The crown of the cap is a high one, and around
the crown is a wide band of dazzling scarlet. He is carrying
a parcel wrapped in brown paper, either side of which is a
little torn. He looks north, south, west, and then, turning
east, he sees the two men in the garden.*]

PORTER [*to the two men*]. Isn't it handy now that I've clapped
eyes on two human bein's in this godforsaken hole! I've
been trudghin' about for hours thryin' to find th' one that'll
claim what's in this parcel I'm bearin', an', maybe, th' two
of yous, or maybe, one of yous, can tell me where I'll find
him. I'm on th' thrack of an oul' fella callin' himself a
Councillor an' a Jay Pee.

MICHAEL. What's his name?

PORTER. That's more than I can say, for th' chit of th' girl
in th' shop who took th' ordher forgot to write down th'
name, an' then forgot th' name itself when she started to
write it down. All I know is that in this disthrict I'm
seekin' a Mr. Councillor So-an'-so; one havin' Councillor
at his head an' Jay Pee at his tail.

MICHAEL [*with importance*]. I'm a Councillor and a Jay Pee.

PORTER [*with some scorn*]. D'ye tell me that now? [*He bends
over the wall to come closer to* MICHAEL.] Listen, me good

man, me journey's been too long an' too dangerous for me
to glorify any cod-actin'! It would be a quare place if you
were a councillor. You'll have to grow a few more grey
hairs before you can take a rise outa me!

MICHAEL [*indignantly*]. Tell us what you've got there, fella,
an', if it's not for us, be off about your business!

PORTER [*angrily*]. Fella yourself! An' mend your manners,
please! It's hardly th' like of you would be standin' in need
of a silky, shinin' tall-hat.

MICHAEL. If it's a tall-hat, it's for me! I'm Mr. Councillor,
Marthraun, Jay Pee—ordhered to be sent express by th'
firm of Buckley's.

PORTER [*with a quick conciliatory change*]. That's th' firm.
I guessed you was th' man at once, at once. That man's a
leadher in th' locality, I said, as soon as I clapped me eye
on you. A fine, clever, upstandin' individual, I says to
meself.

MICHAEL [*shortly*]. Hand over th' hat, and you can go.

PORTER. Hould on a minute, sir; wait till I tell you: I'm sorry,
but th' hat's been slightly damaged in thransit. [*He begins
to take the hat from the paper.*]

MICHAEL. Damaged? How th' hell did you damage it?

PORTER. Me, is it? No, not me, sir. [*He stretches over the wall
towards them.*] When I was bringin' it here, someone shot
a bullet through it, east be west!

MICHAEL. Nonsense, man, who'd be shootin' bullets round
here?

PORTER. Who indeed? That's th' mystery. Bullet it was.
People told me the Civic Guards were out thryin' to shoot
down an evil spirit flyin' th' air in th' shape of a bird.

MICHAEL [*alarmed*]. Th' Cock!

PORTER [*placing the tall-hat on the wall carefully*]. An' seein'
how things are, an' th' fright I got, it's welcome a dhrink
would be from th' handsome bottle I see paradin' on th'
table.

MICHAEL [*in a loud whisper*]. To touch it is to go in danger of
your life—th' bottle's bewitched!

PORTER. Th' bottle bewitched? What sort of a place have me
poor, wandherin' feet sthrayed into at all? Before I ven-
tured to come here at all, I should have stayed at home.
I'm already as uneasy as th' place itself!

[*A shot is heard, and the tall-hat is knocked from the wall
on to the road.*]

Saints in glory, there's another one!

MAHAN [*excitedly*]. It's your hat, man, th' red band on your hat!

PORTER [*to* MICHAEL—*speaking rapidly, picking the tall-hat from the road and offering it to* MICHAEL]. Here, take your hat, sir, an' keep it safe, an' I'll be goin'.

MICHAEL [*frightened and angry*]. Take it back; it's damaged; take it back, fella!

PORTER [*loudly and with anger*]. Fella yourself! Is it takin' th' risk I'd be of a bullet rushin' through me instead of th' oul' hat? [*He flings it towards the two men.*] Here, take your oul' hat an' th' risk along with it! Do what you want with it; do what you like with it; do what you can with it—I'm off!

[*He runs off in the direction he came from, while the two men gaze doubtfully at the hat lying in the garden.*]

MICHAEL [*tremulously*]. The cowards that are in this counthry leavin' a poor man alone in his dilemma! I'd be afraid to wear it now.

MAHAN. Aw, give yourself a shake, Mick. You're not afraid of a poor tall-hat. An' throw away ten good pounds. [*He goes toward where the hat is, but* MICHAEL *holds him by the arm.*]

MICHAEL [*with warning and appeal*]. No, don't touch it till we see further.

[*The* SERGEANT *appears on the pathway outside. He has a rifle in his hands; he leans against the wall looking towards the two. He is obviously anxious, and in a state of fear.*]

SERGEANT. Yous didn't see it? It didn't come here, did it?

MICHAEL [*breathless with the tension of fear*]. No, no; not yet. [*With doleful appeal.*] Oh, don't be prowlin' round here— you'll only be attractin' it to th' place!

SERGEANT [*ignoring appeal*]. Three times I shot at it; three times th' bullets went right through it; and twice th' thing flew away crowing.

MICHAEL [*excitedly*]. Did you get it th' third time, did you get it then?

SERGEANT. Wait till I tell yous: sthrange things an' unruly are happenin' in this holy land of ours this day! Will I ever forget what happened th' third time I shot it! Never, never. Isn't it a wondher an' a mercy of God that I'm left alive afther th' reverberatin' fright I got!

MICHAEL [*eagerly*]. Well, what happened when you shot it then?

MAHAN [*eagerly*]. When you shot it for th' third time?

SERGEANT. Yous could never guess?

MICHAEL [*impatiently*]. Oh, we know we'd never guess; no-one can go guessin' about demonological disturbances.

MAHAN. Tell us, will you, without any more of your sthructural suggestions!

SERGEANT. As sure as I'm standin' here; as sure as this gun is in me left hand; [*he is holding it in his right one*] as sure as we're all poor, identified sinners; when I shot him for th' third time, I seen him changin' into a——

MICHAEL
MAHAN   } [*together*]. What?

SERGEANT [*whispering*]. What d'ye think?

MAHAN [*explosively*]. Oh, we're not thinkin'; we can't think; we're beyond thinkin'! We're waitin' for you to tell us!

SERGEANT. Th' soul well-nigh left me body when I seen th' unholy novelty happenin': th' thing that couldn't be, yet th' thing that was. If I never prayed before, I prayed then —for hope; for holy considheration in th' quandary; for power to be usual an' spry again when th' thing was gone.

MICHAEL. What thing, what thing, man?

MAHAN [*despairingly*]. Thry to tell us, Sergeant, what you said you said you seen.

SERGEANT. I'm comin' to it; since what I seen was seen by no man never before, it's not easy for a man to describe with evidential accuracy th' consequential thoughts flutterin' through me amazed mind at what was, an' what couldn't be, demonstrated there, or there or anywhere else, where mortals congregate in ones or twos or crowds astoundin'.

MICHAEL [*imploringly*]. Looka, Sergeant, we're languishin' for th' information that may keep us from spendin' the rest of our lives in constant consternation.

SERGEANT. As I was tellin' you, there was th' crimson crest of th' Cock, enhancin' th' head lifted up to give a crow, an' when I riz th' gun to me shouldher, an' let bang, th' whole place went dead-dark; a flash of red lightning near blinded me; an' when it got light again, a second afther, there was the demonised Cock changin' himself into a silken glossified tall-hat!

MICHAEL [*horrified*]. A silken tall-hat!

MAHAN. A glossified tall-hat!

MICHAEL [*to* MAHAN—*viciously*]. Now you'll quit undher-
    estimatin' what th' holy Missioner said last night about
    th' desperate an' deranging thrickeries of evil things loose
    an' loungin' among us! Now can you see the significantly
    of things?

MAHAN [*going away as far as he can from the tall-hat lying in
    the garden*]. Steer clear of it; get as far away from it as we
    can! Keep well abaft of it!

SERGEANT [*puzzled*]. Keep clear from what?

MAHAN [*pointing to the hat*]. Th' hat, man, th' hat!

SERGEANT [*seeing the hat beside him, and jumping away from
    it*]. I was near touchin' th' brim of it! Jasus! yous should
    have warned me!

MICHAEL [*close to the* SERGEANT—*in a whisper*]. Does it look
    anything like th' thing you shot?

SERGEANT [*laying a shaking hand on* MICHAEL'S *arm*]. It's th'
    dead spit of what I seen him changin' into durin' th' flash
    of lightning! I just riz th' gun to me shouldher—like this
    [*he raises the gun to his shoulder*] to let bang.

[*The garden is suddenly enveloped in darkness for a few
    moments. A fierce flash of lightning shoots through the
    darkness; the hat has disappeared, and where it stood now
    stands the* COCK. *While the lightning flashes, the* COCK *crows
    lustily. Then the light as suddenly comes back to the garden,
    and shows that the* COCK *and the hat have gone.* MICHAEL
    and MAHAN *are seen to be lying on the ground, and the*
    SERGEANT *is on his knees, as if in prayer.*]

SERGEANT. Holy St. Custodius, pathron of th' police, protect
    me!

MICHAEL [*in a whisper*]. Are you there, Sailor Mahan?

MAHAN [*in a whisper*]. Are you there, Michael Marthraun?

MICHAEL. I'm done for.

MAHAN. We're both done for.

SERGEANT. We're all done for.

MAHAN. Th' smell of th' sulphur an' brimstone's burnin' me.

MICHAEL. Now you'll give up mockin' Shanaar, if it's not too
    late. You seen how Marion's head was ornamented, an'
    it'll not be long till Lorna has them too.

SERGEANT [*now sitting down, so that he is to the left of*
    MICHAEL, *while* MAHAN *sits to the right of him, so fright-
    ened that he must blame someone*]. We'll have to curtail
    th' gallivantin' of th' women afther th' men. Th' house

is their province, as th' clergy's tired tellin' them. They'll
have to realize that th' home's their only proper place.

MICHAEL. An' demolish th' minds that babble about books.

SERGEANT [*raising his voice*]. Th' biggest curse of all! Books
no decent mortal should touch, should never even see th'
cover of one!

MICHAEL [*warningly*]. Hush! Don't speak so loud, or th'
lesser boyo'll hear you!

SERGEANT [*startled*]. Lesser boyo? What lesser boyo?

MAHAN [*whispering and pointing*]. Th' boyo in th' bottle
there.

SERGEANT [*noticing it for the first time*]. Why, what's in it?

MICHAEL. Th' best of whiskey was in it till some evil spirit
put a spell on it, desthroyin' its legitimate use.

SERGEANT [*unbelievingly*]. I don't believe it. Nothin' could
translate good dhrink into anything but what it was made
to be. We could do with a dhrink now. [*He advances
cautiously towards the table.*]

MICHAEL [*excitedly*]. Don't meddle with it, man; don't
stimulate him!

[*The* SERGEANT *tiptoes over to the table, stretches his hand
out, and touches the bottle. He immediately lets out a
yelp, and jumps back.*]

SERGEANT. Oh! Be God, it's red-hot!

MAHAN [*angrily*]. You were told not to touch it! You're
addin' to our dangers.

MICHAEL [*shouting*]. Good God, man, couldn't you do what
you're told! Now you've added anger to its impositional
qualities!

SERGEANT [*nursing his hand*]. Aren't we in a nice quandary
when an evil thing can inscounce itself in a bottle!

MICHAEL. Th' whole place's seethin' with them. You, Sergeant, watch th' road north; you, Sailor Mahan, watch it
south; an' I'll keep an eye on th' house.

[MAHAN *goes to one end of the wall, the* SERGEANT *to the
other, and both stretch over it to look different ways along
the road. During the next discussion, whenever they leave
where they are, they move cautiously, crouching a little,
as if they were afraid to be seen; keeping as low as possible for security.*]

One of us'll have to take th' risk, an' go for Father
Domineer at once. [*He waits for a few moments, but
no-one answers.*] Did yous hear me, or are yous lettin' on
to be deaf? I said one of us'll have to go for Father
Domineer. [*There is no reply.*] Are you listenin' to me by
any chance, Sailor Mahan?

MAHAN. I heard you, I heard you.

MICHAEL. An' why don't you go, then?

MAHAN [*coming down towards* MICHAEL—*crouching low*].
Nice thing if I met th' Cock barrin' me way? Why don't
you go yourself?

MICHAEL. What about th' possibility of me meetin' him? I'm
more conspicuous in this disthrict than you, an' th' thing
would take immediate recognisance of me.

SERGEANT [*coming down towards them—crouching too*]. Me
an' Sailor Mahan'll go together.

MICHAEL [*indignantly*]. An' leave me to grapple with *mys-
teriosa Daemones* alone? [*He turns his face skywards.*]
Oh, in this disthrict there's not a sign of one willin' to do
unto another what another would do to him!

MAHAN [*fiercely*]. That's a lie: there isn't a one who isn't
eager to do to others what others would do to him!

[*The* BELLMAN, *dressed as a fireman, comes in, and walks
along on the path outside. He has a huge brass fireman's
helmet on his head, and is wearing a red shirt and blue
trousers. He has a bell in his hand which he rings loudly
before he shouts his orders. The three men cease their discussion, and give him their full attention.*]

BELLMAN [*shouting*]. Into your houses all! Bar th' doors,
shut th' windows! Th' Cock's comin'! In the shape of a
woman! Gallus, Le Coq, an' Kyleloch, th' Cock's comin'
in th' shape of a woman! Into your houses, shut to th'
windows, bar th' doors! [*He goes out in the opposite
direction, shouting his orders and ringing his bell, leaving
the three men agitated and more frightened than ever.*]

SERGEANT [*frantically*]. Into the house with us all—quick!

MICHAEL [*hindering him—ferociously*]. Not in there, you
fool! Th' house is full o' them. You seen what happened
to the whiskey? If he or she comes, th' thing to do is to
take no notice; if he or she talks, not to answer; and take
no notice of whatever questionable shape it takes. Sit
down, quiet, th' three of us.

[*The three men sit down on the ground—*MICHAEL *to the right, the* SERGEANT *to the left, and* MAHAN *in the centre.*]

MICHAEL [*trembling*]. Now, let th' two of yous pull yourselves together. An' you, Mahan, sing that favourite of
yours, quietly, as if we were passing th' time pleasantly.
[*As* MAHAN *hesitates.*] Go on, man, for God's sake!

MAHAN [*agitated*]. I can't see how I'll do it justice undher
these conditions. I'll thry. [*He sings, but his voice quavers
occasionally.*]

Long time ago when men was men
An' ships not ships that sail'd just to an' fro-o-o,
We hoisted sail an' sail'd, an' then sail'd on an' on to
Jericho-o-o;
With silks an' spice came back again because we'd no-
where else to go!

MICHAEL }
SERGEANT } [*together*]. Go, go!

MAHAN [*singing*].

Th' captain says, says he, we'll make
Th' pirates where th' palm trees wave an' grow-o-o,
Haul down their sable flag, an' pray, before we hang
them all, heave yo-ho-ho;
Then fling their bodies in th' sea to feed th' fishes down
below!

MICHAEL }
SERGEANT } [*together*]. Low, low!

[*A golden shaft of light streams in from the left of the road,
and, a moment afterwards,* LORELEEN *appears in the midst
of it. She stands in the gateway staring at the three men
squatted on the ground.*]

LORELEEN [*puzzled*]. What th' hell's wrong here?

MICHAEL [*in a whisper—motioning* MAHAN *to continue*].
Go on, man.

MAHAN [*singing—with more quavers in his voice*].

An' when we've swabb'd th' blood away.
We'll take their hundhred-ton gunn'd ship in tow-o-o;
Their precious jewels'll go to deck th' breasts of women,
white as snow-o-o;
So hoist all sail an' make for home through waves that
lash an' winds that blow!

MICHAEL   } [*together*]. Blow, blow!
SERGEANT

[LORELEEN *comes into the garden, and approaches the men.
   The golden light follows her, and partly shines on the
   three singers.*]

LORELEEN [*brightly*]. Singin' is it the three of you are? Practisin' for the fancy-dress ball tonight, eh? Ye do well to
bring a spray of light, now and again, into a dark place.
The Sergeant's eyes, too, whenever Lorna or me passes
by, are lit with a light that never was on sea or land. An'
th' bould Sailor Mahan is smiling too; only Dad is dour.
[*She glances at the bottle on the table.*] The song is heard,
th' wine is seen, only th' women wanting.
[*She runs over to the porchway, and shouts into the
house.*]
Lorna, Marion, come on down, come out here, an' join
th' enthertainment!

[LORNA *and* MARION *come trotting out of the house into the
garden. They are both clad in what would be called fancy
dress.* LORNA *is supposed to be a gypsy, and is wearing a
short black skirt, low-cut green bodice, with a gay sash
round her waist, sparkling with sequins. Her fair arms are
bare. Her head is bound with a silver and black ornament,
similar in shape to that already worn by* MARION. *Her legs
are encased in black stockings, and dark red shoes cover
her feet.* MARION *is dressed as a Nippy, a gay one. She
has on a short, bright green skirt, below which a black
petticoat peeps; a low-cut bodice of a darker green, and
sports a tiny black apron to protect her costume. She
wears light brown silk stockings and brown shoes. Outside
the white bandeau round her head she wears the ornament
worn before. The two women stare at the three men.*]

LORNA [*vexatiously*]. Dhrunk is it? To get in that state just
when we were practisin' a few steps for tonight's fancy-
dress dance! [*She notices the bottle*]. Looka th' dhrink left
out in th' sun an' air to dhry! [*She whips up the bottle,
and places it inside on the floor of the porch.*] An' even
th' Sailor Mahan is moody too! [*She goes over to the* SER-
GEANT, *stands behind him, and lays a hand on his head.
She is now in the golden light which shines down on the*
SERGEANT *too.*]

I saw a ship a-sailing, a-sailing on th' sea;
An' among its spicy cargo was a bonny lad for me!

[*The* SERGEANT *rises slowly, as if enchanted, with a foolish look of devotion on his face, till he stands upright beside* LORNA, *glancing at her face, now and again, very shy and uncertain. While this has been happening,* LORELEEN *has gone to* SAILOR MAHAN, *and now stands behind him with a hand on his head.*]

LORELEEN [*down to* SAILOR MAHAN].
I saw a man come running, come running o'er th' lea, sir,
    And, lo, he carried silken gowns
That couldn't hide a knee,
    That he had bought in saucy towns;
An' jewels he'd bought beyond th' bounds
    Of Asia's furthest sea.
And all were lovely, all were fine,
    An' all were meant for me!

[SAILOR MAHAN *rises, as if enchanted, till he stands upright beside* LORELEEN, *slyly looking at her now and again.*]

MARION. Aw, let's be sensible. [*She sees the gun.*] What's th' gun doin? Who owns th' gun?

SERGEANT. It's mine. I'm on pathrol lookin' to shoot down th' demon bird loose among innocent people.

MARION. Demon bird loose among innocent people! Yous must be mad.

SERGEANT [*indignantly*]. We're not mad! It's only that we were startled when th' darkness came, th' lightning flashed, an' we saw Mr. Marthraun's tall-hat turnin' itself into th' demon bird!

LORNA [*mystified*]. Th' darkness came, th' lightning flashed! A tall-hat changin' into a demon bird!

MICHAEL [*springing to his feet*]. Ay, an' this isn't th' time for gay disturbance! So go in, an' sthrip off them gaudy things, an' bend your mind to silent prayer an' long fastin'! Fall prostrate before God, admittin' your dire disthress, an' you may be admitted to a new dispensation!

LORNA [*to* MICHAEL] Nonsense! Your new tall-hat was delivered an hour ago, an' is upstairs now, waitin' for you to put it on. [*To* MARION.] Take that gun in, dear, outa th' way, an' bring down th' tall-hat to show him he's dreamin'.

[MARION *takes up the gun, and goes into the house with it, as* MICHAEL, *in a great rage, shoves* MAHAN *aside to face* LORNA *fiercely.*]

MICHAEL [*loudly*]. Who are you, you jade, to set yourself up against th' inner sight an' outer sight of genuine Christian men? [*He shouts.*] We seen this thing, I tell you! If you knew what you ought to know, you'd acknowledge th' thrained tenacity of evil things. Betther had I left you soakin' in poverty, with your rags coverin' your thin legs, an' your cheeks hollow from mean feedin'. Through our bulgin' eyes, didn't we see th' horrification of me tall-hat turnin' into th' demonised cock? Me tall-hat, you bitch, me own tall-hat is roamin' round th' counthry, temptin' souls to desthroy themselves with dancin' an' desultory pleasures!

MAHAN [*gripping* MICHAEL'S *arm*]. Aw, draw it mild, Mick!

MICHAEL [*flinging off* MAHAN'S *hold*]. Go in, an' take them things, showy with sin, off you, an' dhress decent! [*He points to* LORELEEN.] It's you who's brought this blast from th' undherworld, England, with you! It's easy seen what you learned while you worked there—a place where no God is; where pride and lust an' money are the brightest liveries of life!

[*He advances as if to strike her, but* MAHAN *bars his way.*]
You painted slug!

[MARION *comes from the house, carrying a fresh, dignified tall-hat, noble in its silken glossiness. She offers it to* MICHAEL, *who jumps away from it.*]

No, no, take it away; don't let it touch me.

[MARION *puts the hat on the table, and the three men stare at it as if expecting something to happen.*]

LORNA [*darting into the porch, and returning with the bottle. It has gone back to its former colour*]. Let's have a dhrink to give us courage to fight our dangers. Fetch another glass, Marion.

[MARION *goes in, and returns with a glass.* LORNA *uncorks the bottle, and takes up a glass to fill it.*]

MICHAEL [*warningly*]. Don't meddle with that dhrink, or harm may come to us all!

LORNA [*recklessly*]. If I can't wrap myself in th' arms of a man, I'll wrap myself in a cordial. [*She fills the glass then she fills another one, and gives it to* LORELEEN; *then she fills a third, and gives it to* MARION.] Here, Loreleen. [LORELEEN *takes the glass.*] Here, Marion. [MARION *takes the glass from her.*]

MAHAN [*doubtfully, and with some fear*]. I wouldn't, Lorna, I wouldn't dhrink it—there's some kind of a spell on it.

LORNA. Is there, now? I hope to God it's a strong one! [*Raising her glass.*] Th' Cock-a-doodle Dandy!

MARION ⎫ [*raising their glasses—*   Th' Cock-a-doodle Dandy!
LORELEEN ⎭   *together*].

[*The three women empty their glasses together.* LORNA *fills her glass again, and goes over to the* SERGEANT.]

LORNA [*offering the glass to the* SERGEANT]. Dhrink, hearty man, an' praise th' good things life can give. [*As he hesitates.*] Dhrink from th' glass touched by th' lips of a very fair lady!

SERGEANT [*impulsively*]. Death an' bedamnit, ma'am, it's a fair lady you are. [*He takes the glass from her*]. I'm not th' one to be short in salutin' loveliness! [*He drinks, and a look of delightful animation gradually comes on to his face.*]

LORELEEN [*who has filled her glass again—going over to* SAILOR MAHAN, *and offering him the drink*]. Here, Sailor Mahan, man of th' wider waters, an' th' seven seas, dhrink! [*As he hesitates.*] Dhrink from th' glass touched by th' lips of a very fair lady!

MAHAN [*taking the glass—impulsively*]. Here's a one who always yelled ahoy to a lovely face an' charmin' figure whenever they went sailin' by—*salud!* [*He drinks, and the look of animation gradually comes on to his face too.*]

MARION [*who has filled her glass the second time—going over to* MICHAEL *and offering him the drink*]. Dark man, let th' light come to you be dhrinkin' from a glass touched be th' red lips of a fair young maiden!

MICHAEL [*who has been watching the others enviously— taking the glass from her*]. Gimme it! I won't be one odd. Yous can't best me! [*He drinks it down greedily. A reckless look steals over his face.*]

[*During the last few moments,* LORNA *has been humming a tune, which has been taken up by an accordion, very softly. Then the* MESSENGER *appears on the pathway out-*

*side, and it can be seen that he is the player. He sits side-
ways on the wall, still playing softly a kind of a dance tune.*]

MICHAEL [*to* MARION]. In our heart of hearts, maid Marion,
we care nothin' about th' world of men. Do we now, Sailor
Mahan?

MAHAN [*cautiously—though a reckless gleam is appearing in
his eyes too*]. We all have to think about th' world o' men
at times.

MICHAEL. Not with our hearts, Sailor Mahan; oh, not with our
hearts. You're thinkin' now of th' exthra money you
want off me, Sailor Mahan. Take it, man, an' welcome!
[*Enthusiastically.*] An' more! You can have double what
you're askin', without a whimper, without a grudge!

MAHAN [*enthusiastically*]. No, damnit, Michael, not a penny
from you! We're as good as bein' brothers! Looka th' lilies
of th' field, an' ask yourself what th' hell's money!

MICHAEL [*excitedly*]. Dhross, be God! Dhross, an' nothin'
else! [*To* MARION.] Gimme that hat there!

[*She gives it to him. He puts it on, puts an arm round her
waist, and they begin to move with the beat of the music.
As* MICHAEL *puts his arm around her waist, the ornament
on her head rises into a graceful, curving horn, but he does
not notice it.*

At the same time, the SERGEANT, *having put an arm
round* LORNA, *moves in the dance, too. As he does so, the
ornament on her head, too, becomes a curving horn, but
he does not notice it. Then* MAHAN *goes over stealthily to*
LORELEEN, *who is watching the others, and stabs her shyly
in the ribs with a finger. She turns, smiles, takes hold of his
arm, and puts it round her waist. Then the two of them join
the others in moving round to the beat of the music, the
cock-like crest in* LORELEEN'S *hat rising higher as she begins
to move in the dance.*

*After a few moments, the dance quickens, the excitement
grows, and the men stamp out the measure of the music
fiercely, while the three women begin to whirl round them
with ardour and abandon. While the excitement is at its
height, a loud, long peal of thunder is heard, and in the
midst of it, with a sliding, rushing pace,* FATHER DOMINEER
*appears in the gateway, a green glow enveloping him as he
glares down at the swinging dancers, and as a loud, lusty
crow from the* COCK *rings out through the garden.*

The dancers, excepting LORELEEN, *suddenly stand stock-still, then fall on one knee, facing the priest, their heads bent in shame and some dismay.* LORELEEN *dances on for some few moments longer, the music becoming softer, then she slowly ends her dance to face forward towards the priest, the* MESSENGER *continuing to play the tune very softly, very faintly now.*

FATHER DOMINEER [*down to those in the garden—with vicious intensity*]. Stop that devil's dance! How often have yous been warned that th' avowed enemies of Christianity are on th' march everywhere! An' I find yous dancin'! How often have yous been told that pagan poison is floodin' th' world, an' that Ireland is dhrinken in generous doses through films, plays, an' books! An' yet I come here to find yous dancin'! Dancin', an' with th' Kyleloch, Le Coq, Gallus, th' Cock rampant in th' disthrict, destroyin' desire for prayer, desire for work, an' weakenin' th' authority of th' pastors an' masters of your souls! Th' empire of Satan's pushin' out its foundations everywhere, an' I find yous dancin', *ubique ululanti cockalorum ochone, ululo!*

MESSENGER [*through his soft playing of the accordion*]. Th' devil was as often in th' street, an' as intimate in th' home when there was nor film nor play nor book.

FATHER DOMINEER. There was singin' then, an' there's singin' now; there was dancin' then, an' there's dancin' now, leadin' innocent souls to perjure their perfection. [*To* LORELEEN.] Kneel down, as th' others do, you proud an' dartin' cheat, an' beg a pardon!

LORELEEN [*obstinately*]. I seek no pardon for th' dance that's done.

FATHER DOMINEER [*turning away from her*]. Seek for it then when pardon hides away.

MICHAEL. Oh, what have I done! I've bethrayed meself into a sudden misdoin'!

MAHAN. *Mea culpa*, me, too, Father!

FATHER DOMINEER. Oh, Michael Marthraun, an' you, Sailor Mahan, Knights of Columbanus, I come to help yous, an' I catch yous in th' act of prancin' about with shameless women, dhressed to stun th' virtue out of all beholders!

MICHAEL. It was them, right enough, Father, helped be th' wine, that done poor me an' poor Sailor Mahan in! I should have remembered that a Columbanian knight told

me a brother Columbanian knight told him another brother
has said that St. Jerome told a brother once that woman
was th' gate of hell! An' it's thrue—they stab a man with
a knife wreathed with roses!

FATHER DOMINEER. Get up, get up, an' stand away from me;
an' let ye never be loungers again in th' fight for good
against evil.

[*They all rise up humbly, the women to one side, the men
to the other, and go back some way, as the priest comes
into the garden.* LORELEEN *strolls defiantly over to the table,
and sits sideways upon it. To* MAHAN.]

An' now, Sailor Mahan, a special word for you. On my
way here, I passed that man of yours who's livin' in sin with
a lost an' wretched woman. He dodged down a lane to give
me th' slip. I warned you, if he didn't leave her, to dismiss
him—did you do so? [MAHAN *is silent.*] I have asked you,
Mahan, if you've dismissed him?

MAHAN [*obstinately*]. I see no reason why I should dismiss me
best lorry driver.

FATHER DOMINEER [*coldly*]. You don't see a reason? An' who
are you to have any need of a reason in a question of this
kind? [*Loudly.*] I have a reason, an' that's enough for you!

MAHAN [*defensively*]. He's a fine worker, Father, an' th' nation
needs such as him.

FATHER DOMINEER [*loudly*]. We're above all nations. Nation-
ality is mystical, maundering nonsense! It's a heresy! I'm the
custodian of higher interests. [*Shouting.*] Do as you're told
—get rid of him!

MICHAEL [*wheedling*]. It's all right, Father—he'll do what
your reverence tells him. Sailor Mahan's a thrue Columbanian.

MAHAN [*angrily—to* MICHAEL]. He won't do what his reverence tells him!

[*Down the path outside comes the* LORRY DRIVER, *a man of
thirty years of age. He doesn't look a giant, but there is an
air of independence and sturdiness about him. He is wearing a leather jacket, a pair of soldier's khaki trousers, and
an oily-looking peaked cap. His face is tanned by the
weather, and his upper lip is hidden by a well-trimmed
moustache. He hesitates for a moment when he sees* FATHER
DOMINEER; *but, stiffening a little, he continues his walk to*

the gateway, into the garden. He stands a little away from
MAHAN, *looking at him, evidently having something to say*
to him.]

FATHER DOMINEER [*sneeringly*]. Ah, the gentleman himself has
arrived. [*To the man*]. We were just talking of you, my man.
I have told Mr. Mahan to dismiss you. You know why.
You're a scandal to th' whole place; you're a shame to us all.
Either leave this woman you're living with, or go to where
that sort of thing's permitted. [*Loudly.*] You heard me?
LORRY DRIVER [*surlily*]. I heard you.
FATHER DOMINEER [*impatiently*]. Well?
LORRY DRIVER. I come to speak with Mr. Mahan, Father.
MAHAN [*quickly*]. Me, Jack! Oh, yes; what's the throuble now?
LORRY DRIVER. Plenty, sir. The turf-workers have left th' bog,
an' we've no turf to load. Th' delegate says he sent a tele-
gram to Mr. Marthraun, sayin' th' men would leave th' bog,
if no answer came within an hour.
MESSENGER. He did, an' I delivered it.
MICHAEL. Damnit, but I forgot about it! The tension here put
it out of me mind!
FATHER DOMINEER [*catching the* LORRY DRIVER *by an arm*].
Never mind turf or tension now. Are you going to go from
here?
LORRY DRIVER [*obstinately*]. I'll go, if Mr. Mahan tells me
to go.
FATHER DOMINEER [*in a fury*]. Isn't it a wondher God doesn't
strike you dead! I tell you to give the wretched woman up,
or go, an' that's enough for either Sailor Mahan or you.
[*He shakes the* LORRY DRIVER'S *arm*.] Will you give that
wretched woman up; will you send that woman of yours
away?
LORRY DRIVER [*resentfully*]. Eh, don't be pullin' th' arm outa
me!
FATHER DOMINEER [*his fury growing*]. Did you send that
woman away; are you going to do it?
LORRY DRIVER [*shaking his arm free, and stepping back*]. Aw,
let go! I didn't an' I won't!
FATHER DOMINEER [*in an ungovernable burst of fury*]. You
wretch, would you dare to outface your priest? Get out of
me sight!

[*He lunges forward, and strikes the* LORRY DRIVER *swiftly and*
savagely on the side of the head. The man falls heavily; lies

*still for a moment; tries feebly to rise; falls down again, and
lies quite still.*]

MAHAN [*frightened*]. He's hurted, Father; you hot him far too
hard.

FATHER DOMINEER [*frightened too—with a forced laugh*].
Nonsense! I just touched him. [*He touches the fallen man
with his foot.*] Get up, get up—you're not that much hurt.

MAHAN [*bending over the* LORRY DRIVER, *and placing a hand
on his breast*]. I'm afraid he's either dyin' or dead, Father!

[FATHER DOMINEER *runs over agitatedly to the fallen man,
kneels down beside him, and murmurs in his ear. Then he
raises his head to face the others.*]

FATHER DOMINEER [*to the others*]. Yous all saw what happened. I just touched him, an' he fell. I'd no intention of
hurting him—only to administer a rebuke.

SERGEANT [*consolingly*]. Sure, we know that, Father—it was
a pure accident.

FATHER DOMINEER. I murmured an act of contrition into th'
poor man's ear.

MESSENGER [*playing very softly*]. It would have been far
fitther, Father, if you'd murmured one into your own.

End of Scene 2

Scene 3

[*It is towards dusk in the garden now. The sun is setting, and
the sky shows it. The rich blue of the sky has given place
to a rich yellow, slashed with green and purple. The flagpole stands black against the green and yellow of the sky,
and the flag, now, has the same sombre hue.*

*The big sunflowers against the wall have turned into a
solemn black, too; the house has a dark look, save where
a falling shaft from the sun turns the window above the
porch into a golden eye of light. Far away, in the depths
of the sky, the evening star can be faintly seen.*

*In the distance, for some time, the sounds of drumming,
occasionally pierced by the shrill notes of a fife, can be
heard.*

MAHAN *is sitting at the table, busy totting up figures on*

*papers spread out before him, his face knotted into creases
of anxiety and doubt.*

    LORNA *and* MARION *are leaning against the wall, away
from the gateway, and near the house. Their gay garments
are covered with dark hooded cloaks to temper the coolness
of the evening air.*

LORNA. They all seem to be out on th' hunt—police an' sol-
    diers, with th' bands to give them courage. Th' fools!

MARION. D'ye think they'll get him? Th' place'll lose its
    brightness if th' Cock's killed.

LORNA. How can they desthroy a thing they say themselves is
    not of this world? [*She goes over to* MAHAN, *and stares at
    him for a moment.*] It's cooler. The sun's settin'.

MAHAN [*hardly noticing*]. Is it? I didn't notice. I'm busy.
    Everything thrust through everything else, since that
    damned Cock got loose. Th' drouth now dhryin' everything
    to dust; the turf-workers refusin' to work, th' women
    thinkin' only of dancin' an' dhress. But we'll lay him low,
    an' bury him deep enough to forget he ever came here!

LORNA. Th' men on th' bog work hard; they should get all
    you've got to give them.

MAHAN [*resentfully*]. An' why th' hell shouldn't they work
    hard? Who'd keep th' fires of th' nation burning, if they
    didn't?

LORNA. They work for you, too; an' for Michael. He's got a
    pile in th' bank, an' rumour says you've got one too.

MAHAN [*whining*]. Michael may; I never had, an' I'm losin' th'
    little I had since I lost me best lorry dhriver—blast th' hand
    that hot him!

[*The* COCK *suddenly glides in, weaving a way between* MAHAN
at the table and LORNA, *circling the garden, and finally
disappearing round the gable end of the house; the dance
tune softly keeps time with his movements. Jumping to his
feet.*]

What was that? I thought I saw him prancin' by me!

LORNA [*startled too*]. What was what?

MAHAN. Th' Cock in his black plumage, yellow legs, an'
    crimson crest!

MARION [*who has gone tense*]. You put th' heart across me!
    I thought you meant th' poor dead man. [*She turns to look
    along the road again.*]

LORNA [*To* MAHAN]. There's little use worryin' over figures till
you settle with th' men.

MAHAN [*irritably*]. That's Mick's business, that's Mick's business!

MARION [*running over to whisper excitedly to* LORNA]. Here
they are—Father Domineer an' Mr. Marthraun comin'
along th' road!

MAHAN [*irascibly*]. Aw, what does that Father Domineer want
comin' here when we've so much to think about! Delayin'
things! I want to get away from here before it gets dark.

LORNA. Didn't you know they're goin' to purge th' poor house
of its evil influences?

MAHAN [*irritably*]. Oh, can't they do first things first?

[*Along the pathway outside come* FATHER DOMINEER *and*
MICHAEL, *followed by a lad. The lad is* ONE-EYED LARRY.
*His face is one alternately showing stupidity or cunning,
according to whosoever may be speaking to him. Where his
left eye was is a black cavity, giving him a somewhat sinister
look. He is lanky and rather awkward-looking. He is wearing a black cassock or soutane, piped with red braid, and is
bareheaded. He is carrying a small bell, a book, and an
unlighted candle. He shuffles along after the two men, and
follows them into the garden.*]

FATHER DOMINEER. We'll banish them, never fear, Michael,
before I have to leave th' parish because of that unhappy
accident. I've faced worse. Be staunch. Th' bell is powerful,
so is th' book, an' th' blessed candle, too. [*He glances at
the women.*] Let yous women keep to th' farther end of
th' garden. [*He glances at* MAHAN.] We won't be long,
Sailor Mahan. [*Suddenly, as he,* MICHAEL, *and* ONE-EYED
LARRY *reach the porch.*] Where's that other one?

MICHAEL. Is it Loreleen, me daughter, Father?

FATHER DOMINEER. She's no daughter of yours, Michael.
[*Bending down to whisper warningly.*] Get rid of her, get
rid of her—she's dangerous!

MICHAEL. How get rid of her, Father?

FATHER DOMINEER. Pack her off to America!

MICHAEL [*respectfully—as they are about to go into the
house*]. I'll go first, Father.

FATHER DOMINEER [*setting him gently aside*]. No, no; mine
th' gap of danger.

[*The three of them go in, the priest first, then* MICHAEL, *and, lastly,* ONE-EYED LARRY. MARION *and* LORNA *move over to the farther side of the garden.*]

LORNA. It's all damn nonsense, though Michael has me nerves in such a way that I'm near ready to believe in anything.

MAHAN. Waste of time, too. It'll take a better man than Father Domineer to dhrive evil things outa Eire.

MARION. Messenger says he's only addin' to their number, an' soon a noddin' daffodil, when it dies, 'll know its own way to hell.

[*The roll of a drum is heard and a great booing.* MARION *runs to the wall to look over it, and up the road. Excitedly.*] A girl runnin' this way, hell for leather. My God, it's Loreleen!

[*After a few moments,* LORELEEN *runs along the pathway outside, and dashes in through the gateway to* LORNA, *who catches her in her arms. Clumps of grass and sods of turf, and a few stones follow* LORELEEN *in her rush along the road.*]

LORELEEN [*out of breath*]. God damn th' dastards of this vile disthrict! They pelted me with whatever they could lay hands on—th' women because they couldn't stand beside me; th' men because there was ne'er a hope of usin' me as they'd like to! Is it any wondher that th' girls are fleein' in their tens of thousands from this bewildhered land? Blast them! I'll still be gay an' good-lookin'. Let them draw me as I am not, an' sketch in a devil where a maiden stands!

LORNA [*soothingly*]. Be calm, child! We can't go in, for Father Domineer's inside puttin' things in ordher. [*Releasing* LORE-LEEN.] I'll run along th' road to them disturbers, an' give them a bit o' me mind! [*She catches hold of* MARION'S *arm.*] Come on, Marion! [*She and* MARION *rush out along the road, and pass out of sight.*]

LORELEEN [*staring at the house*]. He's inside, is he? That's not where th' evil is, th' gaum, if he wants to know.

MAHAN [*seriously*]. Come here, Loreleen; nearer, for I've something to say to you. [*As she does not stir, he grips her arm, and draws her farther from the house.*] We might be heard.

LORELEEN [*suspiciously*]. What do you want, Sailor Mahan? You're not of one mind with them who chased me?

MAHAN [*a little embarrassed*]. Aw, God, no! Me sails of love
are reefed at last, an' I lie quiet, restin' in a lonely harbour
now, I'm too old to be flustered with that kinda folly. I just
want to warn you to get outa this disthrict.

LORELEEN [*bitterly*]. Why must I go? Is it because I'm good-
lookin' an' gay?

[*But the bold* MAHAN *isn't indifferent to the charms of* LORE-
LEEN. *So he goes on to show* LORELEEN *the youthfulness
of his old age; that his muscles are still strong, his fibres
flexible. He becomes restless, and walks about, occasionally
glancing at the house, nervous at what may be happening
inside. When he comes to a chair, he nonchalantly swings a
leg over the back of it, turning on the foot of the same leg
to swing the other one back again. These actions, like the
conversation, though not done in a hurry, are done quickly,
as if he wanted to say all he had to say before any inter-
ruption.*]

MAHAN [*swinging a leg over a chair*]. Partly because you're
good-lookin' an' partly because of th' reckless way you
talk. Remember what happened to poor Jack. I'd clear out
if I were you. [*He vaults on to the table, swings round it
on his backside, and vaults from it on the opposite side, a
little stiffly.*]

LORELEEN. How'm I to clear out? I've no money left. Th' forty
pounds I had, Dad put into his bank for me, an' now won't
give me a penny of it, because he says if I got it, I'd go to
England; an' if I went to England, I'd lose me soul, th'
shaky, venomous lout! An' I keep quiet because of Lorna.
[*Hurriedly, as* MAHAN *is stiffly climbing a few feet up the
flagpole.*] Oh, don't be doin' th' monkey on a stick! Maybe
you could help me? Could you, would you?

MAHAN [*sliddering from the pole, swinging a leg over a chair,
and coming closer to her*]. Now that's what I'd hoped you'd
say. This is th' first time I've caught you alone. I'll give you
what you need, an' you can weigh anchor, an' be off outa
this damned place. Listen, darlin': you steal out tonight to
th' Red Barn, west of th' Holy Cross, an' I'll dhrive there
with what'll get you as far as you want to go. [*He suddenly
puts an arm round her in a kind of clutch.*] Jasus, you have
lovely eyes!

LORELEEN [*trying to pull his arm away*]. Oh, Sailor Mahan,
don't do that! Let me go—someone may see us!

MAHAN [*recklessly*]. You deserve to be ruffled a bit! Well, will
you come to th' Red Barn, while th' rest are goin' to th'
dance, an' save yourself? Yes or no!

LORELEEN. Maybe, maybe; yes, yes, I'll go. Let go your clutch!

[*The house shakes; a sound of things moving and crockery
breaking comes from it; several flashes of lightning spear
out through the window over the porch; and the flagpole
wags drunkenly from side to side.*

*MARION and LORNA appear on the pathway outside the
wall, and hurry along into the garden just as ONE-EYED
LARRY comes running out of the house, his face beset with
fear. His one eye takes in the picture of LORELEEN breaking
away from MAHAN. LORELEEN turns aside from ONE-EYED
LARRY, while MAHAN, embarrassed, turns to face him.*]

ONE-EYED LARRY [*excitedly*]. It's startin' in earnest! There's a
death sthruggle goin' on in there! Poor Father Domineer's
got a bad black eye, an' Micky Marthraun's coat is torn to
tatthers!

LORNA [*hurrying into the garden*]. What's happened, what's
happenin'?

MAHAN [*with dignity—to* ONE-EYED LARRY]. Misther Marthraun in your mouth, me lad.

LORELEEN [*mischievously*]. Let th' lad tell his funny story.

ONE-EYED LARRY [*turning on* LORELEEN]. It's funny to you
because you're in league with th' evil ones! [*To the others.*]
One o' Father Domineer's feet is all burned be a touch from
one o' them, an' one o' Micky's is frozen stiff be a touch
from another. [*To* MAHAN.] Maybe you'd ha' liked me to
have lost me other eye while you were warmin' yourself in
that one's arms! [*He points to* LORELEEN.]

MAHAN [*furiously*]. You one-eyed gett, if you had two, I'd
cyclonise you with a box!

LORELEEN [*unmoved—a little mockingly*]. An' how did th'
poor lamb lose his eye?

MAHAN [*indifferently*]. Oh, when he was a kid, he was ham-
merin' a bottle, an' a flyin' piece cut it out of his head.

ONE-EYED LARRY [*venomously*]. You're a liar, that wasn't th'
way! It was th' Demon Cock who done it to me. Only
certain eyes can see him, an' I had one that could. He
caught me once when I was spyin' on him, put a claw over
me left eye, askin' if I could see him then; an' on me sayin'
no, put th' claw over th' other one, an' when I said I could

see him clear now, says he, that eye sees too well, an' on that, he pushed an' pushed till it was crushed into me head.

LORELEEN [*mockingly*]. What a sad thing to happen!

[*The house shakes worse than before, and seems to lurch over to one side. The flagpole wags from side to side merrily; there is a rumble of thunder, and blue lightning flashes from the window. All, except* LORELEEN, *cower together at the far end of the garden. She stands over by the wall, partly framed by the sable sunflowers.*]

MARION [*full of fright*]. Sacred Heart! Th' house'll fall asundher!

LORELEEN [*gleefully*]. Let it! It's th' finest thing that could happen to it!

ONE-EYED LARRY [*trembling violently*]. It's now or never for them an' for us. They're terrible powerful spirits. Knocked th' bell outa me hand, blew out th' candle, an' tore th' book to threads! Thousands of them there are, led be th' bigger ones—Kissalass, Velvethighs, Reedabuck, Dancesolong, an' Sameagain. Keep close. Don't run. They might want help.

[*Screeches like those of barn owls are heard from the house, with the "too-whit too-whoo" of other kinds, the cackling of hens, and the loud cawing of crows. Frantically pushing his way to the back of the others.*]

Oooh! Let me get back, get back!

[*The house shakes again; the flagpole totters and falls flat; blue and red lightning flashes from the window, and a great peal of thunder drums through the garden. Then all becomes suddenly silent. They all hang on to each other, shivering with fear, except* LORELEEN, *who lights a cigarette, puts a foot on a chair, leans on its back, looks at the house, and smokes away serenely.*]

LORNA [*tremulously*]. Why has th' house gone so silent suddenly?

ONE-EYED LARRY [*from the rear*]. They've either killed th' demons, or th' demons has killed them.

MARION. God save us, they must be dead!

LORELEEN [*with quiet mockery*]. Welcome be th' will o' God.

LORNA [*suddenly—with great agitation*]. Get back, get back! Run! There's something comin' out!

[*She,* MARION, *and* ONE-EYED LARRY *race for the gateway, rush on to the sidewalk, and bend down, so that only their heads can be seen peeping over the wall.* MAHAN *shrinks back to the far end of the garden, and* LORELEEN *remains where she is.*

From the house, sideways, through the now lurching porch, come FATHER DOMINEER *and* MICHAEL. *Both are limping,* FATHER DOMINEER *on his left foot,* MICHAEL *on his right one.* DOMINEER *has a big black eye, his coat is awry on his back, and his hair is widely tossed.* MICHAEL'S *coat hangs in tatters on him.* FATHER DOMINEER'S *face is begrimed with the smudges of smoke, and both look tired, but elated.*

ONE-EYED LARRY *at once runs out, and takes his place reverently behind them, standing with his hands folded piously in front of his breast, his head bent towards the ground.* MAHAN *straightens up, and* LORNA *and* MARION *return to the garden.* LORELEEN *remains as she was.*]

FATHER DOMINEER [*as he enters with* MICHAEL]. Be assured, good people, all's well, now. The house is safe for all. The evil things have been banished from the dwelling. Most of the myrmidons of Anticlericus, Secularius, an' Odeonius have been destroyed. The Civic Guard and the soldiers of Feehanna Fawl will see to the few who escaped. We can think quietly again of our Irish Sweep. Now I must get to my car to go home, and have a wash an' brush up. [*To* MARION *and* LORNA.] Off you go into the house, good women. Th' place, th' proper place, th' only place for th' woman. Straighten it out, and take pride in doing it. [*He shoves* MARION *towards the porch.*] Go on, woman, when you're told! [*To* MICHAEL.] You'll have to exert your authority more as head of the house.

MICHAEL [*asserting it at once—to* LORNA]. You heard what Father Domineer said. Go on; in you go, an' show yourself a decent, God-fearin' woman.

FATHER DOMINEER [*trying to be gracious—to* LORNA]. Th' queen of th' household as th' husband is th' king.

[MARION *has gone into the house with a sour-looking face, and* LORNA *now follows her example, looking anything but charmed.*]

FATHER DOMINEER [*turning to* LORELEEN]. And you—aren't you going in to help?

LORELEEN [*quietly*]. No, thanks; I prefer to stay on in the garden.

FATHER DOMINEER [*thunderously*]. Then learn to stand on the earth in a more modest and suitable way, woman! [*Pointing to ornaments on crest of hat and breast of bodice.*] An' do you mind that th' ornaments ye have on of brooch an' bangle were invented be th' fallin angels, now condemned to everlastin' death for worshippin' beauty that faded before it could be clearly seen? [*Angrily.*] Oh, woman, *de cultus feminarum malifico eradicum!*

MICHAEL. That one's mind is always mustherin' dangerous thoughts plundered outa evil books!

FATHER DOMINEER [*startled*]. Books? What kinda books? Where are they?

MICHAEL. She has some o' them in th' house this minute.

FATHER DOMINEER [*roaring*]. Bring them out, bring them out! How often have I to warn you against books! Hell's bells tolling people away from th' thruth! Bring them out, *in annem fiat ecclesiam nonsensio,* before th' demoneens we've banished flood back into th' house again!

[MICHAEL *and* ONE-EYED LARRY *jostle together into the porch and into the house to do* FATHER DOMINEER'S *bidding.*]

LORELEEN [*taking her leg down from the chair, and striding over to* FATHER DOMINEER]. You fool, d'ye know what you're thryin' to do? You're thryin' to keep God from talkin'!

FATHER DOMINEER. You're speakin' blasphemy, woman!

MAHAN. What do people want with books? I don't remember readin' a book in me life.

[MICHAEL *comes back carrying a book, followed by* ONE-EYED LARRY *carrying another.* FATHER DOMINEER *takes the book from* MICHAEL, *and glances at the title page.*]

FATHER DOMINEER [*explosively*]. A book about Voltaire! [*To* LORELEEN.] This book has been banned, woman.

LORELEEN [*innocently*]. Has it now? If so, I must read it over again.

FATHER DOMINEER [*to* ONE-EYED LARRY]. What's th' name of that one?

ONE-EYED LARRY [*squinting at the title*]. Ullisississies, or something.

FATHER DOMINEER. Worse than th' other one. [*He hands his*

to ONE-EYED LARRY.] Bring th' two o' them down to th'
Presbytery, an' we'll desthroy them.

[LORELEEN *snatches the two books from* ONE-EYED LARRY.
ONE-EYED LARRY *tries to prevent her, but a sharp push from
her sends him toppling over.* LORELEEN, *with great speed,
darts out of the gateway, runs along the pathway, and disappears. Standing as if stuck to the ground.*]

Afther her, afther her!

MICHAEL [*astonished*]. Me legs won't move!

MAHAN
ONE-EYED LARRY } [*together*]. Nor mine, neither.

[*As* LORELEEN *disappears, the* COCK *suddenly springs over the
wall, and pirouettes in and out between them as they stand
stuck to the ground.*

*Cute ears may hear the quick tune, played softly, of an
accordion, as the* COCK *weaves his way about. The* SER-
GEANT *appears running outside, stops when he sees the*
COCK, *leans over the wall, and presents a gun at* MICHAEL.]

MICHAEL [*frantically—to* SERGEANT]. Not me, man, not me!

[*Terribly excited, the* SERGEANT *swings the gun till it is pointing at* MAHAN.]

MAHAN [*frantically*]. Eh, not me, man!

[*After the* COCK *has pirouetted round for some moments,
while they all remain transfixed, the scene suddenly goes
dark, though the music continues to sound through it. Then
two squib-like shots are heard, followed by a clash of
thunder, and, when the garden enjoys the light of early
dusk again, which comes immediately after the clap of
thunder, the music as suddenly ceases.*

The returning light shows that FATHER DOMINEER *is not
there; that* MICHAEL *and* MAHAN *are stretched out on the
ground; and that* ONE-EYED LARRY *is half over the wall, his
belly on it, his legs trailing in the garden, his head and
shoulders protruding into the road.*]

MICHAEL [*moaning*]. Shot through the soft flesh an' th' hard
bone!

MAHAN [*groaning*]. Shot through th' hard bone an' th' soft
flesh!

ONE-EYED LARRY [*shouting*]. Mrs. Marthraun, Marion, we're all killed be th' Cock an' th' Sergeant!

[LORNA *and* MARION *come running out of the house over to the two prostrate men.*]

LORNA. What's happened? Where's th' Sergeant?

ONE-EYED LARRY [*sliddering over the wall, frantic with fear*]. I seen him runnin' off when he'd shot us all! I'm goin' home, I'm goin' home! Father Domineer's been carried off be th' Demon Cock—I'm off! [*He runs swiftly down the road, and disappears.*]

LORNA [*bending over* MICHAEL]. Where were you hit? D'ye think there's a chance of you dyin'?

MICHAEL [*despairingly*]. I'm riddled!

LORNA [*feeling his body over*]. I can't see a speck of damage on you anywhere, you fool.

MARION [*who has been examining* MAHAN]. No, nor on this fella either.

MICHAEL. I tell you th' bullet careered through me breast an' come out be me back!

MAHAN. An' then tore through me back an' came out be me breast!

LORNA. What darkness was One-eyed Larry talkin' about? An' Father Domineer carried off be the Cock! Me nerves are all gettin' shatthered. It's all very thryin'. [*She pokes* MICHAEL *roughly with her foot.*] Here, get up, th' both of yous. There isn't a thing wrong with either of you.

MAHAN [*sitting up cautiously, and feeling in his breast pocket*]. What th' hell's this? [*He pulls out a bullet bigger than a cigar.*] Looka, Michael Marthraun, th' size of th' bullet that went tearin' through you an' then through me! [*Very devoutly.*] Good angels musta gone along with it, healin' all at th' same time that it tore our vitals.

MICHAEL [*as devoutly*]. Some higher an' special power musta been watchin' over us, Sailor Mahan. Sharin' a miracle, now, Sailor Mahan, we're more than brothers.

MAHAN [*fervently*]. We are that, now; we are indeed. I'll keep this bullet till th' day I die as a momento of a momentous occasion!

LORNA [*impatiently*]. Get up, get up. An' don't disturb us again while we're practisin' for the fancy-dhress dance tonight in th' hope of winning a spot prize.

MICHAEL [*furiously to her*]. You'll win no spot prize, an'

there'll be no dance till that Demon Cock's laid low! [*To* MAHAN—*piously.*] Thrue men we are, workin' in a thruly brotherly way for the good of th' entire community—aren't we, Sailor Mahan? That's what saved us!

MAHAN [*as piously*]. We are that, Michael; we are indeed; especially now that we've settled th' question finally so long disputed between us.

MICHAEL [*suspiciously, a note of sharpness in his voice*]. How settled it?

MAHAN. Be you arrangin' to give me, not only what I was askin', but twice as much.

MICHAEL [*sarcastically*]. Oh, did I now? That was damned good of me! [*Angrily.*] No, nor what you were askin' either. D'ye want me to ruin meself to glorify you? An' didn't I hear a certain man promisin', nearly on his oath, he'd give his lorries for next to nothin' to serve th' community?

MAHAN [*shouting*]. When I was undher a spell, fosthered on me here! I'm goin', I'm goin'. I'll argue no more!
[*He goes out by the gate and along the road, pausing as he is about to disappear.*] For th' last time, Michael Marthraun, are you goin' to do th' decent for th' sake of th' nation, an' give me what I'm askin'?

MICHAEL [*with decision—quietly*]. No, Sailor Mahan, I'm not. [*He shouts.*] I'd see you in hell first!

MAHAN [*as he goes*]. A sweet good-bye to you, an' take a dhrug to keep from stayin' awake o' nights thinkin' of the nation's needs!

LORNA [*persuasively*]. Be reasonable, Michael. You're makin' enough now to be well able to give him all he asks.

MICHAEL [*savagely seizing her arm*]. Listen, you: even though you keep th' accounts for me, it's a law of nature an' a law of God that a wife must be silent about her husband's secrets! D'ye hear me, you costumed slut?

LORNA [*freeing herself with an effort*]. Don't tear th' arm out of me! If you want to embalm yourself in money, you won't get me to do it!

[*The sound of the wind rising is heard now—a long, sudden gust-like sound, causing* MICHAEL *to do a sudden rush towards the gate, pressing himself back all the time, and gripping the wall when he gets to it. The two women do not notice the wind.*]

MICHAEL. Jasus! that was a sudden blast!

LORNA [*wonderingly*]. Blast? I felt no blast.

MARION [*shaking her head*]. He's undher a spell again.

[ONE-EYED LARRY *comes running along the road outside, excited and shouting. He is holding on tensely to the waistband of his trousers.*]

ONE-EYED LARRY [*without the wall*]. A miracle, a miracle! Father Domineer, outa th' darkness, was snatched from th' claws of the Demon Cock, an' carried home safe on th' back of a white duck!

LORNA [*amazed*]. On th' back of a white duck? When will wondhers cease! They're all goin' mad!

MICHAEL [*clapping his hands*]. Grand news! Was it a wild duck, now, or merely a domestic one?

ONE-EYED LARRY. Wild or tame, what does it matther? It carried him cheerily through th' sky, an' deposited him dacently down on his own doorstep!

MICHAEL [*with deep thought*]. It might well have been one of me own sensible ducks that done it.

ONE-EYED LARRY [*coming to the gate*]. Wait till I tell yous. Th' Demon Cock's furious at his escape, an' he's causin' consthernation. He's raised a fierce wind be th' beat of his wings, an' it's tossin' cattle on to their backs; whippin' th' guns from th' hands of Civic Guard an' soldier, so that th' guns go sailin' through the sky like cranes; an' th' wind's tearin' at the clothes of th' people. It's only be hard holdin' that I can keep me own trousers on!

MICHAEL [*eagerly*]. Th' wind near whipped me on to th' road a minute ago.

[*The* BELLMAN *enters on the pathway outside, and meets* ONE-EYED LARRY *at the gateway, so that the two of them stand there, the one on the left, the other to the right of it. The collar and one arm are all that are left of the* BELLMAN's *coat, and his shirt has been blown outside of his trousers. He is still wearing the brass hat. His right hand is gripping his waistband, and his left carries the bell that he is ringing.*]

BELLMAN [*shouting*]. Get out, get in! Th' Demon Cock's scourin' the skies again, mettlesome, menacin', molestifyin' monsther! Fly to your houses, fall upon your knees, shut th' doors, close th' windows! In a tearin' rage, he's rippin' th' clouds outa the sky, because Father Domineer was snatched away from him, an' carried home, fit an' well, on th' back of a speckled duck!

ONE-EYED LARRY [*startled into anger*]. You're a liar, it wasn't a speckled duck! What are you sayin', fella? It was a pure white duck that carried th' Father home!

BELLMAN [*angrily—to* ONE-EYED LARRY]. Liar yourself, an' you're wrong! It was a speckled duck that done it; speckled in black, brown, an' green spots. I seen it with me own two eyes doin' th' thrick.

ONE-EYED LARRY [*vehemently*]. I seen it with me one eye in concentration, an' it was a duck white as th' dhriven snow that brought him to his domiceel.

LORNA. I'd say white's a sensible colour, an' more apter for th' job.

MICHAEL. I'd say a speckled duck would look more handsome landin' on a doorstep than a white fowl.

MARION [*thoughtfully*]. I wondher, now, could it have been Mr. McGilligan's tame barnacle goose?

MICHAEL [*explosively*]. No, it couldn't have been Mr. Mc-Gilligan's tame barnacle goose! Don't be thryin' to scatther confusion over a miracle happenin' before our very eyes!

[*The* SERGEANT *comes rushing in along the pathway outside the wall, and runs into the garden through the gateway, roughly shoving the* BELLMAN *and* ONE-EYED LARRY *out of his way. His cap is gone, a piece of rope is tied round his chest to keep his coat on; and, when he reaches the gate, all can see that he wears no trousers, leaving him in a long shirt over short pants. He is excited, and his face is almost convulsed with fear and shame.*]

SERGEANT [*shoving* ONE-EYED LARRY *and* BELLMAN *aside*]. Outa me way, you fools!

[*Rushing into the garden—to* MICHAEL.] Give me one of your oul' trousers, Mick, for th' love o' God! Whipped off me be a blast of th' wind me own were. When I seen them goin', me entire nature was galvanised into alarmin' anxiety as to what might happen next.

MICHAEL. A terrible experience! What's to come of us, at all!

SERGEANT [*tearfully*]. Why isn't Father Domineer here to help? He doesn't care a damn now, since he was carried home, safe an' sound on th' back of a barnacle goose!

ONE-EYED LARRY [*dumbfounded and angry*]. A barnacle goose? What are you sayin', man? It was a dazzlin' white duck that brought him home.

BELLMAN [*to* ONE-EYED LARRY]. I'm tellin' you it was a spe-cially speckled duck that done it.

SERGEANT [*emphatically*]. It was a goose, I'm sayin'. Th'
Inspector seen it through a field glass, an' identified it as
a goose, a goose!

LORNA [*amused—laying a hand on* MARION'S *shoulder*]. Look
at him, Marion. All dollied up for th' fancy-dhress dance!

MARION [*hilariously*]. It's lookin' like th' blue bonnets are over
th' bordher!

MICHAEL]*angrily—to the* SERGEANT]. Get into th' house, man,
an' don't be standin' there in that style of half-naked finality!
You'll find some oul' trousers upstairs.

[*Turning on* LORNA *and* MARION *as the* SERGEANT *trots
timidly into the house.*] You two hussies, have yous no
semblance of sense of things past an' things to come? Here's
a sweet miracle only afther happenin', an' there yous are,
gigglin' an' gloatin' at an aspect in a man that should send
th' two of yous screamin' away! Yous are as bad as that one
possessed th' people call me daughter.

[*The sound of the wind now rises, swifter, shriller, and
stronger, carrying in it an occasional moan, as in a gale,
and with this stronger wind comes the* MESSENGER, *saunter-
ing along outside the wall, sitting down on it when he
reaches the end farthest from the house. Nothing in the
garden is moved by the wind's whistling violence, except*
MICHAEL, *the* BELLMAN, *and* ONE-EYED LARRY (*who have
been suddenly hustled into the garden by the wind*). *These
three now grip their waistbands, and begin to make sudden
movements to and fro, as if dragged by an invisible force;
each of them trying to hold back as the wind pushes them
forward. The* MESSENGER *is coaxing a soft tune from his
accordion; while* MARION *and* LORNA *are unaffected by the
wind, and stand staring at the men, amused by their antics.*]

MICHAEL [*a little frantic*]. Listen to th' risin' evil of th' wind!
Oh, th' beat of it, oh, th' beat of it! We know where it
comes from—red wind on our backs, black wind on our
breasts, thryin' to blow us to hell!

BELLMAN [*gliding about, pushed by the wind; holding on to
his trousers with one hand, while he rings his bell with the
other one*]. Fly into th' houses, close th' windows, shut th'
doors!

ONE-EYED LARRY [*gliding in opposite direction*]. We can't, we
can't—we go where th' wind blows us!

MESSENGER. What ails yous? I feel only th' brisk breeze

carryin' the smell of pinewoods, or th' softer one carryin'
the scent of th' ripenin' apples.

MICHAEL [*to the women, while he holds fast to his waistband*].
Get in, an' sthrip off them coloured deceits, smellin' of th'
sly violet an' th' richer rose, sequestherin' a lure in every
petal! Off with them, I say, an' put on a cautious grey, or
th' stated humbleness of a coal-black gown!

[*The* SERGEANT *comes from the house wearing* MICHAEL'S *best
black Sunday trousers. He comes from the porch shyly,
but the moment he steps into the garden, his face flashes
into a grim look, and he grabs hold of the waistband, and
glides about as the others do.* MICHAEL, *seeing the trousers
—with a squeal of indignation.*]

Me best Sunday black ones! Couldn't your damned plund-
herin' paws pounce on something a little lowlier to wear?

BELLMAN. Get into th' houses, shut to th' doors, close th'
windows!

[FATHER DOMINEER *suddenly appears on the pathway outside,
and stands at the gateway looking into the garden. A gust
of wind, fierce and shrill, that preceded him, declines in a
sad wail, and ceases altogether, leaving a sombre silence
behind it.* FATHER DOMINEER'S *hair is tossed about; he has
a wild look in his eyes, and he carries a walking stick to
help him surmount the limp from the hurt he got when
warring with the evil spirits.*]

FATHER DOMINEER [*stormily*]. Stop where yous are! No hidin'
from the enemy! Back to hell with all bad books, bad plays,
bad pictures, and bad thoughts! Cock o' th' north, or cock
o' th' south, we'll down derry-doh down him yet. Shoulder
to shoulder, an' step together against th' onward rush of
paganism! Boldly tread, firm each foot, erect each head!

ONE-EYED LARRY
MICHAEL
BELLMAN   } [*together—very feebly*]. Hurrah!
SERGEANT

FATHER DOMINEER. Fixed in front be every glance, forward at
th' word advance!

ONE-EYED LARRY
MICHAEL
BELLMAN   } [*together—very feebly*]. Advance!
SERGEANT

FATHER DOMINEER. We know where we're goin', an' we know
    who's goin' with us.

MICHAEL. The minsthrel boy with th' dear harp of his country,
    an' Brian O'Lynn.

BELLMAN. Danny Boy an' th' man who sthruck O'Hara.

ONE-EYED LARRY. Not forgettin' Mick McGilligan's daughter,
    Maryann!

[*Sounds of fifing and drumming are heard, mingled with the
    sound of booing, a little distance away.*]

FATHER DOMINEER [*jubilantly*]. Listen to th' band! We're
    closin' in; we're winnin'!

[*He puts a hand up to shade his eyes, and peers forward.*]
They've collared one of them! Aha, a woman again!
[*A pause.*]
A fine, familiar one too. [*He shouts.*] Lead th' slut here,
Shanaar, right here in front of me!

[*He goes through the gateway, and waits in the garden for
    things to come.*

    SHANAAR *appears on the pathway, followed by the two*
    ROUGH FELLOWS *dragging* LORELEEN *along. She is in a sad
    way. Her hair is tumbled about; her clothes are disarranged;
    her bodice unbuttoned, and her skirt reefed halfway up,
    showing a slim leg, with the nylon stocking torn. One of the*
    ROUGH FELLOWS *is carrying her hat with its cock-like crest
    in his hand. A bloodstained streak stretches from a corner
    of an eye halfway down a cheek. Her face is very pale, and
    intense fright is vividly mirrored in it. She is dragged by
    the arms along the ground by the men, led by* SHANAAR, *to
    where the priest is standing. When she is nicely placed
    before him, she hangs her head, ashamed of her dishevelled
    state, and of the way she has been pulled before him. Other
    men and women follow them in, but are checked from
    crowding the pathway by an order from the priest. The*
    MESSENGER *rises from his seat on the wall, and comes near
    to where the men are holding* LORELEEN. *He has placed the
    carrying straps of his accordion over his shoulders, and
    now bears the instrument on his back.* MICHAEL, *the* BELL-
    MAN, *and* ONE-EYED LARRY *stand some way behind the
    priest.* MARION *and* LORNA *have started to come to* LORE-
    LEEN'S *assistance, but have been imperiously waved back
    by* FATHER DOMINEER, *and have retreated back towards the*

house, where they stand to stare at what happens. SHANAAR
stands at the gateway, gloating over the woeful condition of
LORELEEN.]

FATHER DOMINEER [*to those following the men dragging in*
LORELEEN]. Go back; keep back there! Give th' honied
harlot plenty of space to show herself off in.

SHANAAR [*down to* FATHER DOMINEER]. Tell her off, Father;
speak to her in th' name of holy Ireland!

FATHER DOMINEER [*to* SERGEANT]. You go, Sergeant, an' keep
them from coming too close; [*to* SHANAAR] an' you,
Shanaar, stand at the opposite end to keep any others from
pressing in on us.

[*To the men holding* LORELEEN.] Bring her a little closer.
[*The men drag her closer.*]

FATHER DOMINEER. Now, jerk her to her feet.

[*The men jerk her upright.*] Well, me painted paramour,
you're not looking quite so gay now; your impudent confidence has left you to yourself. Your jest with heaven is
over, me lass!

[*To the men.*] How did you ketch her?

FIRST ROUGH FELLOW [*with pride*]. We've been on her tail,
Father, for some time. We ketched her in a grand car with
a married man; with a married man, Father, an' he thryin
to put an arm round her.

SECOND ROUGH FELLOW [*butting in to share the pride of capture.*] So we hauled her outa th' car, and hustled her here
to you.

LORNA [*running over to the man nearest to her, and catching
his arm*]. Let th' poor lass go, you cowardly lout! I know
you: your whole nature's a tuft of villainies! Lust inflames
your flimsy eyes whenever a skirt passes you by. If God
had given you a tusk, you'd rend asundher every woman
of th' district!

FATHER DOMINEER [*angrily—to* LORNA]. Get back to your
place, woman!

[*Shouting, as she hesitates.*] Get back when I tell you!
[LORNA *moves slowly away from* LORELEEN'S *side and goes
into the house.*]

MARION [*as she follows* LORNA *into the house*]. Dastard
Knights of Columbanus, do noble work an' do it well!

LORELEEN [*to* FATHER DOMINEER—*appealingly*]. Make them
let me go, Father, an' let me get into th' house! It was

Sailor Mahan promised me enough to take me away from here that made me go to him. I shouldn't have gone, but I wanted to get away; [*brokenly*] get away, away! Five pounds he gave me, an' they took them off me, with th' last two pounds of me own I had left.

FATHER DOMINEER [*savagely*]. Sailor Mahan's a decent, honest soul, woman! A man fresh for th' faith, full of good works for clergy an' his neighbors. [*He bends down to hiss in her ears.*] An' this is th' man, you sinful slut, this is th' man you would pet an' probe into a scarlet sin!

LORELEEN. I only wanted to get away. I wanted to get away from Sailor Mahan as much as I wanted to get away from all here.

FATHER DOMINEER [*to the two* ROUGH FELLOWS]. Where's Sailor Mahan?

FIRST ROUGH FELLOW. Th' people pelted him back to his home an' proper wife, Father, an' he's there now, in bed, an' sorry for what he thried to do.

LORELEEN [*plaintively*]. Make them give me back th' last few pounds I had.

FATHER DOMINEER [*to the* ROUGH FELLOWS]. You shouldn't have handled Sailor Mahan so roughly. Where's the money?

SECOND ROUGH FELLOW. We tore it up, Father, thinkin' it wasn't fit to be handled be anyone of decent discernment.

LORELEEN [*emphatically*]. They didn't; they kept it. [*Stifling a scream.*] Oh, they're twisting me arms!

FATHER DOMINEER [*cynically*]. Don't be timid of a little twinge of pain, woman, for, afther th' life you've lived, you'll welther in it later.

[*To the two* ROUGH FELLOWS.] Yous should have kept th' money to be given to th' poor.

MESSENGER [*coming over to the* ROUGH FELLOW *on* LORE- LEEN'S *right—calmly*]. Let that fair arm go, me man, for, if you don't, there's a live arm here'll twist your neck instead. [*With a shout.*] Let it go! [*After a nod from the priest, the* FIRST ROUGH FELLOW *lets* LORELEEN'S *arm go. The* MESSENGER *goes quietly round to the* SECOND ROUGH FELLOW.]

Let that fair arm go, me man, or another arm may twist your own neck! Let it go! [*The* SECOND ROUGH FELLOW *sullenly does so.*] Now stand a little away, an' give th' girl room to breathe. [*The two* ROUGH FELLOWS *move a little away from* LORELEEN.] Thank you.

[*To the priest.*]

Now, Father, so full of pity an' loving-kindness, jet out
your bitther blessin', an' let th' girl go. An' thry to mingle
undherstandin' with your pride, so as to ease th' tangle
God has suffered to be flung around us all.

FATHER DOMINEER [*fiercely—to the* MESSENGER]. Keep farther
away, you, for th' crowd is angry and their arms are
sthrong! We know you—enemy to th' glow of tradition's
thruth, enemy to righteous reprobation, whose rowdy livery
is but dyed in rust from th' gates of hell!

[*To* LORELEEN.] An' you, you'd hook your unholy reputa-
tion to a decent man's life. A man, like Sailor Mahan,
diligent in his duty, th' echo of whose last prayer can ever
be heard when another worshipper enters th' church. You'd
sentence him to stand beside you, you shuttlecock of sin!

LORELEEN [*roused to indignation*]. Oh, end it, will you! You
fail in honesty when you won't make them give me back
what they robbed from me. When you condemn a fair face,
you sneer at God's good handiwork. You are layin' your
curse, sir, not upon a sin, but on a joy. Take care a divil
doesn't climb up your own cassock into your own belfry!

FATHER DOMINEER [*furiously*]. You'll dhribble th' blackness
of sin no longer over our virtuous bordhers!

[*He hisses the words out.*] Stipendium peccati mors est!
Get away from here quicker than you came, or it's in your
coffin you'll be—in your coffin, your coffin!

SHANAAR [*from the gateway*]. A merciful sentence, an aysey
one, for a one like her!

LORELEEN [*half defiantly*]. How am I to go where I'd like to
go, when they took all I had off me? How am I to go for
miles with me clothes near rent from me back, an' frail
shoes on me feet?

FATHER DOMINEER [*putting his face closer to hers*]. Thrudge it;
thrudge on your two feet; an' when these burn an' blister,
go on your knees; an' when your knees are broken an'
bruised, go on your belly; crawl in th' dust, as did th'
snake in th' Garden of Eden, for dust is th' right cushion
for th' like of you!

[*He raises himself erect, and commands in a loud voice.*]
Go now!

[LORELEEN *turns away, goes slowly through the gateway, and
along the road outside. As* LORELEEN *reaches the gate,*

LORNA *runs out of the house. She is wearing a dark red cloak, and carries a green one over her arm. She has a fairly large rucksack strapped on her back.*]

LORNA [*calling as she runs out of the house*]. Loreleen!
[LORELEEN *halts but does not turn her head.*] Loreleen, I go with you!
[LORNA *shoves* FATHER DOMINEER *aside at the gateway, nearly knocks* SHANAAR *over, and hurries to* LORELEEN. *Draping the green cloak over* LORELEEN's *shoulders.*] I go with you, love. I've got a sthrong pair of shoes in the sack you can put on when we're free from th' priest an' his rabble. Lift up your heart, lass: we go not towards an evil, but leave an evil behind us!
[*They go out slowly together.*]

FATHER DOMINEER [*taking the* SERGEANT *by the arm*]. Let her go quietly to her own. We'll follow some of the way to prevent anyone from harming her.
[*Down to* MICHAEL.] Be of good cheer, Michael; th' demon is conquered—you can live peaceful an' happy in your own home now.

[*He goes out with the* SERGEANT, *followed by all who may be there, except* MICHAEL, *the* MESSENGER, *and* SHANAAR. *The* MESSENGER *goes back to the wall, sits on it sideways, takes the accordion from his back, and begins to play, very softly, the air of "Oh, Woman Gracious."* SHANAAR *leans on the wall from the outside, looking down at* MICHAEL, *who is now seated gloomily on a chair beside the table, an elbow resting on it, his head resting on the hand.*]

SHANAAR [*down to* MICHAEL]. His reverence never spoke a thruer word, Mick, than that of you'd have happiness an' peace now. You were a long time without them, but you have them now.

MICHAEL [*doubtfully*]. Maybe I have, Shanaar, an', God knows, I need them. [*He pauses for a moment, thinking.*] I wonder will Lorna come back?

SHANAAR [*emphatically*]. Oh, devil a come back! You need have no fear o' that, man. An' fortunate you are, for a woman's always a menace to a man's soul. Woman is th' passionate path to hell!

MESSENGER [*playing softly on his accordion and singing*].
  Oh, woman gracious, in golden garments,

Through life's dark places, all glintin' go;
Bring man, in search of th' thruth tremendous,
Th' joy that ev'ry young lad should know.
Then come out, darlin', in reckless raiment,
We'll dance along through Ireland gay,
An' clip from life life's rich enjoyments,
An' never want for a word to say.

[MARION *has come into the porch, and now stands at the door,*
watching the MESSENGER. *She is covered to her knees by*
a bright blue cloak.]

Cling close to youth with your arms enthrancin',
For youth is restless, an' loth to stay;
So take your share of th' kisses goin',
Ere sly youth, tirin', can slink away!

[MARION *crosses the garden towards the gate, and is about*
to go through it when the MESSENGER *catches her by the*
arm.] Would you leave me here, alone, without a lass to
love me?

MARION [*gently removing the hold of his hand on her arm*].
Your voice is dear to me; your arm around me near seals
me to you; an' I'd love to have—

MESSENGER [*quickly*]. Your lips on mine!

MARION. But not here, Robin Adair, oh, not here; for a
whisper of love in this place bites away some of th' soul!

[*She goes out by the gateway, and along the road taken by*
LORNA *and* LORELEEN. *The* MESSENGER *stays where he is,*
wistful and still. Just before she goes.]

Come, if you want to, Robin Adair; stay, if you will.

SHANAAR [*to the* MESSENGER]. Stay, Messenger. Take a warnin'
from a wise oul' man, a very wise oul' one, too.
[*He turns his head to look peeringly to the left along the*
road.] What's this I see comin'? If it isn't Julia, back from
Lourdes, an' she on her stretcher still! I'd best be off, for
I've no inclination to thry a chatter with a one who's come
back as bad as she was when she went.

[*He bends down nearly double, so as not to be seen, and*
slyly and quietly steals away.
After a pause, JULIA *comes in on her stretcher, carried*
by the two ROUGH FELLOWS *as before, her father, silent and*
stony-faced, walking beside her. The stretcher is laid down

in the garden just inside the gate. JULIA *is covered with a rug, black as a winter's sky, and its sombre hue is enlivened only by the chalk-white face of the dying girl. The* MES-SENGER *has gone from the gateway, and now stands in a half-to-attention, military way, a little distance from the stretcher, looking down at* JULIA. JULIA'S *father stands, as before, behind her head.* MICHAEL *sits, unnoticing, elbow on table, his head resting on his hand.*]

JULIA [*in a toneless voice—to no-one in particular*]. Lorna, I want Lorna.

MESSENGER [*gently*]. She's gone, Julia.

JULIA. Gone? Gone where?

MESSENGER. To a place where life resembles life more than it does here.

JULIA. She's a long way to go, then. It's th' same everywhere. In Lourdes as here, with all its crowds an' all its candles. I want Loreleen.

MESSENGER. She's gone with Lorna, an' Marion's followed them both.

JULIA. Then, there's no voice left to offer even th' taunting comfort of asking if I feel better.

MESSENGER. There's Michael Marthraun there.

JULIA [*after a long look at* MICHAEL]. He, poor man, is dyin' too. No-one left, an' th' stir there was when I was goin'— th' Mayor there, with all his accouthered helpers; th' band playin'; Father Domineer spoutin' his blessin'; an' oul' Shanaar busy sayin' somersaultin' prayers; because they all thought I would bring a sweet miracle back. [*She pauses.*] There was no miracle, Robin; she didn't cure me, she didn't cure me, Robin. I've come back, without even a gloamin' thought of hope. [*She pauses again; with a wan smile.*] I can see your whole soul wishin' you could cure me. Touch me with your questionable blessin' before I go.

MESSENGER [*very softly*]. Be brave.

JULIA. Nothin' else, Robin Adair?

MESSENGER. Evermore be brave.

JULIA [*after a pause*]. Dad, take me home.

[*The* ROUGH FELLOWS *take up the stretcher and carry it out, the stony-faced father following in the rear without a word.*]

MICHAEL [*raising his head from his hand to look at the* MES-SENGER]. Maybe Lorna might come back. Maybe I mightn't have been so down on her fancy dhressin'.

MESSENGER [*tonelessly*]. Maybe she will; maybe you mightn't.

MICHAEL [*tonelessly too*]. It'll be very lonely for me now. All have left me. [*He takes a set of rosary beads from his pocket, and fingers them.*] I've no one left to me but th' Son o' God. [*He notices the* MESSENGER *settling the accordion comfortably on his back, and watches him going to the gate.*] Are you goin' too?

MESSENGER [*shortly*]. Ay.

MICHAEL. Where?

MESSENGER. To a place where life resembles life more than it does here.

MICHAEL [*after a pause*]. What, Messenger, would you advise me to do?

MESSENGER [*turning at the gate to reply*]. Die. There is little else left useful for the likes of you to do.

[*He swings his accordion comfortably before him, and plays a few preliminary notes. Then he starts to sing softly as he goes away along the pathway outside; while* MICHAEL *leans forward on to the table, and buries his head in his arms.*]

MESSENGER [*singing and accompanying himself on the accordion—as he is going off*].
> She's just like a young star out taking the air—
> Let others be good or be clever—
> With Marion gay, a gay flow'r in her hair,
> Life becomes but a pleasant endeavor.
> When building a city or making the hay,
> I'll follow her close as night follows day,
> Or lads follow lasses out nutting in May,
> For ever and ever and ever!

THE END

TUNES FOR COCK-A-DOODLE DANDY
STAR OF THE SEA

Hail, Queen of Heav'n, the o-cean Star! Guide of — the wand-'rer here be-low! Thrown on — life's surge, we claim thy care, Save us — from' per-il and from woe. Mo-ther of Christ, Star of the Sea, Pray for the wan-der-er, pray for me.

WHEN MEN WAS MEN

Long time a-go when men was men An' ships not ships that sail'd just to an' fro, We hoist-ed sail an' sail'd an' then sail'd on an' on to Je-ri-cho — With silks an' spice come back a-gain be-cause we'd nowhere else to go.

LORELEEN'S SHANTY

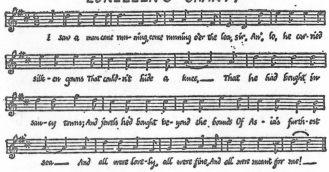

I saw a man come run-ning, come running o'er the lea, sir. An' lo, he car-ried silk-en gowns That could-n't hide a knee, — That he had bought in sau-cy towns; And jewels he'd bought be-yond the bounds Of As-ia's furth-est sea. — And all were love-ly, all were fine, And all were meant for me! —